AF774429

Changing Liaisons

The Dynamics of Social Partnership in 20th Century West-European Democracies

P.I.E. Peter Lang

Bruxelles · Bern · Berlin · Frankfurt am Main · New York · Oxford · Wien

Karel DAVIDS, Greta DEVOS & Patrick PASTURE (eds.)

Changing Liaisons

The Dynamics of Social Partnership in 20th Century West-European Democracies

"Work & Society"
No. 59

This book has been produced in the framework of the research project "The Growth of the Consultation Economy" and with the generous support from the Flemish-Dutch Committee for Dutch Language and Culture (VNC).

No part of this book may be reproduced in any form, by print, photocopy, microfilm or any other means, without prior written permission from the publisher. All rights reserved.

© P.I.E. PETER LANG S.A.
Éditions scientifiques internationales
Brussels, 2007
1 avenue Maurice, 1050 Brussels, Belgium
info@peterlang.com; www.peterlang.com

ISSN 1376-0955
ISBN 978-90-5201-365-7
D/2007/5678/54

Printed in Germany

Bibliographic information published by "Die Deutsche Bibliothek"

"Die Deutsche Bibliothek" lists this publication in the "Deutsche Nationalbibliografie"; detailed bibliographic data is available on the Internet at <http://dnb.ddb.de>.

CIP available from the British Library, GB and the Library of Congress, USA.

Contents

Preface

In the 1990s, the so-called Dutch "polder model" of industrial relations captured the imagination of policy-makers all over the world. Social partnership economies existed in many European countries, however. They have been studied, mainly within a national context, by social and political scientists as well as economists, much less by historians. However, new theoretical insights such as those developed by Colin Crouch, Anton Hemerijck and Jelle Visser, suggest it might be useful to develop a more historical approach, as we intend in the present publication.

This book has been produced within the framework of a research project into the historical development of consultative economies in Flanders (Belgium) and the Netherlands, subsidised by the Flemish-Dutch Committee for Dutch Language and Culture (VNC) and involving scholars from both countries, in particular the Vrije Universiteit Amsterdam, the University of Antwerp, the Katholieke Universiteit Leuven and the Erasmus University of Rotterdam. It offers a number of studies that may help to understand and explain the development of social partnership economies and focuses in particular upon processes of historical change. The countries presented were selected on the basis of concrete interrogation and parallels between the development of consultative economies in Belgium and the Netherlands, who in many ways reflect more general European patterns. Each author was confronted with a particular set of research questions and invited to write a paper. These papers were discussed at a workshop in Leuven on 6-7 February 2004. After further review, they were rewritten and turned into the chapters presented here. Some drafts unfortunately never made it into the publication, one chapter was added later on. We want to express our appreciation to all who have contributed to the process that led to the present book.

We wish to dedicate this book to the memory of Ivan Wijnens, a promising young scholar and a fine human being, who suddenly passed away on a sunny day in May 2006, at the age of 33.

Karel Davids, Greta Devos, Patrick Pasture

INTRODUCTION

"Changing Liaisons"

The Dynamics of Social Partnership in 20th Century West-European Democracies

Patrick PASTURE, Karel DAVIDS and Greta DEVOS

Setting the Stage

The way industrial relations and consultation economies in Western Europe are organised continues to fascinate scholars and policy makers alike from all over the world.[1] At the centre of this interest is the institutionalised relationship between the state and the social partners, i.e. employers and workers, represented by their respective associations, and the consultation mechanisms that associate unions and employers' associations to public policy.

This fascination, however, does not prevent criticism and indeed the European social partnership systems have been blamed as much as they have been credited for the economic vicissitudes of the continent. The successive shifts in appreciation from economic and socio-political scientists and policy makers even came to the fore in the course of the project within which this book has been conceived. Indeed, when we first drew-up its research agenda it was still in the heyday of the so-called "polder" model in the Netherlands, presented as the quintessential

1 With the term "consultation economies" we mean systems of policy making in which public authorities (the state, but also decentralised – e.g. regional – public authorities) jointly with trade unions, employers associations, and occasionally other pressure groups (such as consumers associations) decide upon social and economic policy. The degree of concertation may vary, but it should be more than just an exchange of views (in that case the term pluralist is indicated). The role of the state can vary from determining to limited to establishing a legal framework to bipartite negotiations (as regarding wage formation in Belgium). Compare the concept of "social partnership" used by Berger and Compston (2002) (see the introduction of Compston, 2002). Though the latter term perhaps tends to obscure the continuing importance of different policies and interests among the "partners", we do use both terms interchangeably. Both terms are less ambiguous than neo-corporatism, but the meaning remains virtually the same.

model of successful neo-corporatist policy making and even touted as such to the world by arguably the then most powerful man on the globe, US President Bill Clinton. Since then, the reputed "polder model" has lost much of its appeal. Again, criticism of the institutional overload and inertia of the complex neo-corporatist decision-making processes has taken the upper hand, for which inevitably the trade unions are blamed.

This book's first aim is not, however, to assess the impact of neo-corporatist organisation on the economy, though it is of course impossible to completely ignore questions of economic performance and efficiency, and the first contribution of the present volume explicitly focuses on this issue. Nevertheless, we are primarily interested in the origins and development of different social practices and relations between the state and social partners with regard to the organisation of the economy and the labour market within Western Europe, with a special emphasis on Belgium and the Netherlands. These two countries, of which Belgium remains comparatively understudied, appear at first sight extremely similar. Both small states are blessed with a highly developed social partnership and welfare economies, and possess quite similar political and cultural institutions, traditions, and practices, partly inherited from the strong institutional position of Christianity and Christian democracy which, in contrast to previous generations raised in the paradigm of secularised modernity, we now know was of paramount importance in the shaping of 20th century socio-economic and political institutions (van Kersbergen, 1995). In some ways they appear to represent European societies in pocket-size. Belgium in particular, divided into two linguistic regions that also have important differences regarding socio-economic characteristics, seems to unite features of "Northern" and "Southern" (Latin) traditions. American historian Carl Strikwerda even recently argued that "Belgium, except for its not being a great power, has been the quintessential Western European state" (Strikwerda, 2005: 503). Still, a closer look at these two countries shows striking differences and, above all, extremely relevant ones and representative for Europe as a whole. Hence, understanding the origins of these divergences may contribute to a more general understanding of the development of such systems in general.

There have been many studies since the 1970s that compare different industrial relations systems in Europe and beyond, usually with strong theoretical ambitions of developing models that assess and explain different institutional settings or economic performance.[2] However, far

2 A penetrating assessment of these studies is offered by Anton Hemerijck in chapter 1 below. On the use of the literature relating to Belgium and the Netherlands see Arnoldus *et al.*, 2004.

less common are historical-comparative studies on the history of national industrial relations, on the role of the state and the different relationships developed between the employers' associations and the trade unions that underpin the neo-corporatist systems. A most impressive exception has been written by Colin Crouch with his magnum opus *Industrial Relations and European State Traditions*, in which, within the framework of rational choice theory and the period between roughly 1870 and 1990, he offers a powerful assessment on how the social actors, labour and capital in several non-communist European countries developed and acted within different industrial relations systems, ranging from pluralist to neo-corporatist (Crouch, 1993). Crouch's interest, of course, was merely with the efficiency of the different systems, but he introduced an appropriate historical and cultural perspective into the study of industrial relations in general and into neo-corporatism in particular. Few have really followed him on the road of socio-historical analysis, though the cultural and long term historical dimensions of industrial relations are now more widely acknowledged and are introduced into more theoretical arguments tailored rather to the present and the future (Berger and Compston, 2002). Perhaps the most inspiring theoretical new argument on the development of social partnership has been advanced by Anton Hemerijck and Jelle Visser, using the concept of policy learning as developed by Hugh Heclo (Heclo, 1974) and Peter Hall (Hall, 1993). In contrast to the British case studied by Hall, the learning process as analysed by Hemerijck and Visser applies to the social partners perhaps more than to the political actors, i.e. the trade unions as well as the employers – even if emphasis is mostly on the political actors and in particular governments. Hemerijck and Visser indeed argue that social actors actually may "learn" from past experiences and by sheer strength of will and a determination to unravel problems come to question the basic presumptions of existing policies, which may (or may not) result in fundamental policy changes. The famous "polder model" came into being as the result of just such a process (Visser and Hemerijck, 1997). It has been observed though that Visser and Hemelrijck may well have overstated their case, simply by idealising a particular convergence of circumstances in the Netherlands (Vercauteren, 2007). The cases presented here may help to test the validity of Hemerijck and Visser's model further.

External and Internal Triggers

In the present book, the emphasis is on the origins and development, and the convergences and divergences of consultation economies. It presents and confronts different countries' cases and developments with the aim of deepening our understanding of concrete, topical developments, the "dynamics of the moment", rather than abstract and general processes. The growth of "social partnerships" was indeed far from straightforward, but was a dynamic process nurtured by a continuous interaction with and embedded in a history of political, social and economic developments and practices, as well as socio-cultural traditions. The theory of policy learning suggests that decision making processes on the one hand suffer from path-dependent variables, the "weight of history", but on the other hand can be enhanced by external and internal triggers. Hence, this book focuses on some of those possible triggers on the development of consultative arrangements.

External triggers are, as the name suggests, external to the decision making as such and originate in the wider political and socio-economic environment, such as wars and economic depressions. The economic crises of the 1930s and the 1980s no doubt were important moments of consultation, consideration and reflection, which led to significant policy changes. The question is though how these policy adjustments came about and what exactly made them possible. European integration too can be considered an external trigger, insofar as it incites the economies of the member states – and beyond – to adapt their economic and, to a lesser extent, social policies to common objectives and increases the inter-European competition. The latter can be an external trigger in its own right. In contrast to external triggers, internal triggers are important moments or milestones in the development of social partnerships, which are obviously seldom unrelated to external developments. Indeed, they were arguably often the outcome of the policy reappraisals as a result of reaction to such external triggers. The classic examples include social pacts, major collective labour agreements, and the adoption of social and economic plans, which seem to push policy changes in the direction of greater consultation. One should first of all consider if and to what extent they actually acted as corner- or milestones for the development of consultative arrangements. But perhaps one should also wonder if – from a contrasting perspective – and to what extent "regression" or alternative courses actually were possible. The careful comparison and confrontation of different national cases as presented in this book, intends to offer answers to such questions.

In developing models and studying individual cases, it is easily overlooked that one not only "learns" from one's own experiences, but also from the experiences of others. Hence, attention should also be given to the way information between social partners and across borders circulated and was appreciated. Even if a true transnational Europe still remains a distant chimera, the European integration process, with its institutional framework and the formation of transnational European associations, after 1950 increasingly offered opportunities for the circulation of ideas (Kaiser and Starie, 2005). Both employers and unions set up transnational European associations. Although their actual clout as pressure groups may not have always been as powerful as the affiliated associations (especially in the case of the unions) (Middlemas, 1995; Greenwood, 2003; Pasture, 2005), they did function as transmission belts between them. Indeed, a careful analysis would certainly uncover the fact that the information department was the main office of those associations actually operating efficiently. Also, the European institutions created structures that underpinned European decision-making processes. These were effectively used by the trade unions and employers' associations too. In particular the former established a good working relationship with the European administration, to their mutual benefit (Pasture, 2005).

Any kind of social partnership, be it in the field of industrial relations or consultation with regard to the conception of economic and social policies, involves three – sometimes unwilling – "partners": trade unions as representatives of the workers/ employees, employers' associations, and the state. The exact relationship and degree of involvement may vary considerably between countries – social and political scientists have drawn detailed schemes to situate and compare them, and have established frameworks, models and systems, ranging from contesting over pluralist to neo-corporatist, the latter subdivided further (Compston, 2003). Hence they create "varieties of capitalism", to use the already classic term of Peter Hall and David Soskice, but these relations also change over time. The title of this book, *Changing Liaisons*, suggests that they can both gain and lose intensity. Yet, even though this process has gone through various ups and downs (some of which are discussed in this volume), the 20th century on the whole has witnessed a trend towards increasing socio-economic consultation and cooperation. Moreover, it should be realised that these liaisons are enacted within a *ménage à trois*, in which different alliances and exchanges are possible. Indeed, in contrast with the standard argument of neo-corporatist theory, exchanges do not only take place between the state on the one hand and the representatives of labour and capital on the other (Pizzorno, 1978; Marin, 1990; Visser and Hemerijck, 1997).[3] Any of the social partners can ally with the state and realise mutual beneficial exchanges, as the latter can also do with any of the social partners, and impose exchanges with any third party. Welfare state

---

3 See also Hemerijck, chapter 1 in this volume, as well as Howell, 2006, who's important book on British unions and the state appeared too late for its conclusions to be incorporated in the following analyses.

research has emphasised the role of the middle class and farmers and the importance of cross-class alliances, e.g. in the development of social welfare regimes in Sweden and Denmark (Baldwin, 1990; Swenson, 2002), which contradicts the still prevailing view of corporatism as an outcome of class conflict, such as advanced by Walter Korpi (1983). The history of industrial relations in Belgium illustrates even more clearly the impact of altering alliances between state, unions and employers (see esp. Luyten, 1996a; Luyten, 1996b; Vercauteren, 2007).

In that respect it is useful to insist that the state should not be viewed as simply a neutral, third partner, let alone just the "representative" of general interest as it is in state-centred theories and neo-corporatist analyses. Moreover, in some cases, most strongly – though not necessarily only – in Italy and Belgium, borders between the state and civil society are blurred as social organisations infiltrate public administration and many overlaps exist between different levels of decision-making, while, as Peter Berger and Gregory Vercauteren especially emphasise in their contributions on Austria and Belgium below, informal decision making processes may take place that ignore the theoretical boundaries between state and society. However, as Anton Hemerijck reminds us in the first chapter, neo-corporatism does not necessarily imply a weak state, since associating the main actors to policy may increase not only its legitimacy, but also extend the state's field of intervention. Indeed, that may well be the prime result of corporatist policy making. To which extent the state is able to use this advantage, however, very much depends on the degree to which it manages to develop its own agenda, which in turn is highly dependent on the kind of liaison between the social partners. As especially Fritz Scharpf has argued, these actors can have their own conflicting agenda which carries the risk, particularly in times of economic hardship, of resulting in a deadlock or stalemate, as the state has handed over part of its decision enforcing powers to civil society (Scharpf, 1997).

Similar observations, it should be noted, could be made regarding the social partners as well: neither of them are homogenous units. They all consist of different factions, affiliated unions and associations with sometimes very different, even opposing and conflicting interests. The degree of encompassment, the importance of which has been emphasised by Mancur Olson for the unions (Olson, 1963) is only one dimension of a problem that in practice may have far more consequences. To start with, encompassment is not only relevant for the unions, but for the employers as well, as the Belgian historian Dirk Luyten has demonstrated with regard to the establishment of a Social Pact in Belgium after World War II (see esp. Luyten, 2003; Luyten and Vanthemsche, 1995). Therefore an empirically detailed investigation of the consultation practices and close reading of the interests of all the actors involved are imperative to underpin further, more sophisticated analyses. Like Berger and Compston had done earlier with the explicit aim of drawing "lessons for the 21st century" (Berger and Compston, 2002), the present volume sets out at analysing a number of case studies that, together, will deepen our understanding of a key feature of Western European democracies in the 20th century, and perhaps in the 21st century as well.

Policy Learning and the Corporatist Model

In the first chapter of this book, the Dutch political scientist Anton Hemerijck starts with a wide-ranging and in-depth overview of different approaches to the relationship between social partnership and the welfare state, and the effects of neo-corporatist policy-making on economic performance, culminating in an original and counter-intuitive assessment on the significance of the European Monetary Union for the survival of the welfare state. He indeed recognises in the EMU a way out of the "service economy trilemma" otherwise almost impossible to reconcile in the open modern service economy, between budgetary restraint, earnings equality, and employment growth (compare Iversen and Wren, 1998; Scharpf and Schmidt (2004); Esping-Anderson, 1990; Esping-Anderson, 1999). At first sight, the European nations from the 1980s to the present implemented quite diverse policy responses to the challenges resulting from increased international competition and deregulation. However, the resurgence of corporatist consultation processes expressed in the wake of a wave of social pacts throughout Europe, even in countries with a weak corporatist tradition and a strong inclination to class conflict such as Italy, Portugal and Spain, points to a fundamental common element facilitating this type of decision-making. In his counter-intuitive argument already advanced in his groundbreaking *A Dutch Miracle* (co-authored with Jelle Visser) (Visser and Hemerijck, 1995: 64), Hemerijck indeed argues that the Economic Monetary Union (EMU) was largely responsible for an increase in social and economic concertation in the 1990s, on the one hand by setting an agenda and policy priorities that, according to Hemerijck, proved to be effective in sustaining welfare regimes – and not undermining them as is often argued –, but on the other hand also increasingly (perhaps unintentionally) creating the conditions that allowed the national states to establish favourable frameworks for national consultation and bargaining. The result is a complex yet powerful argument against a model of economic policy assessment as advanced by Peter Hall and David Soskice, which overly stresses path-dependency in economic policy (Hall and Soskice, 2001).

The power of policy learning is also at the heart of Claude Didry's historical-judicial analysis of the establishment of a legislative framework on the collective labour agreements in France which, by focussing on the employment contract, emphasises the central position of the state as legislator in industrial relations and, by doing so, also draws attention to the role of legal advisors and lawyers. Indeed, in France social law specialists formulated solutions to problems on the shop floor far more than the unions as such. Didry's analysis highlights – much more than Paul Dutton's study on the origins of the French welfare state (Dutton, 2002) – both the impact of the "external shocks" to the development of labour legislation, and the different interpretation of employers and unions to the new institutions created by law and the evolution and impact of strategies and tactics that could change prevailing interpretations, such as the use of strikes by unions. The French case studied by Didry also points at the political dimension, reminding that voters can also alter the balance and alliances that underpin industrial relations, because governments and parliaments can modify labour law and thus the conditions under which industrial relations and socio-economic consultation takes place. Politics indeed mattered, as much as the institutional framework left by the Revolution.

Gregory Vercauteren equally assesses the significance of labour legislation on collective labour agreements in Belgium and the Netherlands, and in that respect unveils in particular the lasting effects of the coalition ban (the infamous "*loi Le Chapelier*") on the late development of collective labour relations in Belgium as well as in the Netherlands, as was the case in France. However, in contrast to Didry, Vercauteren pays far more attention to the role of the unions and employers' associations in establishing both the legal framework and the practice of collective bargaining, and in particular to the opposing position of unions and employers and the way their divisions were slowly overcome. The difference in this respect between the Netherlands and Belgium is striking, and Vercauteren's fine comparative assessment lays bare how and why both industrial relations' systems gradually drifted apart, how the Netherlands continued on the path towards increasing collective regulation and social partnership, and Belgium refrained from doing so, even though there was very little difference in the ideological position of workers and employers of both countries and equally little divergence in the balance of power and economic structure. Paradoxically though, while his comparison explains the gradual deviation of paths that the two countries took and the notable remaining differences in role and position of the three agents in the corporatist scheme (unions, employers, and the state), one should all the same note the gradual convergence in the development of collective bargaining in Western Europe in the long run, a conclusion both Colin Crouch and Hartmut Kaelble certainly would endorse (though the latter paid hardly any attention to the issues debated in this volume) (Crouch, 1993; Kaelble, 1987; Kaelble, 2004).

The history of Austrian social partnership in several ways show revealing parallels to both Belgium and the Netherlands. While Didry explicitly denounces the relevance of corporatism in the French case, Peter Berger deals with one of the quintessential European corporatist states. However, his overview of the historical development of Austrian corporatist industrial relations shows that this was far from a foregone conclusion, even if the roots of cooperation between the state bureaucracy and organised interest groups reached back as far as the late 19th and early 20th centuries. World War I worked as an external trigger in pretty much the same way as it did in Belgium and the Netherlands, leading to the establishment of tripartite socio-economic consultation. However it also resulted, considerably more so than it did in Belgium, in political polarisation, extreme fragmentation and the weak central authority of the trade unions and employers' associations, and the subsequent lack of consensus and of an eye for the general interest resulted in the demise of this early social partnership. Inspired by fascist and Catholic views on the organisation of society as well as academic economic theories of the Viennese corporatist economic school, the Dollfuß-Schuschnigg regime from 1934 to 1938 tried to impose a centralised state corporatist economic order – subsequently followed by the nazi New Order – which brought the Austrians, Berger observes, "a marked improvement in their living standard" (!). The establishment of an Austrian social partnership then was a deliberate break from a past of political and social fragmentation, deemed responsible for Austria's tragic demise. It also implied a determination towards the common goal of producing growth, to which, it seems, the legacy of more than a decade of authoritarian and fascist rule made no small contribution. On the one hand it had destroyed the existing structures and associations and so prepared the soil for new and original initiatives that tended to avoid the mistakes of the past (comp. Pasture, 2004). On the other hand it introduced the principles of centralisation and cooperation into the political culture and the economic system. Remarkable, and most interesting to note in a comparison with Belgium and the Netherlands, is the stress on the importance of the informal and personal sphere on the one hand and the recognition of a technical and social scientific paradigm on the other. In the 1970s and 1980s, the tides turned – Berger's assessment offers more keys to understanding why and enables a comparison between both of the "Low Countries", as well as to reassess the impact of European integration.

Actors and Institutional Rules

Berger indeed illustrates the gradual demise of the corporatist model in Austria and the increased interference of public authority at the expense of social partnership and in particular of the unions, a change definitely not welcomed, let alone supported by the latter. In some way the Austrian case resembles the Belgian, though in Belgium the unions managed to retain their high membership – which did not prevent the government after 1981 from shifting economic policy in a neo-liberal economic direction. In the Netherlands though, a policy change was implemented in co-operation with the social partners, which gave a boost to the ideal of social partnership. In two different contributions, Jan Peter van den Toren and Doreen Arnoldus offer new insights and explanations for this move.

Van den Toren places the development of Dutch social partnership – examined in the fields of wage policy and social security – in a long-term perspective, but he focuses on the institutional rules and conditions under which it functions. By doing so, finding inspiration mainly with Fritz Scharpf's *Games Real Actors Play* (Scharpf, 1997), he offers an original and very much needed reappraisal of political and socio-economic pluralism within the corporatist framework, which in the wake of Kees van Kersbergen (1995) he considers conducive to mediation. Therefore he not only refers to particular Christian democratic emphasis on mediation, as Van Kersbergen does, but also, and more originally, on the risk of exclusion which pushes competing social partners, in particular unions, to the negotiation table and incites them to make concessions (an observation, however, which is only valid if the "partners" attach importance to being part of the club, not if they resist integration, as for example French unions as well as the communist union CGT in France and the Socialist unions at times in Belgium). In addition, Van den Toren points at the importance of dealing with contract freedom – the exit option – and of binding and autonomy. This approach proves indeed very effective in explaining the actual development of social partnership in the Netherlands. It makes clear, for example, why social partners could have reached a "near" agreement much earlier, had they not used the Wassenaar agreement of 1982 which they were unable to impose, arguing that the peak organisations were not in a position to guarantee the acceptance of it by their affiliated associations. Equally important in Van den Toren's analysis are the ways in which the government, by using its "shadow of hierarchy", may influence political processes in civil society without directly imposing its decisions, thereby avoiding the risk of inciting public and pressure groups against it.

That social pacts constitute milestones in the development of social partnership economies is something Doreen Arnoldus explicitly endorses, while, as Van den Toren does, at the same time assessing the dynamics that led to the conclusion of the Wassenaar Agreement (1982), the social pact that, departing both in form and in content from existing practices up until that moment, constituted the basis of the famous Dutch polder model in the 1980s and 1990s. While Van den Toren emphasises the institutional conditions for social partnership, Arnoldus, using a conceptual framework proposed by Hugh Compston and John Kingdom (Compston, 2003), concentrates on the question what made the actors opt for a social partnership solution, as they did in 1982 after decades of "immobile corporatism" (Visser and Hemerijck, 1997: 74). In contrast to Compston though (and in a similar way to that which Hemerijck and Visser adapted Peter Hall's concept of policy learning), she directs her attention not primarily to the government, but to all social partners, in particular the unions. Hence, she explains how gradually in the Netherlands a "sense of urgency" arose, as well as a degree of consensus on what was needed to alter the downward spiral of economic development.

Here, incidentally, a comparison with present debates in Belgium, which today appear to be in a very similar position as the Netherlands in 1982, might be most illuminating, since in the Belgian case a variety of institutional and historical factors prevent both a widespread understanding of the urgency of policy reform and the establishment of a consensus on the content of an effective socio-economic policy. On the one hand, one could point at the continuing opposition mentality of at least one of the major Belgian unions, the ABVV-FGTB, the unions' internal fragmentation and the weight of sectoral unions in the major confederations and hence (the Olsonian logic) the lack of an encompassing perspective, which all prevent the acceptance of economic urgency. On the other hand, one should note the striking absence of a common or trusted consensus among social scientific experts. Both Arnoldus regarding the Netherlands and Berger with respect to Austria stress the importance of the unions' acceptance of economic assessments and suggestions made by external parties. In the case of Belgium, by contrast, experts from the social sciences have not shaken off the image of being partisan and, hence, are not equally trusted by all partners (Vercauteren, 2007).

The Wassenaar Agreement in the Netherlands signified the decentralisation of wage formation in an atmosphere of "responsive corporatism", with social consultation enjoying widespread support in society. Remarkably, in contrast to Belgium, the government refrained from direct intervention in wage formation. However, as Arnoldus observes, the state was not entirely absent from the negotiations. On the contrary, using its "shadow of hierarchy", it eased its' way out of the previous stalemate, and proved to be a decisive player in the "changing liaison" between all partners involved.

Planning and Its Failings

Apart from social pacts, social and economic planning can also be considered as an expression of social partnership, although, as it appears from Ruggero Ranieri's contribution, one may wonder if that was indeed the case in Italy. Particular to Italy is the importance of state owned enterprises (SOES) which, notwithstanding political appointments of their management, acted fairly autonomously from the government and hence constituted as intermediary between the state and the private sector. Moreover, Ranieri informs us, trade unions remained very weak and divided and behaved like politically obedient bodies until the late 1960s. In so far as consultation occurred, notably during the fascist regime, it took place between the state and the employers. Hence, it proved extremely difficult to involve unions in the newly established planning mechanism in the 1960s, when the trade union movement was rapidly gaining strength but showed itself reluctant to give up its oppositional stance. Still, the insight that industrial relations also in the (semi) public sector needed to be remodelled following the neo-corporatist example of north and northwest Europe did dawn, partly as result of shop floor militancy that forced the confederations to respond in a way that would enhance their authority and which meant in the direction of centralised collective bargaining. The employers likewise aimed at restoring their authority. In contrast to developments elsewhere in Europe, in Italy social consultation and bargaining increased in the 1970s, though it weakened somewhat in the 1980s, without collapsing completely. An effective model of decision-making could not be put into place. On the contrary, the system contributed to the legendary "politicisation" of the public sector and economic inertia, which fortunately to some extent was neutralised by the development, arguably thanks to government intervention, of a vibrant sector of small and medium enterprises. The latter sector, it should be emphasised, actually benefited from the improvement in social relations, whereby unions effectively acted as conflict avoiding and moderating forces. While national political, economic and social circumstances in the 1970s triggered the movement towards a new industrial relations model, in the 1990s it was largely the European Union that incited a policy change and in particular the demise of the SOES, something both the unions and the sector itself always opposed. As Ranieri concludes, the change heralds a new phase in the history of the Italian economy, but it seems not to really be in the direction Hemerijck would predict in his assessment of the impact of EU on economic policy. Yet as far as economic policy is concerned, Italy remains in Europe an atypical case.

Belgium's economic policy in the 1950s and 1960s is not particularly a showcase of successful economic planning either. In his assessment of the laborious introduction of economic planning in Belgium, Ivan Wijnens emphasises the weight of "path-dependency" or "the legacy of the past", in particular the traditional economic structure dominated by a few powerful, yet conservative holding companies and industrialists, and the pillarised consensus-oriented political culture, which may act as a barrier to innovation. However, the striking differences between the social sphere and the economic domain suggest the relevance of other factors as well. Wijnens also draws attention to the importance of the regional divide in Belgium, a division in which economic, political and linguistic differences largely coincide, increasingly producing a political deadlock and opposition to left-wing radicals within the Socialist union, to the dominance of pragmatic reformers. However, ideas for a different approach were already considered in the 1950s, as for example in the adoption of the Productivity Protocols of 1954 and 1956. Moreover, from the late 1950s onwards, an institutional framework was set up which introduced Keynesian economic planning and tripartite consultation and deliberation. What made this move possible was certainly a sense of urgency but also a shift in economic performance between the north and the south of the country, as well as a change in power between the trade unions (Pasture, 2000). However, the absence of a consensus on this policy change undermined the effectiveness of its implementation and with the economic boom of the 1960s, when Belgium benefited from extensive foreign investments, the need for planning seemed less urgent. Nevertheless, with the establishment of economic consultation and deliberation structures, even without the merger of the main cross-sectoral consultation bodies for social and economic affairs, and after a decade of malfunctioning had created an air of need in the early 1970s, there indeed resulted in new steps being taken to develop economic planning in tripartite consultation and deliberation. This can be taken as yet another illustration of Compston's and Arnoldus' adapted configurational theory of policy concertation to which we might add, pushing Arnoldus' keen observation a bit further, that the very *existence* of a policy framework meant that, in the perception of the participants, *it was* functional and could easily be brought into play (compare Arnoldus' phrasing below).

Striking the Balance

Summarising the results of the essays in this volume, we can conclude that at the end of the day policy learning, transnational influences and the relational dynamics between the state, the employers and the trade unions mattered more for the development of consultation economies in Western European democracies than path dependency and the "weight of history". True, the legacy of the past can certainly make a change in liaisons between social partners a laborious and long-drawn-out affair, as the case-studies on Belgium and Italy show, and formal or informal institutional rules of the game, once established, can display a remarkable degree of persistency, as the studies on France and the Netherlands have demonstrated. Yet, the overwhelming impression that emerges from the historical-comparative essays in this book is rather one of malleability and changeability. No country knows the same pattern of consultation arrangements for long. No set of arrangements is stable for a prolonged period of time. A change in these arrangements can be evoked by any of the parties involved, but can not be entirely shaped or managed by any of them – not even by the state. The timing, rate and direction of change are not only dependent on learning processes on the part of the state, the employers and the trade unions, but also on their mutual dynamic and on influences that transgress national boundaries – notably the impact of European integration. Liaisons change, but no actor can predict or manipulate the outcome.

References

Arnoldus, Doreen, Karel Davids, Gregory Vercauteren and Ivan Wijnens (2004), "De groei van de overlegeconomie in Nederland en België. Een overzicht van ontwikkelingen in het onderzoek", *Tijdschrift voor Sociale en Economische Geschiedenis*, Vol. 1, 1, p. 76-109.

Baldwin, Peter (1990), *The Politics of Social Solidarity. Class Bases of the European Welfare State, 1875-1950*, Cambridge: Cambridge University Press.

Berger, Stefan and Hugh Compston (eds.) (2002), *Policy Concertation and Social Partnership in Western Europe. Lessons for the 21st Century*, Oxford: Berghahn.

Compston, Hugh (2002), "The strange persistence of policy concertation", in: Stefan Berger and Hugh Compston (eds.), *Policy Concertation and Social Partnership in Western Europe. Lessons for the 21st Century*, Oxford: Berghahn, p. 1-18.

Compston, Hugh (2003), "Beyond corporatism: a configurational theory of policy concertation", *European Journal of Political Research*, Vol. 42, p. 787-809.

Crouch, Colin (1993), *Industrial Relations and European State Traditions*, Oxford: Clarendon Press.

Dutton, Paul V. (2002), *Origins of the French Welfare State. The Struggle for Social Reform in France, 1914-1947*, Cambridge: Cambridge University Press.

Esping-Andersen, Gøsta (1990), *The Three Worlds of Welfare Capitalism*, Cambridge: Polity Press.

Esping-Andersen, Gøsta (1999), *Social Foundations of Post-industrial Economies*, Oxford: Oxford University Press.

Esping-Anderson, Gøsta (ed.) (1996), *Welfare States in Transition*, London: Sage.

Greenwood, Justin (2003), *Interest Representation in the European Union*, Basingstroke: Palgrave.

Hall, Peter A. (ed.) (1989), *The Political Power of Economic Ideas: Keynesianism across Nations*, Princeton: Princeton University Press.

Hall, Peter A. (1993), "Policy Paradigms, Social Learning, and the State: The Case of Economic Policy-Making in Britain", *Comparative Politics*, Vol. 25, 3, p. 275-296.

Hall, Peter A. and David Soskice (2001), "An Introduction to Varieties of Capitalism", in: Peter A. Hall, and David Soskice (eds.), *Varieties of Capitalism: The Institutional Foundations of Comparative Advantage*, Oxford: Oxford University Press, 2001.

Heclo, Hugh (1974), *Modern Social Politics in Britain and Sweden: From Relief to Income maintenance*, New Haven: Yale University Press.

Howell, Chris (2005), *Trade Unions and the State. The Construction of Industrial Relations Institutions in Britain, 1890-2000*, New Haven: Princeton University Press.

Iversen, T. and A. Wren (1998), "Equality, Employment and Budgetary Restraint: the Trilemma of the Service Economy", *World Politics*, Vol. 50, 4, p. 507-546.

Kaelble, Hartmut (1987), *Auf dem Weg zu einer europäischen Gesellschaft? Eine Sozialgeschichte Westeuropas 1880-1980*, München: Beck.

Kaelble, Hartmut (ed.) (2004), *The European way: European societies during the 19th and 20th centuries*, Oxford-New York: Berghahn.

Kaiser, Wolfram and Peter Starie (2005), "The European Union as a Transnational European Space. Introduction", in: Wolfram Kaiser and Peter Starie (eds.), *Transnational European Union. Towards a common political space*, London: Routledge, p. 1-14.

Kersbergen, Kees van (1995), *Social Capitalism. A study of Christian Democracy and the Welfare State*, London: Routledge.

Korpi, Walter (1983), *The Democratic Class Struggle*, London: Routledge & Kegan.

Luyten, Dirk (1996a – 2nd edition), *Sociaal-economisch overleg in België sedert 1918*, Brussels: VUB Press.

Luyten, Dirk (1996b), *Ideologisch debat en politieke strijd over het corporatisme tijdens het interbellum in België*, Brussels: Koninklijke academie voor wetenschappen, letteren en schone kunsten van België.

Luyten, Dirk (1997), *Ideologie en praktijk van het corporatisme tijdens de Tweede Wereldoorlog in België*, Brussels: VUB Press.

Luyten, Dirk (2003), "Op zoek naar nationale sociaal-economische consensus. Sociale pacten bij de bevrijding in België, Frankrijk en Nederland", in: Madelon de Keizer *et al.* (eds.), *Thuisfront: oorlog en economie in de twintigste eeuw, Jaarboek van het Nederlands Instituut voor Oorlogsdocumentatie*, Vol. 14, p. 192-205.

Luyten, Dirk and Guy Vanthemsche (eds.) (1995), *Het sociaal pact van 1944: oorsprong, betekenis en gevolgen*, Brussels: VUB Press.

Marin, Bernd (ed.) (1990), *Generalized Political Exchange. Antagonistic Cooperation and Integrated Policy Circuits*, Frankfurt/M.: Campus.

Middlemas, Keith (1995), *Orchestrating Europe. The Informal Politics of the European Union 1973-95*, London: Fontana Press.

Olson, Mancur (1963), *The logic of collective action: public goods and the theory of groups*, Cambridge Mass.: Harvard University Press.

Pasture, Patrick (2000), "Divergent Developments, Regional Alliances and the Need for National Solidarity in Belgium", in: Johan Wets (ed.), *Cultural Diversity in Trade Unions: A Challenge to Class Identity?* Aldershot: Ashgate, p. 35-70.

Pasture, Patrick (2004), "Window of Opportunities or trompe l'œil? The Myth of Labour Unity in Western Europe After 1944", in: Gerd-Rainer Horn and Padraic Kenney (eds.), *Transnational Moments of Change: Europe 1945, 1968, 1989*, Lanham: Rowman & Littlefield, p. 27-49.

Pasture, Patrick (2005), "Trade unions as a transnational movement in the European space 1955-1965", in: Wolfram Kaiser and Peter Starie (eds.), *Transnational European Union. Towards a common political space*, London: Routledge, p. 109-130.

Pizzorno, Alessandro (1978), "Political Exchange and Collective Identity in Industrial Conflict", in: Colin Crouch and Alessandro Pizzorno (eds.), *The Resurgence of Class Conflict in Western Europe Since 1968. Volume 2. Comparative Analyses*, London: Macmillan, p. 277-298.

Scharpf, Fritz W. (1997), *Games real actors play. Actor-centred institutionalism in policy research*, Boulder: Westview Press.

Scharpf, Fritz W. and Vivien A. Schmidt (eds.) (2004), *Welfare and Work in the Open Economy*, 2 Volumes, Oxford: Oxford University Press.

Strikwerda, Carl (2005), "If All of Europe Were Belgium: Lessons in Politics and Globalization From One Country", *Belgisch Tijdschrift voor Nieuwste Geschiedenis/ Revue Belge d'Histoire Contemporaine*, Vol. 35, 4, p. 503-522.

Swenson, Peter A. (2002), *Capitalists against Markets. The Making of Labor Markets and Welfare States in the United States and Sweden*, Oxford: Oxford University Press.

Vercauteren, Gregory (2007), *In naam van de sociale vooruitgang. De rol van de overhead in het sociaal overleg in België*, Leuven, Acco.

Visser, Jelle and Anton Hemerijck (1997), *'A Dutch Miracle'. Job growth, welfare reform and corporatism in the Netherlands*, Amsterdam: Amsterdam University Press.

CHAPTER 1

Corporatist Governance, the Welfare State, and European Integration

Anton HEMERIJCK

Introduction

Both the commitment to the welfare state and social partnership participation in economic policy making can be observed as distinctive features of Europe's social market economies, characteristics which set them apart from other geo-political regions of the world, like North America and South-East Asia. The relationship between the social partnership and the welfare state in the European political economy goes well beyond mere overlap and co-existence. Both social partnership participation in policy-making and the welfare state are based on state-defined and protected rights and status categories, ensuring that economic transactions are "embedded" in a set of industrial and social citizenship rights (Esping-Andersen, 1990). Industrial rights, established under labour law, collective bargaining and employee participation, define the position of workers and their representative corporate actors, like work councils and trade unions, who are employed in organisations. Social rights are politically disengaged from the labour market, as they serve to protect the non-working population – the aged, the sick, and the unemployed – by providing them with source of income, social security, and public assistance, which helps them to make ends meet without necessarily relying on the labour market (Visser and Hemerijck, 1997). The welfare state and social partnership are not only meant to negatively protect workers and inactive citizens from adverse market externalities; it is widely believed that *social justice and social partnership can contribute to economic efficiency and competitiveness*. This line of reasoning contradicts the alleged big "trade offs" among economic competitiveness, social cohesion, and political stability. In the words of Wolfgang Streeck, as "beneficial constraints", social and industrial rights serve to reduce uncertainty and help to mitigate social conflict, which in turn enhances adjustment capacities and the readiness to accept change, helping citizens to bear social risks, acquire specialised skills, and pursue long-term investment opportunities (Streeck, 1997). Patterns of social partnership based on high trust industrial relations, by the same token, encourage concerted problem solving and give collective actors the necessary social capital to overcome particularistic interests (Swank, 2001).

A core feature of today is that national systems of social partnership and social protection are becoming increasingly embedded in practices and EU regulation and coordination. National welfare states and institutionalised patterns of social partnership reached their full development in the post-war decades, when advanced industrial democracies were in practically full control of their national economic boundaries. This is no longer the case. Issues of work and welfare since the mid-1980s become ever more intertwined with the Single Market and EMU. It is fair to say that we have entered an era of *semi-sovereign welfare states* in the early 21st century. Many observers believe that as a result of intensified European economic integration, the basic "market correcting" functions of Europe's highly diverse national welfare systems and patterns of industrial relations are negatively affected. With integrated markets and a single currency, adequately functioning industrial relations with proper social protection is no longer a matter for national political economies only.

My contribution to the analysis of the "changing liaisons" between corporatist governance, the welfare state, and European economic integration for this volume is primarily historical. Before turning to the historical narrative, I start off in section 2, highlighting the theoretical nature of the relationship between social partnership and the welfare state in comparative institutional analysis. For heuristic purposes, I will next trace the evolution of post-war social policy and industrial relations development in terms of a stylised narrative of four periods from: (1) the "Golden Age of welfare" capitalism (section 3); to (2) the period of the resurgence of class conflict, the 1970s oil crisis and corporatist crisis management (section 4); (3) the 1980s episode competitive adjustment and the resurgence of "new" social pacts (section 5); to (4) the episode of welfare reform in the shadow of EMU in the 1990s (section 6). Next, in section 7, I will address the dynamic of intensified European economic integration since the mid-1980s which increasingly infringes upon the core competencies of national welfare states and domestic social partners and elected governments. Finally, I will provide a number of theoretical lessons for comparative institutional analysis in the concluding section 8.

The Tie that Binds Corporatism to the Welfare State

Probably the most successful attempt to bring political institutions into the study of comparative political economy as relatively independent factors shaping economic performance and social policy progress has been developed by the students of modern corporatism in the 1970s and 1980s (Schmitter, 1979; Berger, 1981; Lehmbruch and Schmitter, 1982; Goldthorpe, 1984). The central argument corporatist theorists put forward was that the ability of advanced industrial societies to manage social conflict and enhance economic performance was highly contingent on an institutional infrastructure which incorporated the societal interests of organised capital and organised labour into nation-wide economic policy formation.

Reasoning from the perspective of actor centered institutionalism (Scharpf, 1997), corporatism is perhaps best understood as a close and highly structured form of (generalised) "political exchange" between the democratic state and the formal representatives of the organised interests of capital and labour, facilitated by the state and conditional upon substantive outcomes, over issues of social and economic policy-making under the primacy of the democratic constitutional state (Pizzorno, 1978; Marin, 1990; Visser and Hemerijck, 1997). By defining the exchange relationships among the social partners and the state as a form of political exchange, the formal representatives of organised capital and labour, and public officials alike, are credited with definite measures of autonomy and voluntarism in their respective cooperative conduct within state sponsored bi- and tripartite institutions that play important roles in nationwide social and economic policy making. A fundamental recognition of functional interdependence among the interests of organised capital and labour and the state in a capitalist economy, lies at the heart of corporatist political exchange (Lehmbruch, 1984: 62). The famous Swedish Saltsjöbaden accord of 1938 is a case in point. Employers agreed upon an increased level of wages; a relatively expansionary fiscal policy, and a growth of welfare services in exchange for the acceptance and continuation of private control over property and capital markets; labour peace, refraining of strikes, openness to world economy, on the part of employees (Katzenstein, 1985).

Highly structured forms of political exchange can only develop if all three participant collective actors are sufficiently comprehensive and coherent to engage in an ongoing liaison. Next to a unitary state, able and willing to share policy authority with organised interests, also organised capital and labour require high levels of internal organisational unity in order to engage in corporatist governance structures. Through the practice of corporatist exchange, the formal representatives of the producer groups of organised capital and labour, ideally, trade their capacity to mobilise constituent membership – i.e. forego the use of their political and economic power for short-term, self-interested gains – in exchange for political participation in public policy-coordination oriented to the long-term national economic interest. The expected gain of political exchange for organised interests is preferential access to public policy-making processes together with an increased ability to affect market outcomes and protect their monopoly status.

The dominant "society-centred" line of reasoning in the corporatist literature is that the success of corporatist political exchange depends largely on the strategic capacity of large, centralised, and monolithic functional organised interests. Cross-national research suggests that especially "encompassing" or "inclusive", large, centralised and disciplined, trade unions tend to set priorities which correspond to macroeconomic requirements (Calmfors and Driffill, 1988; Bruno and Sachs, 1985; Layard *et al.*, 1991). Although the empirical value of "associational encompassiveness" should not be exaggerated, it does serve as a valuable heuristic device for comparative analysis. "Associational encompassiveness" relates to the two main functions of interest group representation, which pertain to the organisational capabilities of the organised interests to represent workers and managers' demands in corporatist arrangements, and the ability of the leadership to instruct membership to comply with agreements reached at the level of national policy making. There is an inherent tension between Schmitter and Streeck have called the "logic of influence" and the "logic of membership"; when the strain between these two outward-and inward-oriented logics is not successfully managed by the social partners, a "representation crisis" is likely to result, which could jeopardise the entire edifice of social partnership institutions (Streeck and Schmitter, 1984; 1999).

By admitting private economic interests to the administrative level of the state, democratic government, committed to the political goals of economic growth, full employment, monetary stability, and balance of trade, seek to enhance the effectiveness of their social and economic policies in exchange for organised interest support for agreed public policies. The key advantage of corporatist exchange practice for the democratic state is *Staatsentlastung* in highly complex and politically sensitive areas of policy making. By placing the responsibility of economic policy-making on those immediately affected, the democratic state does not need an unwieldy bureaucracy to achieve support for public policies and policy implementation. In exchange for public status and increased access to public-policy formation and implementation, voluntary associations share in the burden of public administration, thereby becoming *staatsträgende Kräfte*, or "state-supporting powers".

At the same time, by bestowing private interests with circumscribed public authority, the state is able to expand its sources of information and professional expertise, resolve problems of public-policy implementation, and overcome dilemmas of policy coordination (Crouch, 1993). Favourable economic performance and social stability, in turn, reinforces the overall legitimacy of the political and economic order (Hemerijck, 1993).

The defining feature of the corporatist state lies in its willingness to share political authority with organised interests, with which it develops complex, reciprocal relationships, a dynamic which Colin Crouch has aptly termed the "sharing of political space" (Crouch, 1993). Effective "sharing of political space" is crucially dependent upon a number of other institutional preconditions which cannot be taken for granted. For example, the role of bi- and tripartite institutional structures, which bring together state officials and the social partners, often with independent experts, for policy analysis, deliberation, and negotiation, is critically important. Two examples stand out in the European experience; the tripartite Sociaal Economische Raad (Social and Economic Council) in the Netherlands, and the Paritätische Kommission für Preis- und Lohnfragen (the Joint Commission for Prices and Wages) in Austria. Both institutions, established respectively in 1950 and 1957, have a public law status, and a legal right to be consulted during the legislative process over broad to issues of social and economic policy-making (Hemerijck, 1993). Sharing political space can also take the form of the state lending public authority to collective agreements reached between social partners through legislative and administrative provisions, a rule of procedure in many European political economies since the mid-1930s. By the same token, annual centralised consultation rounds between the state and social partners contribute to tacit coordination in managing general assent over wage policy.

In his classic study *Industrial Relations and European State Traditions*, Colin Crouch has shown in great detail how organised interests define their strategies of collective action within an institutional setting involving distinctive state traditions and complex linkages between state and society (Crouch, 1993). Crouch's study reveals that nearly all aspects of corporatist political exchange practices are profoundly affected by the state. First, the state is an institutional regulator providing *Ordnungspolitik*, the legal framework and ground rules that govern corporatist negotiation processes. Second, the state's autonomous legislative capacity in economic, social, and labour market policy-formation has a direct influence on relations among the government, trade unions, and employer organisations. Third, beyond facilitating the initial institutional infrastructure for corporatist encounters, the state frames and facilitates corporatist exchange, whether through side-payments or, ultimately, by threats to bypass bi- and tripartite institutions. As new policy pressures and challenges arise over time, state involvement in each of these functions is required to sustain a responsive system of meaningful corporatist exchange and to counter protracted immobilism. In this respect, the multifarious role of the state in corporatist governance corresponds to Scharpf's notion of the "shadow of hierarchy" in strategic games, as the ultimate availability of hierarchical intervention and state ratification of agreements among private interests helps to curb distributive conflict and opportunistic "rent-seeking" among bargainers (Scharpf, 1997).

Reasoning from a state-centred perspective, it is therefore misleading to view corporatist governance as inherently associated with state weakness. On the contrary, corporatist political exchange practices may well enhance the state's capacity to secure its policy objectives by mobilising associational, administrative and cognitive resources from the social partners and other stakeholders. Effective corporatist governance, therefore, requires state actors not merely to create and maintain a framework for political exchange among organised interests, but also to retain important capacities to guide policy outcomes. The state's authority to positively approve and ratify also implies the power to negatively nullify undesirable agreements, enabling it to ensure bona fide processes of negotiation.

Corporatist governance concerns a particular political exchange practice whereby industrial relations actors gain leverage over a wide range of aspects of social and economic policy making, far beyond the narrow margins of the wage bargain. Ongoing policy exchanges within bi- and tripartite consultative arrangements encourage the transformation of short-run, parochial interests into more "public regarding" or solidaristic interaction orientations across the bargaining table, and, over time, the emergence of a shared understanding of political-economic problems and desirable and feasible policy solutions. Repeated encounters in due course are likely to produce a dense policy network of overlapping self-organising semi-public bodies, extending beyond mere issues of industrial relations to increasingly embrace various issues of larger public concern, including, next to wages, prices, labour legislation, and social welfare expenditures (Hemerijck and Vail, 2003). The large body of literature on comparative industrial relations since the mid-1960s, offers extensive catalogue of corporatist tradeoffs ranging from wage agreements, macro-economic policy, public expenditure, wage indexation, price guidelines, tax liabilities and benefits, industrial restructuring, social protection, pension policy, vocational education and training, and industrial democracy, and many more.

While wage formation still constitutes the "core domain" or the "frontpiece" of corporatist governance (Lehmbruch, 1984; Kenworthy, 1996), Jelle Visser and myself found that especially since the mid-1990s, major industrial conflicts, notably in France, Italy, Germany, Belgium and the Netherlands, increasingly involved disputes over welfare reform and labour market flexibility, throwing into question the standard academic division of labour between industrial relations studies and comparative social policy analysis (Visser and Hemerijck, 1997).

According to Peter Katzenstein the intimate linkage between the spheres of industrial relations and social policy is a distinctive feature of corporatist political economies. In his richly documented study *Small States and World Markets*, Katzenstein demonstrated how seven small corporatist political economies have come to employ sophisticated, stable and highly institutionalised strategies of "flexible adjustment" to changing external conditions in the course of the 20th century (Katzenstein, 1985). Flexible "corporatist" strategies of adjustment in this context features two commitments: first, a dedication to international trade liberalisation; and second, a commitment to domestic compensation, or the development of a variety of welfare programs aimed at an acceptable distribution of social costs associated with economic change. In a mildly functionalist line of reasoning, Katzenstein contends that the "double bind" of foreign economic exposure and domestic compensation have historically compelled the small European political economies to expand their welfare states. Indeed, Esping-Andersen's quantitative assessment of welfare state effort in terms of levels of "decommodification", i.e. the degree to which individuals, or families, can uphold a socially acceptable standard of living independently of market participation', across eighteen OECD countries, corroborates the argument that small and open European economies have developed extensive welfare programs, as they are the largest de-commodifiers in the world (Esping-Andersen, 1990: 37; 52).

The manner to which international economic exposure and sustained social protection are linked to corporatist policy making institutions, of course, varies extensively across countries. In some countries, especially in Scandinavia, the sphere of industrial relations is, for instance, relatively autonomous from state intervention, whereas as social protection, more narrowly understood, falls within the jurisdiction of the state. In other countries there is a strong tradition of state intervention both in industrial relations and the welfare state, as in Belgium and France. In Bismarckian continental regimes, as a corollary of payroll financing, there is a strong tradition of associational self-regulation by the social partners in the area of social security. In most corporatist political economies political authority over labour market policy is often "shared" by the state and the social partners (Scharpf and Schmidt, 2000).

In this context, the works of Gøsta Esping-Andersen assume importance. Esping-Andersen's landmark study *The Three Worlds of Welfare Capitalism*, published in 1990, completely changed the prevailing policy paradigm of idiosyncratic self-contained national systems of social protection. In an effort to reduce complexity, Esping-Andersen reclassified national welfare states into distinctive regime clusters or "worlds", based on various criteria such as their principles of eligibility, structure of benefits, sources of funding, and organisational arrangements (Ferrera 1996; Esping-Andersen 1990; Esping-Andersen 1999; Huber and Stephens 2001). According to his typology, for example, in the "liberal" or "Anglo-Saxon" world, tax-funded public welfare benefits and services are largely residual, flat-rate, and means-tested, with a predominant role reserved for private provision through the market and the family. In the "social democratic" or "Nordic" world, by contrast, tax-funded public welfare benefits and services are generous, extensive, and largely universal, with a limited role for private market provision. In the "conservative-corporatist", "Christian democratic", or "Continental" world, relatively generous earnings-related welfare benefits are financed through employment-based social insurance schemes, often administered by the "social partners" themselves, with a more limited role for public service provision and active labour market policies.

The crucial issue with the strong interdependencies between the areas of industrial relations and the welfare state in both Scandinavian and continental welfare regimes is how policy interdependencies are politically managed. The upshot is that for areas where policy-making authority is shared between the state and non-state corporate actors, adjustment requires the explicit or tacit political agreement of all parties involved, which obviously constrains unilateral state action. In an elementary fashion, we can distinguish between "loosely" and "tightly" coupled political economies (Hemerijck and Schludi, 2000). Loosely coupled political economies are characterised by a high degree of mutual indifference at the level of decision-making. Tightly coupled political economies are, by contrast, characterised by decision-making institutions that enable policy makers to coordinate policy interdependencies. Historically, the Swedish model of the 1960s and 1970s is a perfect example of a "tightly coupled", highly interdependent, political economy. The Swedish policy profile revolved around four tightly connected policies: a loose fiscal and monetary policy, supported by centralised wage moderation, an active labour market policy pushing workers to new job opportunities and out of unemployment, and a solidaristic wage policy, in line with egalitarian normative principles, to speed up structural change by not allowing inefficient firms to stay in the market. To be sure, the manifold interdependencies among the different policy areas of the Swedish welfare state required positive issue-linkage across labour market-social policy nexus and among the key players in the Swedish model. It should be emphasised, however, that there is not necessarily a direct link between the degree of functional interdependency at the level of policy systems and problems and the degree of issue linkage at the level of decision-making structures.

Effective policy adjustment in tightly coupled corporatist political economies requires "positive coordination", on the basis of a common agreement on overarching policy goals and also with an eye on balancing different interests. This because policy changes in one part of highly interactive systems alter the efficiency of other parts. In an ideal-typical fashion, policy actors in different areas coordinate their behaviour across interlinked policy domains in such a way that each can cope adequately with sector-specific constraints while at the same time contributing to joint problem-solving at the macro-level of the economy and the polity. Thus, effective policy adjustment in tightly coupled welfare is the product of coordinated change and issue-linkage across different policy areas. If positive coordination can be reached, tightly coupled welfare states are able to pursue effective adjustment by widening the space for policy and issue linkage beyond the narrow scope of merely "negative coordination". Tightly coupled systems allow for the raising of policy issues within more than one jurisdiction, thereby making it less likely that political interests controlling one jurisdiction can keep emerging policy issues from the political agenda.

Although strong policy interdependencies require overarching institutions of policy coordination, this does not guarantee that positive coordination does in fact take place. "Tightly coupled" political economies always run the risk of institutional self-blockage and gridlock, thereby foreclosing any possibility of effective policy responses being elaborated, adopted, and implemented (Scharpf, 1997). It should not be forgotten that by sharing public decision-making authority with civil society, the state devolves a portion of its most distinctive resources – namely legitimate coercion and the capacity to enforce binding agreements – to organised groups that it does not fully control administratively. Especially in times of economic crisis and uncertainty, participant actors in corporatist exchange practices are likely to pursue contradictory goals, based on different (institutional) interests and divergent cognitive and normative orientations. In such a situation, the representatives of capital and labour may opt to pursue their own versions of the national economic interest, and their respective strategies are influenced not only by divergent ideologies and economic doctrines, but also by perceptions of their respective roles in the political economy and their self-regarding concerns with organisational survival and growth. And the more participants (each with their own objectives and divergent understandings of the problems at hand) partake in the adjustment process, the greater the controversy over the direction of policy adjustment is likely to become. In the case of profound conflicts over the content of policies among the social partners within corporatist institutional framework, which they cannot easily undo, corporatist arrangements thus may become unstable and ineffective in accommodating the collective interests of capital and labour in concertation with democratic government, a situation to which Fritz Scharpf aptly refers as a "joint-decision trap" (Scharpf, 1988). The state will inevitably be confronted with tensions between recognised social partners, whose needs to represent rank-and-file demands effectively and regulate these demands are in constant tension. Given that it is forced to rely upon the often-self-interested social partners for policy implementation, the government's capacity to respond creatively to changing external demands can become constrained in such a scenario. The advantages accruing from *Staatsentlastung*, or the state's sharing of policy responsibilities with the social partners, thus comes at a price, and much depends upon the institutional capacity of "consensus engineering" to generate, maintain, and adjust agreements in the face of changing political-economic circumstances and divergent interests, goals, and perceptions. Under such conditions of "corporatist immobilism", the state becomes imprisoned in an institutional setting that no longer functions as intended (Hemerijck and Vail, 2003). While enjoying a certain autonomy to address problems in an authoritative fashion, state actors will at first be reluctant to break out of the stagnant corporatist policy framework or dismantle corporatist institutions in favour of untried alternatives, as they believe themselves to be in need of broad based societal consensus in hard times.

The Post-War Compromise and the "Golden Age" of Welfare Capitalism

Over the past fifty years, depending on prevailing social, economic, and geopolitical conditions, the institutional ties between social partnership, the welfare state, and European economic integration have been significantly redrawn. Moments of fundamental institutional change, often associated with consecutive waves of economic adjustment, social pressures and political crises, provided important windows of opportunity for policy redirection and institutional change. The interactive dynamic between various modes of social partnership and patterns of social policy development in the second half of the 20th century, can generally be divided into four periods: (i) the post-war compromise and the "Golden Age" of welfare capitalism, the long period of economic growth in Western Europe and North America (1945-1968); (ii) corporatism and crisis management (1968–82); (iii) competitiveness and the new logic of "social pacts" (1982–92); and, finally, (iv) renegotiating the welfare state in the shadow of EMU (1995–2003).

World War II marks a critical watershed in 20th century European economic history. An entire new set of institutions was created to manage disrupted economies. In the period of the expansion of welfare capitalism under the post-war compromise, between 1945 and 1968, the foundations were laid for new ground rules of national unity, economic order, collective action, and social citizenship. After the Liberation a deeply felt consensus over the urgency of social and economic reconstruction materialised in a virtual explosion of corporatist institutional building. Within half a decade, a wide range of tripartite and bipartite boards were built into European political economies. The hegemony of reformist social democracy in the Scandinavian countries, together with the predominance of Christian democracy, with its organicist conceptualisation of social order, in Austria, Germany, the Netherlands, and Belgium, provided propitious ideological bases for stable corporatist political exchange practices between the social partners and the state. The imperative of post-war reconstruction, the commitment to full employment, economic growth, and the welfare state by centrist democratic governments, and the participation of the trade union movement in social and economic policy formation constituted the so-called "post-war compromise", accommodating world market dependency and expanding standards of social protection.

The Keynesian paradigm shift in economics was a crucial element of the "post-war compromise", as Keynesian economics allowed democratic governments to endorse political responsibility for full employment without affecting the primacy of the free market economy (Hall, 1989). With the help of Keynesian economics, reformist social democracy was able to make its "reluctant peace" with capitalism after 1945. Keynesian style macro-economic management promised social democrats full employment, economic growth, expansion of public services, without recurring economic crises (Scharpf, 1991). As such, it provided an economic rationale for social democracy's abandonment of the traditional socialist aspiration for the socialisation of the economy. While Keynes' economic recommendations justified a coordinating role for the democratic state in managing the economy against old *laissez-faire* arguments, David Marquand observes that Keynes himself did not develop a theory of the state, or rather a theory of political institutions linking the state and economic agents in whose activities Keynes felt politics should intervene (Marquand, 1988). William Beveridge, the founding father of the so-called Keynesian welfare state, declared "freedom from want" in his report on Social Insurance and Allied services as the central aim of the welfare state (Beveridge, 1994 (1942)). In his second report, *Full Employment in a Free Society*, "freedom from idleness" was raised to the status of the central purpose of economic policy (Beveridge, 1945). In other words, full employment became the very purpose of the post-war democratic state. Fighting unemployment was considered relatively simple in the initial post-war era of self-contained political economies. As lack of effective demand, industrial change and the need for economic relocation were the main causes of unemployment, the policy responses included public outlays to raise effective demand and mobility incentives with an emphasis of bringing jobs to men not *vice versa* (Schmid and Gazier, 2002). However, Beveridge did concede that a combination of full employment and sectional wage bargaining could produce an inflationary spiral that was likely to undermine the very policy objective of full employment which Keynesian economics made possible. Because wage and price stability was an essential condition vital to success of a Keynesian employment policy, it required a political vision of cooperation between government, business, and labour, an institutional feature which Keynesian economic theory in itself lacked.

Taking heed from Beveridge, the democratic state, especially on the European continent, took on an active role in orchestrating consensual industrial relations and collective bargaining. Many governments to invited trade union representatives alongside business leaders to participate in the formulation, administration and implementation of social and economic policy decisions. Tripartite incomes policies were considered especially effective in promoting growth and employment. The prevalent post-war emphasis on output and growth triggered what Cherles Maier has called the "politics of productivity" (Maier, 1987: 121-52). Moderate governments and pragmatic organised interests assumed responsibility growth and productivity by endorsing incomes policies based on wage restraint, keeping pay increases below productivity growth.

To be sure, the labour movement emerged as a strong political force from the depression and World War II. Strategic cooperation between the interwar antagonists, organised capital and labour, constitutes another prominent political-institutional characteristic of the emerging post-war welfare state. It has been argued that the concerted effort of the social partners and the democratic state to administer responsible incomes policy stood as the basis of the so-called "golden age" of welfare capitalism (Marglin and Schor, 1990). The so-called "post-war settlement" between workers and employers can be viewed as the pragmatic and concerted post-war response to the disruptive, political and social crisis of the interwar period. Both organised capital and labour supported the welfare state and the Keynesian mixed economic order, which offered the prospect of a positive spiral of full employment, high wages, rising demand, increased productivity, and, finally, a higher standard of living (including social protection) for everyone. Employers came to appreciate trade unions as the legitimate representatives in collective bargaining. Meanwhile, organised labour came to recognise the prerogative of private ownership and the legitimate authority of management over crucial economic decisions, especially investment. In exchange of social peace, the state rewarded labour with minimum wage legislation and the expansion of the welfare state, within which the labour movement gained significant measures of administrative authority.

While social services indeed were no longer the exclusive domain of the charities, breadwinner job security of males with dedicated housewives, allowed welfare state responsibilities could be kept at bay (Esping-Andersen, 1990). In this respect, the post-war welfare state very much consolidated conventional family structures. With the consolidation of the traditional nuclear family, professional social services only came into play at the beginning (education) and at the near the end (old-age pensions) of individual life-cycles, with only rare and brief intermittent periods of dependence on social security and state-sponsored assistance. In other words, social protection was coupled to standard or Fordist employment relationships, which reinforced traditional gender-relationship of male bread-winner and female housewives. The central social policy objective of full employment came to be defined in terms of the achievement of full-time jobs for male workers only; 48 hours a week, with 48 working-weeks in a year, for a period of 48 years.

At the level of the international political economy, the post-war welfare state effort was backed by what John Gerard Ruggie has called a regime of "embedded liberalism" (Ruggie, 1982). A multilateral commitment to open international trade remained "embedded" in the recognition of an extensive role for the state in governing national economies. The establishment of the relatively flexible international monetary system of Bretton Woods stood at the heart of the long-term success of the "Golden Age" of welfare capitalism. The monetary system of Bretton Woods supported a key element of political relaxation of the doctrine of price stability in order to sustain multilateralism and domestic social policy expansion and economic stability. The regime of embedded liberalism was contingent upon the hegemony of the United States in the international political economy. By pegging the dollar to gold at a fixed price, agreed to at Bretton Woods, the United States allowed individual polities free convertability of currencies and stable exchange rates at levels that enabled competitiveness in world markets without undermining domestic welfare efforts of sovereign nation-states.

The "Golden Age" of welfare capitalism was a tremendous success. Expanding world markets, high growth rates, low inflation, and increased productivity and investment activity went hand in hand with full employment, decent wages, high standard of living for everyone and a significant reduction of inequality, were the corollary of the "post-war compromise". Far from being polar opposites, competitiveness and solidarity were almost in perfect harmony. Based on the success of the post-war settlement, many academic observers believed that advanced industrial societies were converging in the direction of highly organised political economies dominated by large industrial firms, increasingly fluid social structures, activist welfare states, declining inequalities, consensual industrial relations, Keynesian technocratic macro-economic policy, together and a diminishing importance of ideology in politics.

Corporatism and Crisis Management

The movement of May '68, the Vietnam War, the breakdown of the Bretton Woods monetary system in 1971, the steep rise in oil prices between 1973 and 1979, the erosion of American hegemony in the world markets, brought an end to the happy dialectic between social policy and economic performance of the "Golden Age". The first oil crisis of 1973 simultaneously accelerated inflation and pushed unemployment to unprecedented levels, which in turn led to a dramatic increase in social security outlays. All of a sudden, European political economies seemed no longer able to guarantee industrial full employment, and thus preserve generous welfare standards. In the midst of the allegedly ungovernable 1970s, a number of comparative scholars advanced the claim that advanced industrial societies, employing institutional devices integrating business and labour elites in public policy making platforms, were best able to alleviate the destructive impact of social and political crisis, international conflict, and economic shocks from the late 1960s through to the early 1980s. In this respect, the oil crisis thus prompted a paradigm shift in comparative political economy studies, away from the outdated "functional imperatives" of modernisation theory, towards "middle range" analyses centred around domestic political institutions and power resources. Partisan control over governments and bi- and tripartite bodies took pride of place in the expanding literature of comparative political economy as relatively independent variable in explaining economic performance. However, in his earliest ramifications on the modern corporatist phenomenon in the classic essay *Still the Century of Corporatism?*, Philippe C. Schmitter, the founding father of corporatist scholarship, was still keen to formulate a "general theory" of a secular trend of "creeping corporatism" in late capitalism (Schmitter, 1974; 1979).

In the wake of the early 1980s, most corporatist scholar shied away from speculation over an allegedly corporatist evolution of advanced capitalism, including Philippe Schmitter (Goldthorpe, 1984: 315-43). Ever since corporatist researchers have centred their arguments predominantly around the organisational attributes of functional interests. Especially, centralised "peak" organisations of employers and workers were held to be crucial for mastering the predicament of stagflation through tripartite incomes policy as an indispensable tools of crisis management. In particular, so-called "encompassing organisations", or highly centralised and concentrated functional interests, were believed likely to pursue responsible strategies of collective action supportive of the public goals of full employment and price stability. The theoretical contribution on the macro-effect of "encompassing" unionism is from Mancur Olson. In his *The Rise and Decline of Nations*, Olson advanced the idea that interest organisations which "encompass" large segments of society regard the overall consequences of their collective action and will, consequently, favour socially responsive and co-operative macro-policies (Olson, 1982). By the same token, employing advanced correlational methods, the economists Michael Bruno and Jeffrey Sachs, found strong correlations between corporatism and a relatively low rise in the Okun "misery-index" – the sum of unemployment and inflation – in a cross-national survey of seventeen advanced industrial societies during the first seven oil-shock years, from 1973 to 1980. They emphasised both the importance of real wage moderation for achieving low unemployment after a supply shock and the significance of corporatist institutions for the moderation of union wage demands (Bruno and Sachs, 1985; Kenworthy, 2002).

Subsequently, the economists Lars Calmfors and John Driffill have challenged the main proposition of Bruno and Sachs that the more corporatist a system of collective bargaining, the higher the level of employment (1988). Rather than employing the ambiguous concept of corporatism, Calmfors and Driffill considered different levels of collective bargaining and their consequences for real wage restraint. In their survey, they distinguish three groups of countries: centralised economies, intermediate economies and decentralised economies. In the centralised economies of Austria, Denmark, Finland, Norway, and Sweden wage agreements are settled between national employers associations and union federations. In intermediate economies of Germany, the Netherlands, and Belgium, negotiations take place at industry level. Finally, in the decentralised economies of Canada, the United States, France, and Italy, wage bargaining occurs at company level. Contrary to Bruno and Sachs, Calmfors and Driffill argue that the relation between union centralisation and employment is U-shaped rather than monotonic. The best performance was obtained under fully centralised (the Scandinavian solution) or fully decentralised (the US or UK example) conditions. Both high levels of centralisation and far-reaching decentralisation contribute to real wage restraint, while intermediate degrees of centralisation produce the worst outcome in terms of real wages and employment. The logic behind Calmfors and Driffill's U-shaped curve is that where collective bargaining is highly decentralised, the capacity of small unions to raise nominal wages is severely constrained by product market competition. Conversely, where bargaining is heavily centralised, large "encompassing" union organisations are constrained by the fear of inflation. The intermediate cases are too politicised to adhere to market discipline, but not enough to favour an optimal outcome. In other words, for the intermediate countries wage setting is, on the one hand, too centralised to allow market mechanisms to freely operate freely, on the other hand, too decentralised to allow bargaining parties to take macro-economic concerns into account.

The findings of Calmfors and Driffill to some extent concur with the conclusions established by the political scientist David Cameron, who suggests that social democratic government together with inclusive and centralised trade union federations tends to contain unemployment. He found that corporatism, social democratic hegemony, and labour quiescence, a combination of low strike activity and wage moderation, were positively related (Cameron, 1984: 143-78).

Peter Lange and Geoffrey Garrett also validated support for a kind of U-shaped relation between corporatism and economic performance. Next to level of organisation of the labour movement, Lange and Garrett also included party political variables in their analysis. They found that large "encompassing" unions will only moderate their behaviour where the political Left is in power. Moderation on the part of unions was also found under the condition where both the Left and the trade union are weak. With respect to the intermediate "hybrid" cases, where either Left-wing governments face a fragmented trade union movement or large encompassing unions face Right-wing governments, Lange and Garrett hypothesised that unions pursue militant strategies. The interactive effect between the organisational resources of trade union movement and the political power of partisan parties for hybrid cases thus concludes in the worst of all possible world in terms of high levels of industrial conflict and inferior aggregate economic performance (Lange and Garrett, 1985; Alvarez, Garrett, and Lange; 1991; Garrett, 1998).

Numerous quantitative researchers have since expanded and refined an impressive string of advantageous affinities between corporatism and social order and political stability, on the one hand, and aggregate economic performance, on the other. David Soskice (2000) argues that policy-makers in corporatist political economies worry less about wage cost inflation. This, in turn, engenders a positive effect upon their willingness to pursue growth oriented macro-economic policies and more activist labour market policies (Kenworthy, 2002). Other researchers have been able to establish a positive association, well into the 1990s, of corporatist governance and low levels of earning inequality (Rueda and Pontussen, 2000; Wallerstein, 1999). Walter Korpi and Gosta Esping-Andersen underscored the beneficial interrelation between corporatist institutions and the achievements of the welfare state (Korpi, 1983; Esping-Andersen and Korpi, 1984; Esping-Andersen, 1990). By linking indicators of economic stability, full employment, and economic growth, to a "social wage" component, provided by the welfare state, Frank Castles was able to establish, with a little more sophistication than most economists on the subject, that:

> Neocorporatism [...] appears to pay off, not by offering the best of all possible worlds of full employment, low inflation and high social wage outcomes, but rather by providing a favourable trade-off between these three objectives, which vary from country to country in a way which reflects a balance between the preferences of trade unions and other organisational actors (Castles, 1987: 390).

While there is no denying that much of the variance of economic performance in the wake of the 1970s oil shocks can be explained by political factors and institutional features, such as the relative strength of the labour movement and the existence of 'corporatist' institutions facilitating peak-level wage bargaining, a great deal is left unexplained. Moreover, the causal claims of the sanguine impact of corporatism on economic performance are highly sensitive to the selection of countries included in the set, the periodisation of the data, the choice of economic performance measures and, of course, the choice of indicators for the independent variables representing political resources and institutional structures in simple univariate regression analysis (Scharpf, 1984). More troublesome, I find is that the majority of scholars measuring the effects of political institutions, like neo-corporatism, on economic performance, inevitably fall pry to a method of "comparative statics" in addressing highly dynamic questions of policy adjustment in hard times.

Without denying the immanent value for understanding the impact of corporatist institutions on economic performance across a fair number of affluent democracies, using pooled time-series cross-section analysis, Martin Schludi and I, looking back on what is generally been thought of as the heyday of corporatism, in taking a more qualitative comparative case study perspective of corporatist responses to the perils of stagflation, were able to find only two forthright corporatist-exchange success stories to the perils of stagflation: Austria and Sweden (Hemerijck and Schludi, 2000). To be sure, practically all over Western Europe, the dominant macro-economic policy response was up until the early 1980s inspired by Keynesianism. In the majority of advanced European political economies national policy debates revolved around incomes policy. The success or the failure, respectively, in containing stagflation, was critically dependent on the ability of political actors to organise a high level of "positive coordination" between monetary, fiscal and wage policy actors. Although Austria and Sweden differed with respect to monetary policy, with Austria following a "hard" and Sweden a "soft" monetary policy, both owe their superior performance to the combination of wage restraint on the part of encompassing unions and fiscal reflation on the part left-leaning governments.

When Austria faced the first oil-price shock, the Socialist government was determined to defend full employment. Austrian policy actors (including also employers' organisation and the conservative opposition party) adhered to a Keynesian diagnosis of the ensuing recession. This shared understanding of the crisis helped Austrian policy makers to pursue a common policy strategy, coined "Austro-Keynesianism": Expansionary fiscal and monetary policies were deployed to stabilise effective demand and employment, and a hard currency policy was adopted as the appropriate instrument to curtail inflation. Although the peg to the D-Mark meant a continuous effective appreciation of the schilling after 1976, the social partners took responsibility for competitiveness by way of adopting a moderate wage policy. Wage increases were only slightly above productivity increases. In retrospect, compared to most other West European countries, Austria seemed to have escaped the polarising impact of the resurgence of class conflict after 1968.

Like Austria, also Sweden proved very successful in orchestrating a smooth interplay between monetary, fiscal and wage policy in the 1970s. The initial Swedish response to the first oil-shock centred on fiscal stimulation to boost demand and maintain full employment. As a result, growth rates were comparatively high in 1974 and 1975. The expansive macro-economic policy package included large state subsidies to ailing industries and extensive labour market training programs. The government also reduced income taxation in 1974 in an attempt to lower the pressure on wage increases. When the Swedish economy went into a recession in 1977, the Krona was devaluated in 1976 and 1977 to restore international competitiveness. Most important, the Swedish system of highly centralised wage bargaining was able to revive a strategy of wage moderation, whereby the gains from strategic devaluations in terms of improved international competitiveness were not eaten up by higher wage demands from the unions. Moreover, the modest fall in employment within the exposed sectors was over-compensated for by a swift expansion of the public sector, resulting in a massive increase of labour intensive "women friendly" social services in child care, elderly care, education etc. With high and increasing levels of employment, the Swedish social security system was relatively unaffected by the recession-prone 1970s.

The British experience of the 1970s is exemplar of a complete failure in tackling the problem of stagflation along the lines of Keynesian demand management. Britain entered the 1970s in a state of sluggish growth, low profitability, accelerating inflation and sharply rising unemployment. Moreover, British political actors adopted an incoherent and inconsistent policy mix and thus failed to break with the typical "stop-go" pattern in macro-economic decision-making. Moreover, the British system of voluntarist and adversial industrial relations with its strong but highly decentralised militant unions and its weakly organised employers, counteracted the policy of full employment by triggering a disastrous wage-price spiral (Rhodes, 2000). Successive British governments tried to persuade the unions to pursue wage moderation in support of maintaining full employment. However, due to Britain's scattered union structure, wage inflation could not be brought under control.

Also Italian governments in the 1970s sought the support of the trade unions in their attempt to manage the recession by persuading the unions to moderate wage claims. In exchange, the trade unions were offered increased limitations on overtime and an expansion of social protection, especially as regards disability pensions. However, strong speculative attacks forced the lira to devalue in the wake of the collapse of the regime of Bretton Woods. This exacerbated already spiralling inflation. When the first oil-price shock brought Italy into a recession, the system of automatic indexation of wages in line with inflation (*scala mobile*) reinforced the vicious cycle of self-sustaining inflationary expectations. In Belgium, under conditions of the resurgence of class conflict already in the 1960s, relations between trade union and employers' associations were at a post-war low. An elaborate indexation system prevented Belgian social partners and the government from developing a responsive incomes policy to the predicament of stagflation. The same is true for the Netherlands. Successive governments felt obliged to intervene a number of times in wage setting procedures. After the mid 1970s, the government gave up its demand-side policies of job creation, which had not produced any positive results. As the attempts by the government to bring about centralised wage moderation failed, it imposed a number of wage freezes to contain the wage-price spiral. Only Germany came to grips with the predicament of inflation, exactly because it stayed clear of Keynesian macro-economic management at an early stage (Manow and Seils, 2000).

The counter-intuitive point I want to make is that in the period that has generally been thought of as the heyday of corporatism, only two political economies have been able to resolve the crisis of stagflation, Austria and Sweden, through an effective corporatist exchange package, trading wage moderation for fiscal or monetary reflation. Except for Germany, most other governments did try to orchestrate corporatist crisis deals along the lines of demand stimulation in exchange for wage restraint, but practically all failed to muster effective societal support to do so effectively.

With the introduction of a political perspective to comparative political economy studies, corporatist scholars have arguably made a landmark contribution to the study of contemporary capitalism. To be sure, the "Golden Age" of welfare capitalism concealed many important cross-national political and institutional differences across Western Europe and North America. However, there is ample room for criticism. My problem with the standard claims of corporatist scholarship is that explicitly or implicitly corporatism is perceived of as the institutional outcome of class conflict in relatively closed political economies. Walter Korpi, the main proponent of the so-called "power resources" school, adheres to a distinctively Leftist account of corporatism. Katzenstein correctly contends that Britain's weak corporatism and the Netherlands' strong corporatism cannot be predicted from the strength of their respective labour parties and the density of the respective trade union movements. Shared interests concerted by government rather than institutionalised class conflict drive the development of democratic corporatism. Equally important is the distinctive party system of corporatist polities, which offers strong mechanisms for integrating the working class movement into corporatist arrangements. Party systems of small states mobilise a greater part of the electorate as compared to large states with strong links between political parties and organised interests. In this respect, also proportional representation, has served to integrate labour, business and government into firm collaborative arrangements (Katzenstein, 1985: 171). Moreover, by taking the extent Left power or union centralisation as key indicator for corporatism, Korpi, Castles,

Lange and Garrett, somehow obscure that effective social policy and crisis management is critically dependent on private economic activity to create employment, wealth and a tax base for social policy expansion. There are obvious limits to disengaging politics from economics under welfare capitalism in increasingly open economies. Furthermore, the narrow focus on domestic institutional features, irrespective of the substance of crisis management, embodies a tendency of overrating national sovereignty at the risk of underestimating the effects of the international economy on the domestic political economy. The fist oil price shock seriously undermined the efficacy of domestic social and economic policy. By the same token, by placing the primacy of crisis management so close to domestic politics, the possibility of international coordination and European integration are easily overlooked. Initiatives of European market integration have decisively contributed to the creation of regulatory institutions above and beyond the traditional nation-state, which since the mid-1970s have become ever more important. In retrospect, the crisis of the 1970s reveals that the welfare state, sheltered by Keynesian economic policy, had somehow disengaged itself during its post-war expansion from the economic area of production. Wealth creation and economic efficiency were taken for granted.

Competitiveness and the Logic of New "Social Pacts"

In the wake of the second oil price shock in 1979, many observers believed that corporatist governance had lost its rationale. Many corporatist political economies ran into serious employment, fiscal, and monetary difficulties. This provided clear ammunition for the neo-liberal critique of political "interference" with market mechanisms. As the structural recovery of West European economies seemed increasingly elusive, a number of arguments were advanced for the putative demise of corporatism. As a result of important qualitative changes in economic and labour market conditions, some authors were ready to predict "the end of organised capitalism" (Lash and Urry, 1987). Others discovered the "challenge of flexibility" (Baglioni and Crouch, 1990), arguing that pressures to decentralise collective bargaining and the shift from Fordist, standardised mass production toward craft-based, diversified methods of production were difficult to reconcile with corporatist interest intermediation, with micro-level wage drift at firm- or plant-level increasingly undermining coordinated wage settlements at macro-level (Priori and Sabel, 1984). The decline of heavy manufacturing, the expanding service industry, growing strains between the trade union movement and its allied political parties, internal strife between domestic and export oriented trade unions, all seriously weakened the trade union movement as a key, or perhaps even "the" key actor in the corporatist wage bargain. Highlighting the historical correlation of corporatist success with Keynesian macro-economic intervention, other observers suggested that the liberalisation of international capital markets in the 1980s sharply curtailed the political capacities of national governments to offer full employment, in exchange for wage restraint, through the use of fiscal and monetary policy (Scharpf, 1991). It is fair to say that the second oil price shock marks the transition from full employment to low inflation as the central purpose of economic policy making. With the shift worldwide to a "hard currency" regime, strategies of fiscal and monetary reflation became more difficult to pursue (Boix, 2000). The liberalisation of capital markets in the late 1980s, moreover, has stepped up pressures on firms to move to other countries. Increased exit option from the domestic political economy, have increased the leverage of employers to demand wage moderation *vis-à-vis* trade union, irrespective of the availability of corporatist wage setting and social partnership participation in social and economic policy platforms. In short, by the 1980s it was truly questionable whether the 20th century still was the "century of corporatism" as Schmitter claimed in his opening essay to the debate (Schmitter, 1979). Carlo Dell'Aringa and Bruno Lodovici advanced the thesis, in retrospect wrongly, that corporatist strategies played an important role during the years of stagnation between 1974 and 1982, but that they were no longer relevant (Dell'Arringa and Lodovici, 1990).

But to everybody's surprise, the 1980s saw a remarkable resurgence of "social pacts", which began in the Netherlands with the 1982 "Wassenaar" Agreement. Subsequently, Denmark established more informal norms of wage moderation under the D-Mark zone in 1987. And also Ireland embarked on a series of tripartite accords in the late 1980s, beginning with the "National Recovery" accord in 1987. To be sure, economic internationalisation and imperative of competitiveness rekindled the urge to find co-operative, positive-sum solutions to the predicament of adjustment in these small political economies, in retrospect, especially in countries that failed to respond effectively to the first oil price shock.

This is where the puzzle of the "Dutch disease" turning into a "miracle", that Jelle Visser and I tried to answer in our 1997 monograph on the Netherlands, assumes importance. Given that the Dutch political economy was and still is furnished with an exceptional and firmly institutionalised apparatus of accommodating employers, workers, and government interests, this edifice should, following standard corporatist theory, have incited an effective response to the first oil price shock. Yet, put the test, Dutch corporatism failed as an effective device for crisis management. Then, in the wake of the early 1980s recession, when, following received wisdom, corporatism should not be relevant, a typical bipartite social accord stood at the basis of the miraculous recovery of the Dutch political economy in the 1980s and 1990s. Under the threat of government-imposed austerity and mandated liberalisation, the social partners chose to negotiate, with unions wishing to limit the pain resulting from reform and employers hoping to forestall a government takeover of the policy-making process. The resulting Wassenaar Agreement, concluded in late 1982, provided for the de-indexation of wages, negotiations over work-time reduction and job creation, and the partial decentralisation of wage bargaining. This agreement ushered in a period of vibrant, negotiated reform in the 1980s and early 1990s that underpinned the celebrated "Dutch miracle" of rapid job growth. The Dutch experience reveals that wage restraint, as it lowers wage costs, not only helps to boost competitiveness in the exposed sector, but that it also creates room, albeit indirectly, for job growth in domestic private services. When investments picked up in the second half of the 1980s, the Dutch jobs machine came to operating at full pitch, adding over 100,000 jobs a year during a period lasting more than 15 years (Visser and Hemerijck, 1997)! How do we explain this paradoxical turn of events? The answer should begin with a focus on the relevant economic and social challenges of the 1980s, before turning to variation in institutional conditions and action resources.

In the wake of the second oil crisis of 1979, the international economic environment once more changed again significantly. While the problem of stagflation lost its salience, increasing levels of economic internationalisation and the sharp rise of real interest rates became the key challenges for advanced welfare states in this decade. The question of international competitiveness and profitability gained the upper hand in the policy debate. Rising unemployment and low growth were increasingly perceived as the consequence of policy failures rather than the unhappy but unavoidable consequence of exogenous shocks. This profound sense of dissatisfaction with past policies led to changes in government in a large number of European polities, irrespective of the political colour of ruling parties. In Britain, the Netherlands, and Belgium, mismanagement of the crisis of stagflation through fiscal relation, triggered a shift to a tight fiscal and a hard currency policy in the early 1980s under conservative governments. Policy makers themselves had learnt some tough lessons from the previous decade. First, they realised that their economies were in the midst of a structural transformation rather than cyclical downturn. In the 1980s increasing pressures on the public budget, mainly caused by rising unemployment, led to cut-backs in social expenditures and active labour market policies. In many countries benefit levels were reduced, replacement rates lowered, duration of social insurance benefits shortened, eligibility criteria tightened and more effective eligibility controls introduced. Second, policy makers came to recognise that any effective Keynesian incomes policy requires high degrees of trust between left-leaning governments and encompassing trade union associations, capable of foregoing the short-term profit of high wage increases in exchange for the long-term gains in terms of employment and price stability. While macro-economic and wage policy remained important throughout the 1980s, the direction shifted from an Keynesian incomes policy, which only worked in Austria and Sweden anyhow, to an incomes policy under the shadow of a non-accommodating fiscal and monetary policy.

Under conditions of open capital markets firms came increasingly under pressure to raise rates of return at a level corresponding to the real interest rate available in international capital markets. Many countries embarked on different strategies to meet the requirement of raising profitability. However, raising the international competitiveness in the exposed sectors is only one dimension of successful adjustment: In the face of shrinking employment in the industrial sectors and increasing fiscal constraints on the public budget the need to create more employment possibilities in the private service sector became evident.

Domestic responses to the 1980s challenge of competitiveness did not simply follow a path-dependent pattern of linear extrapolation of developments in the 1970s. As a consequence of the shift to a hard currency, the burden of adjustment was increasingly shifted onto the labour market and different systems of industrial relations. Policy makers have had to refocus their attention on competitiveness, bringing a decisive shift towards supply-side measures, especially in employment policy. Along with deregulating labour markets, many mature welfare states tried to contain open unemployment by reducing labour supply, mainly through early retirement and disability pensions. Interestingly, some of the countries that clearly failed to solve the problem of stagflation, underwent a remarkable recovery in the 1980s, partly as a result of hard lessons learned from past mistakes. Broadly speaking, we can distinguish one may distinguish two different basic strategies in macro-economic adjustment: The majority of countries had switched to a hard currency policy by the mid 1980s. Only Sweden still deployed strategic devaluations to boost competitiveness in the first half of the decade. While this strategy initially paid off in increased competitiveness, rising employment and improved public finances. Toward the end of the 1980s, increasingly tight labour markets and a credit boom (resulting from the liberalisation of the domestic capital market) leading to a disastrous overheating of the Swedish economy.

Within the hard-currency group, those countries that were able to credibly stick to a non-accommodating monetary policy and a tight fiscal policy while bringing about wage restraint, earned the profits of subsiding inflation and falling interest rates. In Denmark this clearly had a stimulating effect on the economy, outweighing the contractionary effects of restrictive macro-policy choices, which also paid off in terms of employment growth. In those countries that adopted a non-accommodating stance in monetary policy, wage moderation became the key instrument to profitability and competitiveness. However, wage moderation was achieved through very different strategies. In the United Kingdom wage discipline was primarily achieved by rising unemployment, radical labour market deregulation, and reductions in unemployment compensation. However, the price paid for deregulation and retrenchment was a sharp rise in inequality. Countries that were successful through a strategy of vertical and explicit coordination by way of novel "social pacts" were Austria, Denmark, Ireland and the Netherlands. But in contrast to the United States and United Kingdom, employment growth in the Netherlands did not come at the expense of major hikes in incomes inequality. International competitiveness of the German economy was strong for much of the 1980s, based on a high wage/ high quality production. Moreover, Germany was able to deliver a responsible incomes policy through horizontal and more covert coordination, in which wage demands of the trade unions were synchronised across sectors (rather than being part of a central agreement) and essentially mirrored the publicly announced growth in the money supply to which the Bundesbank committed itself (Hemerijck and Manow, 2001). Earlier than elsewhere, institutionalised monetarism in Germany refocused the political agenda away from demand management and towards supply-side strategies of cooperative systems of vocational training and education, jointly run by the social partners.

Countries that failed to orchestrate a responsible incomes policy based on explicit or implicit coordination, such as Belgium and France (in the first half of the 1980s) switched to a pattern of imposed wage restraint, which in combination with rising unemployment, brought about wage discipline, but – in combination with relatively high minimum wages – failed to provide for a sufficient level of flexibility at the lower end of the labour market, resulting in an inferior employment performance.

For Denmark, the Netherlands, and Ireland, it seemed that the effects of economic internationalisation helped to rekindle the urge to find co-operative, positive-sum solutions to the predicament of adjustment, bringing the social partners closer together. Danish, Dutch and Irish governments rewarded the willingness of unions to pursue wage restraint by delivering various kinds of side payments ranging from work-time reduction, tax cuts, increased spending for active labour market policy and vocational training. Increasingly important is the manner and extent to which the social partners managed to combine decentralised bargaining autonomy with macroeconomic considerations in wage setting. The Danish and Dutch (as well as the Austrian) experiences suggest that two-level wage bargaining systems, placing sectoral or decentralised negotiations within the confines of a broader national framework accord, were comparatively successful in combining macro-economic objectives with micro-level adjustment. Profitability criteria, as well as the expansion of the service sector have put a premium on wage flexibility at the meso- and micro-levels. Agreements in two-level systems allow sectoral bargainers to strike decentralised deals over productivity, training, and job opportunities for less productive workers within the framework of a longer-term commitment to macroeconomic stability (Rhodes, 2001). The Danish and Dutch systems of "organised decentralisation" (Crouch and Traxler, 1995) – involving high levels of regained trust, not only between the social partners at the national level, but even more so between sectoral negotiators and central leadership – were important for their success.

In the comparative literature, a new form of level-headed, more nuanced, institutionalist perspective was brought into the corporatist debate, both in economics and political science. The leading economist David Soskice took on Calmfors and Driffil analysis of the superiority of either fully centralised or fully decentralised bargaining, arguing that while theoretically the Calmfors and Driffil thesis relates to economy-wide coordination of wage setting, the empirical institutional variable they use is the degree of centralisation of bargaining institutions, defined as the actual location of wage setting. To be sure, where bargaining institutions are highly centralised, wage setting is likely to be coordinated across the economy, as in the experiences of Austria, Norway, and Sweden show. However, the reverse is not necessarily true. Less centralised patterns of wage determination may in fact be highly coordinated. For instance, in the well-performing decentralalised economies of Japan and Switzerland effective institutional mechanisms ensure a high degree of economy-wide coordination, prompted by a small group strong employers' organisations. Similarly, also the Netherlands and Germany are wrongly classified by Calmfors and Driffil. For both Germany and the Netherlands collective bargaining formally takes place at the level of industry; regionally in Germany and in large multinational firms as well as in the key metal and construction industries in the Netherlands. With powerful employers organisations in both countries, and tacit union coordination across the economy through wage-leadership practices, the degree of effective coordination should thus be considered as relatively high (Traxler and Kittel, 2000).

Follow up analysis, taking account of international trade and the interaction with the new hard currency regime, showed that bargaining at intermediate (sectoral) levels, if combined with some degree of coordination, might be just as effective. Surely, most European corporatist countries are very open economies, where international cost competitiveness is under pressure when wages and prices rise relative to world market prices. Especially, if economies opt for fixed exchange rates, as in the cases of Austria, Germany, and the Netherlands. Soskice and others contend that economic modelling should thus allow for a correction of the minimum sustainable unemployment rate, one that is sustainable with a medium current account equilibrium (Soskice, 1991: 51).

Newer analysis has focused on the manner and extent to which wage-setting arrangements interact with central bank independence in determining labour cost developments. Especially forms of implicit coordination between the social partners in the shadow of central bank independence have been found critically important by a fair number of comparative political economists (Hall and Franzese Jr., 1998; Iversen 1999).

In political science, a number of scholar recognising the neglect of the state in earlier approaches, embarked on a separate strain of research since the mid-1980s, developing a more complex, "state-centred" perspective, emphasising the state as an autonomous actor that critically affects the ways in which corporatist political economies adjust to shifting economic, social, and political challenges. In all corporatist political economies, policy adjustment invariably entails a significant and continued level of involvement by the state, whose purview for autonomous action is critical to promoting needed reforms and institutional adjustment. In fact, especially in hard economic times, when the relative scarcity of resources engenders competition among social groups and increases discrepancies between private interests and public weal, the state's coordinating functions are particularly important (Compston, 1998). Such adverse economic contexts tend to intensify pressures on policy-makers, not only to formulate just and viable policies that reduce economic uncertainty, but also to promote negotiation between social partners whom strained circumstances have made more likely to dig in their heels. During the past fifteen years, many governments in corporatist political economies have been instrumental to promoting reform and compensating for the policy failures of corporatist "joint-decision traps". As the economic picture has darkened, the same corporatist institutions that had once been credited with underpinning national prosperity came to be seen as the sources of sclerosis and failed adjustment. In response, the state in corporatist economies like Denmark, Germany, and the Netherlands, employed a variety of forms of intervention in an effort to fix dysfunctional corporatist policy-making structures in the 1980s and 1990s. At times, both states have used administrative and financial pressure to coerce the social partners into undertaking desired policy changes. At others, they have bypassed corporatism and imposed policies of its own devising, while in a few instances they have suspended corporatist bargaining or even dismantled it altogether. The Netherlands is a case in point (Hemerijck, 1993). Nationally distinct patterns of state intervention provide clear support for the two central arguments. First, they demonstrate that careful attention to the state's dynamic and shifting role in remedying political-economic problems is crucial to a more nuanced account of the dynamics of corporatist politics, particularly in periods of reform, fiscal austerity, and slowed economic growth. Second, they illustrate that corporatism is a dynamic and evolving process of dialogue and political exchange between the state and social partners, rather than a fixed institutional structure producing stable and predictable political patterns and policy trajectories. While corporatism works best when there is a credible commitment on the part of the state not to intervene, however, accumulated failures on the part of the social partners to perform delegated policy functions create both opportunity and political pressure for the state to do just that. In short, neither the resurgence of social pacts nor the suspension of corporatist institutions is predetermined, and, in the event of corporatist failure, a succession of carrots, sticks, and threats of the state may or may not encourage the participant actors to return to a negotiated process of reform (Hemerijck, 1995).

Renegotiating the Welfare State in the Shadow of EMU

In the final decade of the 20th century, international economic conditions and internal societal dynamics continued to pose tough challenges to mature welfare state and comprehensive systems of social partnership. *From without*, especially intensified European economic integration, most notably the introduction of EMU, put an extra lid on the redistributive scope of national welfare states. In addition, the swift liberalisation of capital markets in the 1980s pre-empted the kind of reflationary fiscal and monetary policy strategies that were pursued in the 1970s. Rapid economic integration both in Europe and the world economy led to increased structuring, raising the demand for social protection. However, increased factor mobility, of especially capital, put a lid on the supply of social protection, because of difficulties of welfare financing in increasingly open economies.

From within, individualisation, ageing populations, de-industrialisation, changing gender roles in labour markets and households, and new technologies in the organisation of work, trigger path-breaking efforts to recalibrate prevailing social policy repertoires and modes of social partnership. New life-styles, the transformation of the organisation of work and changing gender-relations were undermining traditional workplace and class-solidarities. Women's revolutionary role change in the labour market is arguably a leading dynamic behind service employment growth, new household forms and new gender relations. The open economy and post-industrial societies require more labour market flexibility in terms of work patterns, wages and working time. Flexible working hours are often a requirement for family friendly employment, and there is a clear relation between the ratio of part-time jobs and female employment growth. But the ability of part-time employment to harmonise careers with family depends very much on regulation, whether part-time work is recognised as a regular job with basic social insurance participation, and whether it offers possibilities for career mobility. Next, demographic ageing constitutes one of the most pressing policy problems throughout the European Union (Clark and Whiteside, 2003). In the area of pension policy, the challenge lies in how to allocate the additional expenditures that inevitably accompany population ageing. Increasingly it is understood that pension reform must be coupled to employment policy (Myles, 2002).

The upshot of the internal and external challenges of the 1990s was that the causes of unemployment, especially long-term unemployment were now far more complex than in the post-war decades of Keynesian welfare state. As a consequence, the standard repertoire of policy responses favoured in the days of Beveridge with its emphasis of demand management turned out to be ineffective to the perils of intensified economic internationalisation, modern labour markets, and gender relations. Policy attention and policy reform efforts increasingly gravitated, under the heading "to make work pay", to the core areas of the welfare state, i.e. social policy and labour market regulation, with specific attention to the removal of obstacles that hinder labour market participation (for the low skilled, women, and elderly men). In an environment of free capital movement, low inflation and budgetary discipline have become necessary background conditions for a stable economy. Persistently high public deficits and inflation rates are undesirable in themselves and incompatible with global financial markets. Moreover, high public deficits increase the debt burden of the state. As a result, the room for fiscal manoeuvre may become seriously constrained as interest payments on public debt rise.

Until the late 1980s the macro-economic environment was, by and large, relatively favourable. In most European political economies inflation and public deficits could be brought under control, while economic growth picked up. However, the reunification of Germany prevented a soft landing of European economies. As the Bundesbank feared, that monetary unification and sharply rising budget deficits might endanger price stability, it switched to a very restrictive monetary policy in 1991-1992. Pegged to the D-Mark, in part via the EMS, the other European economies had to follow suit. However, some countries were not able to credibly abide by the constraints on monetary policy imposed by the EMS. As a consequence Italy, Sweden and the United Kingdom had to devalue their currencies substantially. Partly as a result of the currency crisis, most European countries went into recession in the early 1990s, marking another rise in unemployment. As a result of high interest payments on the public debt and rising unemployment, public debt rose considerably in large number of European economies, notably Belgium and Italy.

In the wake of the Maastricht Treaty, policy makers became more willing to adopt cost-containment measures, often connected to a shift from passive compensation of social risks to the active promotion of employability. The Maastricht convergence criteria clearly operated as a trigger helping to overcome political resistance to welfare reform. The need to qualify strengthened the relative position of finance ministers and central bankers at the expense of other national actors. However, this has not provided windows of opportunity to launch labour market deregulation and welfare retrenchment. The fiscal strain brought by the Maastricht criteria, the promise to meet standing commitments, and the need to address new social risks curtailed the immanent danger of regime competition. With nominal exchange rate adjustments ruled out and fiscal stimulation greatly constrained by the Stability and Growth Pact, policy makers were pressed to seek national solutions within the heart of the welfare state. The large-scale endorsement of early retirement and other forms of paid inactivity was therefore seen as increasingly destabilising. This is why access to social security was made more selective, social rights increasingly took on a conditional character, and social payments were reduced. The underlying normative philosophy of "activating" social security reforms is one of reciprocal obligations: Welfare recipients must be obliged to accept employment or training in order to receive benefits, while the state has the obligation to enhance the employability of benefit claimants. Finally, the financial and institutional composition of national welfare states was reformed. Despite EMU pressure for policy convergence and other more endogenous challenges, ranging from the rise of a service economy, and population ageing, policy responses still diverged widely among different welfare-state types.

As a result of pervasive variations in substantive policy design and political institutional conditions across welfare clusters, universal trends like economic internationalisation and post-industrial differentiation confront each cluster of national welfare states with a distinct constellation of regime-specific adjustment problems (Hemerijck and Schludi, 2000). A particularly insightful version of this thesis is the "service economy trilemma", originally formulated by Torben Iversen and Anne Wren (1998), but elaborated in closely related forms by other leading comparative social policy scholars like Fritz Scharpf (Scharpf and Schmidt, 2000; Scharpf, 2001) and Gøsta Esping-Andersen (1996; 1999). The nub of this trilemma is the difficulty for national governments of simultaneously attaining budgetary restraint, earnings equality, and employment growth in an open economy, where international competition and technological innovation restrict job creation in the exposed (mainly manufacturing) sector, capital mobility inhibits fiscal expansion, and relative productivity remains low in the labour-intensive sheltered service sector. Employment growth in advanced economies, on this view, may be achieved either in well-paid public services, thereby undercutting budgetary restraint, or in low-paid private services, thereby sacrificing earnings inequality; hence governments may pursue any two of these goals but not all three at the same time. Since each of the three major types of welfare regime occupies a different position in relation to this trilemma, each accordingly faces a distinct set of policy adjustment problems. Thus the social democratic welfare states of Scandinavia have sustained high levels of both employment and equality by expanding public-sector service jobs, but encounter increased difficulties in financing the ensuing costs through taxation and borrowing. Liberal welfare states in Anglo-Saxon countries like the US and the UK, conversely, have created large numbers of private-sector service jobs without threatening the stability of public finances, but experience widespread problems of poverty and social exclusion among low-wage workers and their families. The conservative or Christian democratic welfare states of continental Europe, have maintained their commitments to both budgetary restraint and earnings equality, but only at the cost of low levels of employment in both public and private services. With social insurance benefits and funding closely tied to stable jobs, this third configuration confronts not only growing divisions between labour market insiders and outsiders, but also a vicious spiral of increasing payroll charges, rising indirect costs, and declining employment, which could eventually undermine the financial sustainability of the continental welfare states themselves. Finally, in Southern Europe, which according to Maurizio

Ferrera (1996) is best considered as a fourth regime cluster, the continental "inactivity trap" is intensified by strict labour market regulation. As a consequence, there is a growing gap between job market "insiders" and "outsiders", resulting in the social exclusion of the young and women (especially young women with children) in Southern European welfare states (Ferrera, Hemerijck and Rhodes, 2000).

Thus, similar external pressures and internal challenges facing existing welfare state models resulted in quite different employment and other social policy problems. No single best remedies seem available: only welfare regime-specific endeavours. This underscores the continuing importance of national political and socio-economic institutions, in spite of – or perhaps because of – the EU's increasingly prominent role in macroeconomic and social policy. The emphasis on variation in regime specific problems and policy responses should however nut blind us from an important element of convergence, namely the proliferation of new types of "social pacts". In addition to the 1980s examples in the Netherlands (1982) and Ireland (1986), we may cite the examples of Finland (1996), Germany (1999), Greece (1997), Italy (1993), Norway (1992), Portugal (1997), and Spain (1996). Not all of these pacts were equally comprehensive; some dealt only with one particular issue or missed the signature of important actors; some ended without significant results (see Streeck 2003 for the case of Germany). Attempts to negotiate national social pacts failed in Belgium (1993; 1996), France (1996-1997) and Germany (1996). In Sweden the attempt to establish a so-called Euro-norm for wage rises (1995-1996) also foundered, but one year later several unions and employers associations in industry reached a path-breaking agreement on conflict regulation and economic forecasting, preparing Sweden's membership in the EMU.

The proliferation of broad agreements between trade unions and employers' associations, usually at the central (national) level and often with involvement of or under pressure from the government, served to renegotiate existing structures or procedures for wages, working time and so on, and to promote wage moderation in line with the cost discipline and competitiveness norms imposed by the new hard currency regime of EMU. More important, many of the pacts also sought to obtain union cooperation over structural reforms of social security (pensions, sickness, unemployment insurance) and employment protection (Ebinghaus and Hassel, 2000; Rhodes, 2003; Regini, 1997). The real surprises are the Southern European social pacts, where the institutional preconditions for national pacts are particularly weak, and the potential for conflict – over both labour market and social policy reform – especially high (Ferrera, 1996). In Italy, the first pact was the "National Agreement" on the *scala mobile* in 1992, followed by pension reform in 1995 and the "Social Pact for Growth and Employment" of 1998. In Portugal a number of agreements were reached throughout the 1990s (without consent from the largest union). In Spain important agreements include the "Toledo Pact" of 1996, and the "Stability of Employment and Bargaining Pact" of 1997. All these national "social pacts" aimed both at strengthening national competitiveness (by means of macro-economically and micro-economically responsible pay settlements) and the promotion of social cohesion (by means of painful but not necessarily unjustified regime-specific adjustments in social security, pensions and labour market regulation).

Critics have often portrayed EMU as a Trojan horse for a full-fledged neo-liberal policy shift that will erode the underpinnings of the European social model (McNamara, 1998). Many believe that EMU, given its restrictive mandate, will reinforce low growth and high unemployment and thus increase pressures on welfare financing. Some even argue that EMU could undermine Europe's growth potential by triggering a vicious cycle of deflationary "beggar-thy-neighbour" strategies of internal devaluation through social dumping and competitive wage moderation. In these perspectives, EMU, like the single market, will greatly constrain the viability of Europe's mature welfare states. However, I contend that the EMU fixed exchange rate regime is not necessarily incompatible with welfare state sustainability and may indeed enhance it. A relatively strict fiscal policy helps to bring down interest rates, which (over time) may stimulate the economy, reduce the public debt burden, and strengthen the confidence of consumers and potential investors in the economy. This has already happened in some of the most chronically indebted European states, of which Italy is a prime example. There, EMU has been critical in allowing a more rational and controlled management of the public accounts (Ferrera and Gualmini, 2000). Moreover, if the structural budget deficit is low on average, there is more leeway to activate the stabilising function of fiscal policy in periods of low economic growth. Far from being a threat, as Ton Notermans (2000) has argued, EMU provided European countries with a favourable institutional set up for avoiding in the future the main problem that threw their welfare states into crisis in the 1970s and 1980s – their inability to prevent inflation in tight labour markets. To be sure, the paradigm shift in macro-economic policy allowed social democratic parties (back in power in most European countries at the time of writing) to underpin a new growth-oriented macro-economic policy with a new redistributive bargain, without the fear that this project will be undermined by an uncontrollable wages and price spiral.

In the 1990s, surprisingly Sweden, the corporatist social market economy par excellence, broke with its institutional legacy of seeking social partnership solutions to pressures of external adjustment. After a successful devaluation in the early 1980s, from 1988 onwards, inflationary pressures grew rapidly again, reaching two-digit levels in 1990. A range of different factors had contributed to that: The deregulation of the domestic capital market in the mid 1980s led to a speculative housing boom pushing domestic demand massively. In combination with a more expansionary fiscal policy, such as an improvement of pensions and sickness benefits, and increasingly tight labour markets it became extremely difficult to maintain wage restraint. International competitiveness deteriorated quickly which also became manifest in a sharply rising current account deficit. Rising tensions within the trade union camp had contributed to a gradual erosion of the centralised wage bargaining system and aggravated wage competition between the public and the private sector, undermining their capacity to bring about coordinated wage restraint under conditions of tight labour markets (Jochem, 1998). Confronted with an overheated economy by 1989, Sweden was faced with the choice between cooling down the economy in an attempt to regain control over inflation or to restore competitiveness by another round of devaluation. The government responded by a major shift in Swedish macro-economic policy priorities, whereby full employment was replaced by price stability as the primary macro-economic target and pegged the krona to the ECU in 1991, resulting in a sharp drop in domestic demand and the worst unemployment crisis since the 1930s.

With respect to the effectiveness of social pacts under the endogenous pressures of post-industrial differentiation and constraints of monetary integration, it is important to underline that the conditions for successful corporatist adjustment had changed considerably tremendously since the late 1970s. The revitalised social pacts of the 1980s and the 1990s, first of all, take place in the context of high unemployment, internationalised capital markets, and non-accommodating fiscal and monetary macro-economic policies. Under these conditions, wage policy not only has to be in line with price stability but also has to allow for profitability and competitiveness (Iversen, 1999). Under high levels of unemployment and increased exit options for employers, unions and firms face a different incentive structure, which made the unions have become the weaker partner. The uncertain reward for unions is that social pacts may fend off the prospect of uncontrolled deregulation. For their good behaviour unions receive work-time reduction and the promise of jobs and apprenticeship places. Governments seem to have gained political backing, lower levels of conflict and perhaps more fine-tuned regulation in lieu of legal intervention. Employers seem to prefer the slow calm of negotiated reform over the risk and upheaval of sudden political reversals, especially if the new deals they support competitiveness and allow for greater flexibility of working conditions.

Second, while EMU made national co-ordination, on the one hand, far more difficult to achieve broad macro-economic corporatist exchanges as a consequence of the loss of domestic exchange rate policy, on the other hand, a hard currency regime did reinforce the need to co-ordinate the rewards to be gained from monetary integration. Forced to abide by the euro-zone, in the face of widely varying levels of productivity and external liabilities, domestic labour market organisations capable of providing minimal co-ordination at national level seem vital. Social pacts thus provided, as Colin Crouch infers, a functional equivalent of devaluation in a period when this is no longer available (Crouch, 2002).

Third, governments have been taking the lead is persuading unions and employers to engage in social pacts. The presence of the state, as a provider of incentives or coercion is more strongly felt than was common in traditional Scandinavian and Continental corporatism. The anchoring of price stability and fiscal consolidation by an independent central banks and the Stability and Growth Pact, empowered the state in this respect, while unions have seen the scope for exercising political power reduced. They had to shelve their earlier drive for a more egalitarian income distribution. However, as modern social pacts aim not only at wage restraint but also at structural welfare reforms, policy initiatives of issue linkage and the co-ordination of reform efforts across various areas of social and economic regulation have assumed increased importance. Typically, the 1990s pacts try to engage the social partners in introducing more (negotiated) flexibility in labour markets and revising the incentive structure of social security systems.

Fourth, the 1990s social pacts no longer revolve around the dichotomy of centralisation or decentralisation. In many countries, for instance Austria, Denmark, the Netherlands and Ireland, social partners had already learnt that centralisation or decentralisation may be less important than co-ordination among the major players in the 1980s. Thus while the 1970s agreements were generally based on a centralised logic of political exchange, in which unions traded their cooperation for guarantees on public spending, job creation, social security or worker rights, neither of these tendencies lies at the root of the 1990s social pacts (Regini, 1997). The new social pacts tend to substitute informal consensual norms and moral suasion for formal centralisation of wage bargaining in a situation when the general development towards lower-level bargaining makes centralisation less likely.

Fifth, under the shadow of employer exit options and state threats, the institutional preconditions of the new social accords are perhaps far less demanding than in the case of Keynesian corporatism in the 1970s, which would explain the relative successes in atypical countries like Ireland, Italy, Portugal, and Spain. The institutional logic of the 1990s social pacts is indeed quite different from the 1970s corporatist incomes policy packages. They are more fragile, less institutionalised and less based on strong organisational leadership or authority, and, as a consequence, more dependent of effective consensus engineering. Regini (1997) highlights the degree of uncertainty and internal dispute surrounding these pacts. Emergency conditions (a looming national crisis; threatened exclusion from the EMU) play a significant role in bringing the unions on board.

In retrospect, the new macro-economic constraints of EMU and Stability and Growth Pact (1997) have not provided policy makers with a "window of opportunity" to launch bold strategies of labour market deregulation, hoped for by the architects of monetary integration. To the contrary, EMU seems to have spurred a resurgence of competitive corporatist solutions ensuring labour market flexibility and welfare state sustainability (Fajertag and Pochet, 2000; Ebbinghaus and Hassel, 1999).

Beyond the "Double Bind" of Social Europe

The democratic legitimacy of the European welfare state states is closely associated with the historical achievements of domestic social policy and consultative social partnership institutions. The national welfare state reached its full development in the post-war decades, when advanced industrial democracies were still in full control of their national economic boundaries. This is no longer the case. Work and welfare policy issues have since the mid-1990s become ever more intertwined with the Single Market and EMU. The current reform agenda in advanced welfare states in Europe reveals the increased importance of the European Union in areas like competition and trade policy, monetary and wage policy, pension and labour market reform, equal opportunity, education, immigration and social inclusion. European economic integration has changed the structures of markets and, as a consequence, the room for manoeuvre of national welfare states and domestic social partners.

To many observers, the Single Market, EMU, and Eastward Enlargement, reveals a clear tendency of "uneven growth" between the EU's economic and social policies: market-correcting "positive integration" does not keep up with market-expanding "negative integration" (Scharpf,

1999). Even worse, in the longer run European economic integration is likely to undermine the basic foundations of European welfare state. From this pessimistic reading, European integration creates a problem-solving gap (Scharpf, 2001: 362). As a result of market integration, the loss of national exchange rate and interest rate policies from EMU and the accompanying budgetary restrictions of the Stability and Growth pact, member states will increasingly be deprived of their capacity to maintain the kind of protective social and industrial citizenship arrangements, as they find themselves in a vicious cycle of deflationary "beggar-thy-neighbour" strategies of internal devaluation, "social dumping" and a "race to the bottom" process of competitive corporatism and welfare retrenchment. Ultimately, through the backdoor, in short, European economic integration will ultimately forge a fully-fledged "disembedded" neo-liberal European political economy.

I would like to make four comments on the argument that the European market integration is likely to destroy the edifice of the welfare state and social partnership. First of all, the empirical evidence suggests that "social dumping" and "race to the bottom" tax competition has so far been limited (Garrett, 1998; Swank, 2001). Second, EMU surely has brought about greater macro-economic stability in the single market. I believe that the margins for national monetary and budgetary of policy under EMU should be viewed of as "beneficial constraints", laying down established limiting conditions that encourage national policy-makers to concentrate on reforming and modernising industrial relations, labour market regulation and social security on the supply side of the labour market. The extent to which a consistent and independent monetary policy has in fact meant a liberation from national and international macro-economic political dilemmas is, I believe, clearly demonstrated by the re-emergence of social pacts and other more employment-friendly reforms in social security across Europe in the 1990s under the shadow of the introduction of EMU. Following this line of reasoning, Maurizio Ferrera and Elisabetta Gualmini content that EMU saved the Italian welfare state from complete ungovernability with the help of the social partners (Ferrera and Gualmini, 2000). This is not to say, in the third place, that the framework of EMU and the Stability and Growth Pact (SGP) already provides for an optimal macro-economic regime for the European economy. There are in fact (let us hope temporary) flaws in the architecture of EMU which become visible in adverse economic times. European Monetary Union and the Stability Pact came about in a situation of strong economic growth in the European member states during the 1990s. The key problem is that regime of EMU and the SGP does not do justice to the differences in economic circumstances across the member states. The European Central Bank (ECB) set interest rates in accordance with European-wide averages and development in the trade cycle, rather than nation-specific shocks. Under the Growth and Stability Pact, an unduly limited budget deficit threshold of 3 per cent of GDP (for three successive years) was adopted for the purposes of national fiscal policy. The architects of the SGP rightfully wished to discipline spendthrift governments, taking a free ride of EMU's low interest rate policy, thus punishing countries with sound fiscal policy with relatively high interest rates. Today, five years after the introduction of the euro, in Germany, France and Italy, the agreements to which the member states committed themselves under the Stability Pact are being observed less strictly than agreed to in the mid-1990s. Although fiscal discipline is in the self-interest of member states, it is nonetheless understandable (and up to a certain point even advisable) for governments to resort to anti-cyclical fiscal and budgetary measures when faced by a severe economic headwind. Inconsiderate and bold reforms of labour market regulation and social protection in a downturn stifle the market and is likely generate social unrest. And once a recession hits it is already too late to tinker with employment regulation and social protection. Moreover, it should not be forgotten that social security provisions like unemployment benefits have historically been designed to act as an automatic anti-cyclical economic stabilisers in a downturn. The policy lesson that can be drawn from the recent experience with the EU's macro-economic policy regime is that domestic fiscal policy should resume to play a key role in the stabilisation of the economy. Stability is a must, but a little more flexibility is called for. With the unduly restrictive limits on government deficits of the Stability Pact on top of the common monetary policy, individual member state have too little macro-economic room for manoeuvre left to stabilise their economies in times of low growth, as recent experience reveals. Future alternatives for the Stability Pact should allow for more flexibility in this respect, with possibly higher country-specific deficit thresholds. Perhaps new rules should be targeted more at the structural deficit and/ or the pace of debt reduction.

In the fourth place, empirically, I very much question the claim that beyond macro-economic constraints "negative integration" at the level of the EU will inevitably overrun domestic "positive integration". In the dynamic interaction between the EU market-making commitments and domestic social protection arrangements new forms of "embeddedness" have emerged over the past decades, as a consequence of the "political", not per se "functional" spill-over effect of European economic integration.

The Single European Act (SEA), ratified in the 1987, signalled the formal commitment of the Europe's then twelve Member States to a comprehensive market model and economic strategy that would foster increased trade and capital flows linked later in 1992 to an equally formal commitment to EMU in the Treaty on European Union (TEU), agreed at Maastricht. Both SEM and EMU served to symbolise the fact that member governments' capacities to shape economic policy making have been seriously constrained.

Towards the end of the 1980s, with the entry of Greece (1981) and of Portugal and Spain (1986), it became increasingly clear that accommodating so many policy traditions, systems of finance and enforcement, and decision-making styles was no longer feasible on a pan-European basis. This stimulated the development of more innovative, flexible institutional solutions in the 1990s. Ultimately, it was not regime competition between the residual welfare state of Southern European and the mature continental and Scandinavian social market economies, but the political confrontation between the European Commission and the United Kingdom (with other "unwilling" countries in its wake) that forced the issue of institutional flexibility on the EU agenda. During the negotiations for the Treaty of Maastricht, attempts to include the objectives of this Charter as Article 117 in the text of the Treaty failed because of a British veto. In a sense, the British opt-out from the "social protocol" marked the first step towards greater differentiation in European social policy development. With this compromise over the closer social policy coordination of eleven countries, acceptable to all twelve member states, it was possible for the group of eleven to impose guidelines concerning labour conditions, consultation of employees, and equal opportunities for men and women by qualified majority voting.

A second feature of institutional flexibility, ingrained in the social protocol, pertained to the formalisation of the European social dialogue between the social partners at the community level, as it allowed the European social partners to sign collective agreements. Through decisions of the Council, these agreements are capable of attaining the public status of fundamental guidelines, with minimum standards that permit much freedom of policy at the national and sectoral levels. Ultimately the social dialogue was introduced into the body of the Treaty (new Articles 138 and 139) at Amsterdam in 1997. The Social Dialogue provide an important institutional infrastructure for tripartite co-regulation and bipartite self-regulation as central features of the institutional architecture of social Europe. Since Maastricht, the social dialogue, an example of horizontal subsidiarity, has led to four accords on parental leave (1995), part-time work (1997), temporary work (1999), and more recently telework (2002). Moreover, with the encouragement of the Commission, at the sectoral level some 27 sectoral social dialogue committees have been established.

From the second half of the 1990s we are witnessing a third form of institutional flexibility EU employment and social policy initiatives. The ultimate goal of Europe's internationally-oriented business class, EMU had to be endorsed by national parliaments, and by the 1990s social and employment policy issues had begun to find their ways onto the European agenda. Moreover, despite welfare reforms in member states, persistently high levels of unemployment opened debate on common European strategies to promote employment and social inclusion. Finally, with a shift to the centre-left in the balance of political power across the European Union, a third institutional breakthrough contributed to a building and deepening of social Europe.

By explicitly recognising the legitimate diversity of national welfare states and domestic social partnership institutions, at the European level, new ways of coordinating national reform trajectories based on broadly formulated common social goals were ventures, following the logic of the Broad Economic Guidelines' surveillance procedure. At the Amsterdam Summit, the European Council unanimously supported the creation of a separate chapter on employment in the Treaty (Articles 125-130 EG [formerly Article 109n-109s]). In addition, the United Kingdom, under "New Labour", signed the Social Protocol (Articles 136-143 EG [formerly Articles 117-120]), which made it an integral part of the EC Treaty.

The introduction of a separate employment chapter in the Treaty of Amsterdam has to be understood as an effect of "political" spill over. At the time of the European Council in Amsterdam, June 1997, no fewer than 13 out of 15 member states had social-democratic or socialist governments, giving the Europeanisation of social policy a vital impulse. Through their combined efforts to tackle unemployment, they wanted to show that Europe was about more than just "a market and money". In a political sense, the Amsterdam Treaty should be seen as a "correction" of Maastricht. The European Employment Strategy (EES) was accepted on condition that no national authority would be transferred to Brussels, there would be no extra cost, and EMU rules would be fully respected. Every member state agreed to develop an annual National Action Plan (NAP) for employment to translate the common guidelines into clear-cut national policy measures, supplemented by – often multi-annual – policy goals. There is also an annual multilateral inspection procedure, in which member states evaluate each other's NAPs (peer review – see Article 128 EG). The social partners on the national and European levels are involved in developing plans to improve employment on their respective levels. The Commission plays a facilitating role by defining indicators, exchanging information, and producing comparative analyses. The (Social) Council can make recommendations to member states based on qualified majority voting and at the proposal of the Commission, but it cannot impose sanctions. The Council can also adjust EES pillars and guidelines on the basis of the insight and suggestions of the Commission. These substantive guidelines have increasingly been made more specific: at the Lisbon Summit, agreement was reached on an overall employment level of 70 per cent (60 per cent for women) by 2010. In Stockholm, the EES was further strengthened by the setting of interim objectives and the introduction of a target employment rate of 50 per cent among older employees (55-64 years of age) in 2010.

With the launch of the European Employment Strategy, institutionally, a new model of cross-national policy making through monitoring and benchmarking was inaugurated: the so-called Open Method of Co-ordination (OMC). OMC is a procedure which involves defining EU-wide goals, translating these into national action plans and evaluating them on the basis of commonly understood indicators and benchmarks. While accepting commonly agreed guidelines national and EU-policy makers take inspiration from "best practices" abroad with respect for national diversity through policy dialogue, peer review and policy experimentation. OMC delineates a procedure for fostering a "learning-friendly" environment in employment and social policy innovation and experimentation (Hemerijck and Visser, 2001) and it may provide a way to cope with the problems and constraints resulting from European integration in areas where national differences in interests and policy legacies limit common European solutions (Scharpf, 2002). The core advantage of the OMC is its potential for reconciling national diversity and democratic accountability at national level with common EU policy ambitions and measures of effectiveness through benchmarking and monitoring (Zeitlin, 2003). OMC facilitates policy initiatives in areas where EU competencies are relatively weak, where regulation is infeasible and impracticable. Open co-ordination has the potential to develop into a valuable addition to the modes of governing now available in the European polity. The objective is not per se to achieve common policies or to transfer power to the European level, but rather to share policy experiences and practices with an eye of effective policy learning. OMC is imminently more flexible than "joint decision procedures" or "intergovernmental negotiations". Policy choices remain at the national level, but are no longer pursued in isolation. Specific policy problems are defined as common concerns, and government agree to have them compared and evaluated in organised iterative processes. Clear and mutually agreed objectives are defined, which enable member states to examine and learn from the best practices in Europe through peer review, organised by the European Commission. OMC not only allows for diversity nut still exerts pressure on laggards and offers examples of "good practice" to poor performers. Not shared ontological aspirations, but rather common objectives in terms of prudent policy concerns, are essential. This allows policy makers to translate the much discussed but underspecified "European social model" into a set of agreed policy objectives (Vandenbroucke, 2002).

The central aim of the EES was to raise the level of employment participation throughout the European Union, allowing for different national strategies to contribute to this aim. Every Member State agreed to develop an annual National Action Plan (NAP) for employment to translate the common guidelines into clear-cut national policy measures, supplemented by – often multi-annual – policy goals. Based on evaluations of the EES we are able to draw a few tentative conclusions with respect to the effectiveness of the open method of coordination (Zeitlin, 2003).

In terms of outcomes, in the late 1990s and 2000, the European Union experienced slightly higher annual rates of employment growth while unemployment decreased somewhat. Although it is very difficult to isolate the effect of the EES on relative labour market performance, David Cameron suggests, on the basis of expectation of prior employment levels and growth rates, that normative and cognitive changes in domestic employment policy orientations, together with the "Europeanisation" of employment policy, in part do explain higher than predicted levels of employment, especially for women, and lower levels of unemployment in some if not all member states of the European Union.

In terms of agenda-setting, we clearly observe the increased political salience and ambition to increase employment rates, rather than reduce levels of unemployment, with a strong emphasis of activation, lifelong learning, gender mainstreaming, active ageing, inclusive labour market integration, through integrated partnership approaches. At the Cologne summit, in June 1999, raising employment, rather than fighting unemployment, was singled out as Europe's "most important objective of economic and social policy". Ministers and civil servants are being kept alert, and an activating approach towards social policy is diffused. In the process, national ambitions have been raised and translated in a large number of concrete targets concerning employment, education and training. Much more attention is paid to activation, and there is a strong focus on increasing labour participation (rather than subsidising inactivity) and better preventive adjustment between work and household responsibilities in young families. In committing the Union to become the "most competitive and dynamic knowledge-based economy in the world, capable of sustainable economic growth and more and better jobs and greater social cohesion", the Council set a concrete target for the overall employment rate in the EU (about 63 per cent at the time) at a figure as close to 70 per cent and it stated that the employment rate for women should increase from the current 53 per cent to more that 60 per cent by 2010. At Stockholm in 2001, the Council added a target employment rate of 50 per cent for workers aged 55-64 from the current low of 35 per cent. The widespread adoption of the above priorities reflects a broad shift in policy ideas in a fair number of countries where activating ambitions were rather weak before, like in most Continental and Southern European welfare states. Practically everywhere, we can observe much improved horizontal coordination of interdependent policy areas of social protection, labour market policy and regulation, collective bargaining and macro-economic steering. Also the integration of various "stakeholders" in processes of open coordination has been much improved. This, in turn, seems to have led to enhanced awareness of (similar) problems and (different) policy responses in other member-states across the Union. As a consequence, domestic policy makers increasingly use European frames of references rather than being exclusively bogged down by national preoccupations.

In 2003, the employment guidelines were revised. In June 2003, the Council invited the Commission to establish a European Employment Task Force, headed by former Prime Minister Wim Kok of the Netherlands, in order to re-energise the Employment Strategy. In November 2003, the Employment Taskforce, echoing the title of its report – "Jobs, Jobs, Jobs" – Kok reported that the Union was in danger of missing its employment targets. Creating more and better jobs was the most urgent issue facing the member states. In elaborating "best practices", the Task Force tried to strike a balance between the need for reform and the need to ensure social justice and fair opportunities, balancing flexibility and security as mutually supportive, not contradictory, policy objectives (Employment Task Force, 2003).

Conclusion

Looking back on past policy experience reviewed in this contribution, the doomsday scenario of the demise of the welfare state and its associated decline of social partnership, predicted in the 1980s, has not been borne out by the turns of events in the 1980s and 1990s. Especially in the 1990s, we observe a manifest convergence of substantive employment and social policy objectives, supported by the bi- and tripartite social pacts, with much greater attention to proactive strategies, a marked focus on increased labour force participation for women and older workers, and improved coordination between employment and social protection.

Throughout the period, the pace of reform has been very high, especially since the late 1970s. Thus far, the corporatist literature and the neo-institutionalist approach to comparative social and employment policy have assumed a relatively tight and fairly static connection between path-dependency and policy inertia: there are "lock in" effect, whereby policy choices made in the past become difficult to reverse, even in the face of serious external pressures. Institutional arrangements become resistant to reform because of high sunk costs, reduced co-ordination and transaction costs, and ingrained popular expectations. It is true: welfare adjustment and labour market reform offers an example of path-dependent policy change.

However, on the basis of high pace of reform observed in above tour d'horizon, it is my contention, that welfare adjustment should be studies as a dynamic transformative process. Much of Europe's welfare states and social partnership institutions have proven to be adaptive – not maladaptive – to external pressures and endogenous challenges.

A large body of comparative institutional analysis continues to ignore the transformative capacity of the welfare state. Contemporary research in comparative institutional analysis has thus focused primarily on institutional differences between national political economies and welfare systems or regimes, with reference to institutional equilibria that have become anchored over time through various kinds of feedback mechanisms (Pierson, 2000). In these models, state and non-state policy actor tend to conform to ingrained patterns of behaviour because it is in their institutional self-interest to do so. The emerging literature on "Varieties of Capitalism" founded by Peter Hall and David Soskice (2001) is a case in point. Hall and Soskice tend to view policy trajectories of both "Coordinated Market Economies" (CMEs), such as Germany, and "Liberal Market Economies" (LMEs), like the US and Britain, as particularly self-reinforcing and highly path-dependent. I take issue with this vision of policy inertia, which continues to plague much of the literature of comparative political economy (Thelen, 1999). Over the past two decades, many European states have – with varying success, but also failure – taken measures in order to redirect industrial restructuring by pushing through adjustments in macro-economic policy, industrial relations, social security, labour market policy and employment protection legislation, public administration, and policy implementation. Mainstream institutional explanations miss out on two crucial dimensions of policy development. First, institutional change and policy innovation is often triggered by substantive pressures and vulnerabilities, which call into question the institutional status quo and prevailing policy paradigms. Second, and irrespective of policy content, institutional capacities and power resources, the adoption of substantive policy choices is still an act of creative policy choice. Also power resources and institutional feasibility do not, by themselves, generate effective substantive policy choices (Scharpf, 1984). There is no straightforward relationship between institutional structures and strategic choices. Policy adjustment is neither simple nor instantaneous. Particularly, in policy environments that are rapidly changing and highly sensitive politically, policy adjustment is not a smooth process. Variation in institutional conditions does explain a great deal of cross-national variation in domestic social and economic policy making. However, external economic pressures and internal societal challenges are not automatically translated into regime-specific policy responses. Domestic responses to environmental pressures are not institutionally bounded, they are also shaped by changing cognitive and normative orientation in the face of high cost policy problems. Explanatory models of transformative policy change must account for how and why cognitive orientation and normative preferences change, so as to offer a more realistic and comprehensive account of social and economic policy making. This calls for a theoretical perspective on institutional learning in comparative political economy studies. This suggest, in contrast to rational choices theorising, that actors update their beliefs, cognitive and normative orientation, in response to information about the changing circumstances they find themselves in. In short, if we really wish to understand the substantive and political dynamic of welfare reform, we therefore need to identify the cognitive and normative orientations of policy actors in political exchange practices (Scharpf, 1997). Policy innovation is the outcome of puzzling – diagnosing the nature and magnitude of the problems at hand, setting priorities and identifying potentially effective solutions – and of powering – organising the political and societal support for the selection of particular solutions (Heclo, 1974). Policy reform is not merely "a contest for power" but depends also on "playing with ideas", the extent to which policy actors agree over the cognitive definition of policy problems, and the normative benchmarks for effective policy solutions.

Institutional perspectives on social learning, which currently experience something of a revival, have for a long time been neglected in comparative political economy analysis. This as a consequence of the contradictory influences of rational choice theory, which relies of actors with fixes preferences, and historical institutional analysis, which overlook dynamics of policy change and institutional evolution, other than through episodic institutional crisis, as a consequence of their over-institutionalised understanding of human behaviour. Preferences are not fixed, they are a critical part of dynamic adjustment processes, as institutional change effects the evolution of wants and desires. Social and economic policy making are based on fundamental cognitive and normative premises. Normative orientations define the objectives of public policy, i.e. the purpose of political authority (Lindvall, 2004). This is what the state is expected to do in response to social problems. As we have observed, the purpose of economic management has shift from full employment to low inflation objectives. Normative orientations concern, in the words of Margaret Weir, "the programmatic set of statements about cause and effect relationship and a method for influencing those relationships" among policy elites (Weir, 1992). To be sure, the normative decline of macro-economic management as the principal tool to secure full employment, is inherently bound up with the cognitive logic of discovery that fiscal and monetary reflation is ineffective in the face of worldwide stagflation.

Since the mid-1970s, macro-economic instability stimulated a sequential learning process through which the hard currency EMU was established. When domestic policy makers gave up fiscal and exchange rate policy to fight unemployment, this triggered new ways of thinking about effective social partnership. As macro-economic choices are inherently bound up with other social and economic policies, the decision to alter the objectives macro-economic policy has important implication for other policy areas. The imperatives of monetary integration put pressure on systems of industrial relations, leading to new adaptations in wage setting. New bargaining procedures, in turn, encouraged a search for more active labour market policies, as well as "activating" social security provisions. Politically, most of the steps in path-dependent policy innovation were outcomes of lengthy processes of transformative (re-) negotiation between political parties, governments and often also the social partners. The resurgence of social pacts since the early-1980s in countries like Denmark, Ireland, the Netherlands, Italy, and Spain reveals that reform processes are guided by far more than path-dependency in substantive policy legacies, formal political institutions and class politics. Before policy alternatives are placed on the political agenda, to be sure, the status quo must be considered unsatisfactory. Institutional learning occurs when the incentives for change are strong. Typically, reforms are preceded by deep political crises, major hikes in unemployment, government deficits, exchange rate pressures, and irresistible economic and political imperatives like EMU participation. An appropriate conception of policy making is to conceive of policy mistakes or failure as relative deviations from the rational expectations, and to view the correction of mistakes in a dynamic perspective. To be sure, Italy's political and economic crisis in the early 1990s, which led to a comprehensive redesign of the Italian pension system, was to a large degree fostered by the irresistible economic and political imperatives of EMU (Ferrera and Gualmini, 2000). Also the cathartic experience of the "Dutch disease" in the early 1980s is a good example of how policy mistakes generate positive learning effects: After a lengthy and painful period of immobilism, a process of self-correction in the Netherlands spurred a remarkable economic recovery without sacrificing core welfare goals (Visser and Hemerijck, 1997). The resurgence of corporatist concertation in the Netherlands is, of course less surprising than proliferation of effective "social pacts" in Ireland in the 1980s and 1990s, a country that is generally not considered to belong to the usual suspect of corporatist analysis. In 1986, the Irish government and social partners prepared their first central agreement for economic recovery, when the Irish economy was said to have reached its nadir. In an evaluation of the Irish experience of social pacting, the National Economic and Social Forum attributes five main effects of social learning to concertation: a shared understanding of the key mechanisms and relationships in the formulation and implementation of policy; a better understanding of the interdependence between the organised actors; a greater sense of fairness and sharing of benefits; a problem solving approach in which various interest groups address joint problems; and a deepening of participation at all levels. Social partnership concertation "involves the players in a process of deliberation which has the potential to shape and reshape their understanding, identity and preferences".

The nature of external stimuli, policy failures and effective sequencing are surely not sufficient conditions for policy change. The capacity to translate a crisis into policy innovation depends on changes in normative and cognitive orientation, triggered by high cost policy problems, power resources and institutional factors. Surely there is a major caveat to effectiveness of trial and error policy learning, and that is the adaptability of formal institutions and ingrained policy legacies. However, this suggests that institutional arrangements that allow for trial and error and reversibility are likely to be more adaptive than those requiring conformity and central direction. Political institutions may limit the repertoire of feasible policy options, but they may also act as critical resources, encouraging particular styles of decision-making (Scharpf, 1997). Consociational democracies and corporatist systems of industrial relations encourage the consensual or problem-solving styles of decision-making, characteristic of Scandinavian and Austrian systems of industrial relations. This contrasts the self-interested bargaining style in more fragmented systems, or the confrontational style in statist systems of industrial relations, like the French, with its deeply divided trade union movement and weak employers organisations. In the typology of Hirschmann (1970), the learning logic of policy concertation and social pacts is founded in the deployment of "voice". Participants are obliged to explain, give reasons and take responsibility for their decisions to each other, to their rank and file, and to the general public. Participants give up flexibility. In retrospect, the corporatist literature of the mid-1970s have tended to vastly and exaggerate the benign consequences of social partnership institutions and underestimated potential rigidities of social partnership involvement in economic policy-making. This because of its institutionalist bias. How well problems of economic and social policy coordination are solved, decisively depends as much on existing institutions as upon the normative motivations and strategic orientations of participant actors and their respective cognitive abilities to make sense of the complexity of the decision-making environment. Only naive academics and rash politicians would today claim that social partnership and the welfare state is directly, either positively or adversely, related to economic performance and social progress. The relationship between social partnership, the welfare state and competitiveness is contingent. There are certain welfare provisions and social partnership arrangements which do negative affect economic development and social progress. To be sure, excessively generous social security benefits, not backed by activating labour market policies, do undermine work incentives, contribute to a high tax burden and lead to high gross labour costs, which in turn impedes flexible adjustment and hamper necessary economic and employment growth. By the same token, in the long run comprehensive systems of collective bargaining create privileges for core "insiders" in the labour market, with high wages, job security and generous social benefits, at the expense of "outsiders" (Lindbeck and Snower, 1988). It cannot be denied that Europe's mature welfare states have over the course of post-war era been captured by organised interests who, given their institutional self-interests and those of their clienteles are increasingly in a position to resist reform (Pierson, 1994; 2001). Especially in corporatist political economies, the government's capacity to respond creatively to changing external pressures and internal demands can be severely constrained by social partnership institutions, given that it is forced to rely upon the often-self-interested social partners for reasons of societal support and policy implementation. Without effective consensus engineering, social partnership can become a barrier to effective economic performance and social progress. Under such conditions of a corporatist "joint-decision trap" or "immobile corporatism", the state becomes imprisoned in an institutional setting that turns out to counterproductive in social, economic, and political consequences (Scharpf, 1988; Hemerijck, 1995).

The historical comparative analysis surveyed in this contribution reveals that there is not, nor has there ever been, one single route to superior economic performance through social partnership and the welfare state. The belief that "coordinated" versions of continental capitalism perform "better" than "liberal" Anglo-Saxon welfare states counterparts holds true in some cases and periods, but not in others. The Swedish model was considered economically efficient and socially effective model to copy in the 1970s. In the 1980s the German social market economy took the lead. Towards the mid-1990s the Dutch "polder" model was considered a viable alternative. Subsequently, the Celtic Tiger and the Danish Lego-model proved turned into examples of a "third way" between neo-liberal deregulation and traditional social democracy. While the Dutch today envy the Belgians, the rest of us have turned to studying the merits of the more knowledge-intensive Irish and Finnish version of the social market economy. The overriding lesson of the comparative literature in political economy, industrial and social policy, produced over the past three decades, is that any assessment of welfare provision and social partnership as productive factors heavily relies on case-by-case comparisons and historical analysis. There are no models of eternal bliss to copy. Because national political economies, as consequence of institutional diversity in terms policy profile and modes of governance, there is an overriding need to consider the "fine" structures of the welfare state and social partnership institutions (Ferrera, Hemerijck and Rhodes, 2000).

The majority of scholars in the tradition of historical institutional analysis, reasoning as they do from the vantage point robust and self-contained national welfare states, remain profoundly sceptical about the prospects of somehow balancing social policy and economic regulation at the level of the EU. Since the Single Market Program, domestic adjustment processes can no longer be explained without reference to specific European initiatives that did not play garners a decisive impact on processes of policy development in the earlier decades of "embedded liberalism". To be sure, fully-fledged redistributive social policies on the European level are not to be expected. The EU will continue to focus of a "regulative" social policy. However, European social policy integration has come a long way since six Continental welfare states set out to establish a common market. Although social policy remains deeply entrenched in national politics, the social dimension of the European Union no longer merely holds a "Cinderella status" of good intentions (job growth, social dialogue), high principles (improving living standards, working conditions, solidarity and adequate social protection), but little action. While over time, the "hard" social acquis has surely "deepened", since the mid-1990s new, "softer" forms of EU involvement, such as the social dialogue and OMC, have become institutionalised so as to balance common concerns and legitimate diversity. The pace of change in European social and employment policy during the 1990s clearly rebuts the bias towards negative integration. Persistently high unemployment in the run-up to the EMU raised the urgency of a common European strategy. All the member states are today explicitly dedicated towards raising employment, promote social inclusion, invest in the productivity and skills of future workers, and enhance innovation in the pursuit of a competitive knowledge-based economy, with a distinct preference for social partnership involvement in the process.

Social policy reform and institutional change continue to be replete with contingencies, policy failures, learning processes, co-ordination and implementation problems and, obviously, shifts in the balance of political and economic power. This surely makes the nature of policy prescriptions necessarily conditional. There are no quick fixes. We are best to direct our attention more closely to particular combinations of policies, institutions, and economic development at different points in time, if we wish to say anything about the relative proficiency of corporatist governance and the welfare state under shadow of European economic integration.

References

Alvarez, R. M., G. Garret and P. Lange (1991), "Government Partisanship, Labor Organization, and Macroeconomic Performance", *American Political Science Review*, Vol. 85, p. 539-556.

Baglioni, G. and C. Crouch (eds.) (1990), *European Industrial Relations: The Challenge of Flexibility*, London: Sage.

Berger, S. (ed.) (1981), *Organizing Interests in Western Europe: Pluralism, Corporatism, and the Transformation of Politics*, Cambridge: Cambridge University Press.

Beveridge, W. H. (1995 [1942]), *Social Insurance and Allied Services*, Reprint, London.

Beveridge, W. H. (1945), *Full Employment in a Free Society*, New York: W. W. Norton and Company.

Boix, C. (2002), "Partisan Governments, the International Economy, and Macroeconomic Policies in Advanced Nations, 1960-93", *World Politics*, Vol. 53, p. 38-73.

Bruno, M., and J. D. Sachs (1985), *Economics of Worldwide Stagflation*, Cambridge, Mass.: Harvard University Press.

Calmfors, L. and J. Driffill (1988), "Bargaining Structure, Corporatism and Macroeconomic Performance", *Economic Policy*, April, p. 14-61.

Cameron, D. R. (1984), "Social Democracy, Corporatism, Labour Quiescence, and the Representation of Economic Interest in Advanced Capitalist Society", in: J. H. Goldthorpe (ed.), *Order and Conflict in Contemporary Capitalism*, Oxford: Oxford University Press.

Cameron, D. R. (2000), "Unemployment, Job Creation and EMU", in: N. Bermeo (ed.), *Unemployment in the New Europe*, Cambridge: Cambridge University Press.

Castels, F. G. (1987), "Neo-corporatism and the Happiness index", *European Journal of Political Research*, Vol. 15, p. 381-393.

Clark, G. L. and N. Whiteside (eds.) (2003), *Pension Security in the 21st century*, Oxford: Oxford University Press.

Compston, H. (1998), "The End of National Policy Concertation? Western Europe since the Single European Act", *Journal of European Public Policy*, Vol. 5, p. 507-526.

Crouch, C. (1993), *Industrial Relations and European State Traditions*, Oxford: Clarendon Press.

Crouch, C. and A. Pizzorno (eds.) (1979), *The Resurgence of Class Conflict in Western Europe since 1968*, London: Macmillan.

Crouch, C. and R. Dore (eds.) (1990), *Corporatism and Accountability: Organized Interests in British Public Life*, Oxford: Clarendon Press.

Crouch, C. and F. Traxler (eds.) (1995), *Organized Industrial Relations in Europe: What Future?*, Brookfield, Vt.: Avebury.

Crouch, C. (2002), "The Euro and labour market and wage policy", in: L. Magnusson and J. Ottoson (eds.), *Europe – One Labour Market*, Brussels: P.I.E.-Peter Lang.

Dell'Aringa, C. and L. Lodivici (eds.) (1990), "Industrial Relations and the Role of the State in EEC Countries", Brussels: European Commission, DG V.

Ebbinghaus, B. and A. Hassel (1999), "Striking Deals: Concertation in the Reform of Continental European Welfare States", MPIfG Discussion Paper 99/3, Cologne: Max Planck Institute for the Study of Societies (MPIfG).

Employment Taskforce (2003), *Jobs, Jobs, Jobs. Creating More Employment in Europe*, Brussels: European Communities.

Esping-Andersen, G. (1990), *The Three Worlds of Welfare Capitalism*, Cambridge: Polity Press.

Esping-Andersen, G. (1999), *Social Foundations of Post-industrial Economies*, Oxford: Oxford University Press.

Esping-Anderson, G. (ed.) (1996), *Welfare States in Transition*, London: Sage.

Esping-Andersen, G. and W. Korpi (1984), "Social Policy as Class Politics in Post-War Capitalism: Scandinavia, Austria, and Germany", in: J. Goldthorpe (ed.), *Order and Conflict in Contemporary Capitalism*, Oxford: Oxford University Press.

Esping-Andersen, G. *et al.* (2002), *Why We Need a New Welfare State*, Oxford: Oxford University Press.

Fajertag, G. and P. Pochet (eds.) (2000), *Social Pacts in Europe – New Dynamics*, Brussels: ETUI.

Ferrera, M. (1996), "The southern model of welfare in social Europe", *Journal of European Social Policy*, Vol. 1, p. 17-37.

Ferrera, M. and E. Gualmini (2000), "Italy: Rescue from Without?", in: F. W. Scharpf and V. A. Schmidt (eds.), *Welfare and Work in the Open Economy, Volume II. Diverse Responses to Common Challenges*, Oxford: Oxford University Press.

Ferrera, M., A. Hemerijck and M. Rhodes (2000), *The Future of Social Europe: Recasting Work and Welfare in the New Economy*, Oeiras: Celta Editora.

Garrett, G. (1998), *Partisan Politics in the Global Economy*, Cambridge: Cambridge University Press.

Goldthorpe, J. H. (ed.) (1984), *Order and Conflict in Contemporary Capitalism*, Oxford: Clarendon Press.

Hall, P. A. (ed.) (1989), *The Political Power of Economic Ideas: Keynesianism across Nations*, Princeton: Princeton University Press.

Hall, P. A. (1993), "Policy Paradigms, Social Learning, and the State", *Comparative Politics*, Vol. 25, April, p. 275-296.

Hall, P. A. and R. J. Franzese, Jr. (1998), "Mixed Signals: Central Bank Independence, Coordinated Wage Bargaining, and European Monetary Union", *International Organization*, Vol. 52, p. 505-535.

Hall, P. A. and D. Soskice (2001), "An Introduction to Varieties of Capitalism", in: P. A. Hall and D. Soskice, *Varieties of Capitalism: The Institutional Foundations of Comparative Advantage*, Oxford: Oxford University Press.

Heclo, H. (1974), *Modern Social Politics in Britain and Sweden: From Relief to Income Maintenance*, New Haven: Yale University Press.

Hemerijck, A. (1995), "Corporatist Immobility in the Netherlands" in C. Crouch and F. Traxler (eds.), *Organized Industrial Relations in Europe: What Future?*, Brookfield, Vt.: Avebury.

Hemerijck, A. (1993), *The Historical Contingencies of Dutch Corporatism*, D. Phil. diss., Oxford: Balliol College, Oxford University.

Hemerijck, A. and P. Manow (2001), "The experience of negotiated reforms in the Dutch and German welfare states", in: B. Ebbinghaus en P. Manow (eds.), *Comparing Welfare Capitalism, Social policy and political economy in Europe, Japan and the USA*, London – New York: Routledge, p. 217-239.

Hemerijck, A and M. Schludi (2000), "Sequences of Policy Failures and Effective Policy Responses", in: F. W. Scharpf and V. Schmidt (eds.), *Welfare and Work in the Open Economy – From Vulnerability to Competitiveness*, Oxford: Oxford University Press.

Hemerijck, A. and M. Vail (2003), "The Forgotten Center: the State as a Dynamic Actor in Corporatist Political Economies", unpublished manuscript, Berkeley: University of California.

Hemerijck, A. and J. Visser (2003), "Policy Learning in European Welfare States", unpublished manuscript, Amsterdam: University of Amsterdam.

Hirschman, A. O. (1970), *Exit, Voice, and Loyalty: Responses to Decline in Firms, Organizations, and States*, Cambridge, Mass.: Harvard University Press.

Huber, E. and J. D. Stephens (2001), *Development and Crisis of the Welfare State: Parties and Policies in Global Markets*, Chicago: Chicago University Press.

Iversen, T. (1999), *Contested Economic Institutions. The Politics of Macroeconomics and Wage Bargaining in Advanced Democracies*, Cambridge: Cambridge University Press.

Iversen, T. and A. Wren (1998), "Equality, Employment and Budgetary Restraint: the Trilemma of the Service Economy", *World Politics*, Vol. 50, 4, p. 507-546.

Jochem, S. (1998), *Die skandinavischen Wege in die Arbeitslosigkeit. Kontinuität und Wandel der nordischen Beschäftigungspolitik im internationalen Vergleich*, Opladen: Leske + Budrich.

Katzenstein, P. J. (1985), *Small States in World Markets Industrial Policy in Europe*, Ithaca NY: Cornell University Press.

Kenworthy, L. (1996), "Unions, Wages, and the Common Interest", *Comparative Political Studies*, Vol. 28, p. 227-268.

Kenworthy, L. (2002), "Corporatism and Unemployment in the 1980s and 1990s", *American Sociological Review*, Vol. 67, June, p. 367-388.

Korpi, W. (1983), *The Democratic Class Struggle*, London: Routledge & Kegan.

Lange, P. and G. Garrett (1985), "The Politics of Growth: Strategic Interaction and Economic Performance in the Advanced Industrial Democracies", *Journal of Politics*, Vol. 47, p. 792-828.

Lash, S. and J. Urry (1987), *The End of Organized Capitalism*, Oxford: Polity Press.

Layard, R., S. Nickell and R. Jackman (1991), *Unemployment: Macroeconomic Performance and the labour Market*, Oxford: Oxford University Press.

Lehmbruch, G. (1984), "Concertation and the Structure of Corporatist Networks", in: J. H. Goldthorpe (ed.), *Order and Conflict in Contemporary Capitalism*, Oxford: Oxford University Press.

Lehmbruch, G. and P. C. Schmitter (eds.) (1982), *Patterns of Corporatist Policy-Making*, Beverly Hills, Calif.: Sage.

Lindbeck, A. and D. J. Snower (1988), *The Insider-Outsider Theory of Employment and Unemployment*, Cambridge, Mass.: MIT Press.

Lindvall, J. (2004), *The Politics of Purpose. Swedish macroeconomic policy after the Golden Age*, Göteborg: Department of Political Science, Göteborg University.

McNamara, K. (1998), *The Currency of Ideas. Monetary Politics in the European Union*, Ithaca NY: Cornell University Press.

Magnusson, L. and J. Ottoson (eds.) (2002), *Europe – One Labour Market?* Brussels: P.I.E. Peter Lang.

Maier, C. S. (1987), "The politics of productivity: foundation of American international economic policy after World War II", in: C. S. Maier (ed.), *In Search of Stability, Explorations in Historical Political Economy*, Cambridge: Cambridge University Press, p. 121-152.

Marglin, S. A. and J. Schor (eds.), *The Golden Age of Capitalism: Reinterpreting the Postwar Experience*, Oxford: Clarendon Press.

Marin, B. (ed.) (1990), *Generalized Political Exchange. Antagonistic Cooperation and Integrated Policy Circuits*, Frankfurt/M.: Campus.

Marquand, D. (1988), *The Unprincipled Society*, London: Fontana.

Mayntz, R. and F. W. Scharpf (1975), *Policy Making in the German Federal Bureaucracy*, Amsterdam: Elsevier.

Myles, J. (2002), "A new social contract for the elderly", in: G. Esping-Andersen (ed.), *Why We Need a New Welfare State*, Oxford: Oxford University Press, p. 130-172.

Notermans, T. (2000), *Money, Markets, and the State: Social democratic economic policies since 1918*, Cambridge: Cambridge University Press.

Olson, M. (1982), *The Rise and Decline of Nations: Economic Growth, Stagflation, and Social Rigidities*, New Haven, Conn.: Yale University Press.

Pierson, P. (1994), *Dismantling the Welfare State? Reagan, Thatcher, and the politics of retrenchment*, Cambridge: Cambridge University Press.

Pierson, P. (1998), "Irresistible Forces, Immovable Objects: Post-Industrial Welfare States Confront Permanent Austerity", *Journal of European Public Policy*, Vol. 5, 4, p. 539-560.

Piore, M. J. and C. F. Sabel (1984), *The Second Industrial Divide: Possibilities for Prosperity*, New York: Basic Books.

Pizzorno, A. (1978), "Political Exchange and Collective Identity in Industrial Conflict", in: C. Crouch and A. Pizzorno (eds.), *The Resurgence of Class Conflict in Western Europe Since 1968. Volume 2. Comparative Analyses*, London: Macmillan, p. 277-298.

Regini, M. (1984), "The Conditions for Political Exchange: How Concertation Emerged and Collapsed in Britain and Italy", in: J. H. Goldthorpe (ed.), *Order and Conflict in Contemporary Capitalism*, Oxford: Clarendon Press.

Regini, M. (1997), "Still Engaging in Corporatism? Recent Italian Experience in Comparative Perspective", *European Journal of Industrial Relations*, Vol. 3, 3, p. 259-278.

Rhodes, M. (2001), "The Political Economy of Social Pacts", in: P. Pierson (ed.), *The New Politics of the Welfare State*, Oxford: Oxford University Press.

Rhodes, M. (2003), "National 'Pacts' and EU Governance in Social Policy and the Labor Market", in: J. Zeitlin and D. M. Trubek (eds.), *Governing Work and Welfare in the New Economy. European and American Experiments*, Oxford: Oxford University Press.

Rueda, D. and J. Pontussen (2000), "Wage Inequality and Varieties of Capitalism", *World Politics*, Vol. 52, p. 350-383.

Ruggie, J. G. (1982), "International Regimes, Transactions, and Change: Embedded Liberalism in the Postwar Economic Order", *International Organization*, Vol. 36, 2, p. 379-415.

Scharpf, F. W. (1984), "Economic and Institutional Constraints of Full-Employment Strategies: Sweden, Austria, and West Germany, 1973-1982", in: J. H. Goldthorpe (ed.), *Order and Conflict in Contemporary Capitalism*, Oxford: Clarendon Press.

Scharpf, F. W. (1988), "The Joint Decision Trap. Lessons from German Federalism and European Integration", *Public Administration*, Vol. 88, p. 239-278.

Scharpf, F. W. (1991 [1987]), *Crisis and Choice in European Social Democracy*, trans. R. Crowley and F. Thompson, Ithaca NY: Cornell University Press.

Scharpf, F. W. (1997), *Games Real Actors Play*, Boulder, Colo.: Westview.

Scharpf, F. W. (1999), *Governing in Europe: Effective and Democratic?*, Oxford: Oxford University Press.

Scharpf, F. W. (2000), "Economic Changes, Vulnerabilities and Institutional Capabilities", in: F. W. Scharpf and V. Schmidt (eds.), *Welfare and Work in the Open Economy – From Vulnerability to Competitiveness*, Vol. 1, Oxford: Oxford University Press, p. 21-124.

Scharpf, F. W. (2001), "Democratic legitimacy under conditions of regulatory competition: Why Europe differs from the United States", in: K. Nicolaidis and R. Howse (eds.), *The Federal Vision – Legitimacy and levels of governance in the United States and the European Union*, Oxford: Oxford University Press, p. 355-374.

Scharpf, F. W. and V. A. Schmidt (eds.) (2000), *Welfare and Work in the Open Economy*, 2 Volumes, Oxford: Oxford University Press.

Schmid, G. and B. Gazier (eds.) (2002), *The Dynamics of Full Employment. Social Integration through Transitional Labour Markets*, Cheltenham: Edward Elgar.

Schmitter, P. C. (1977), "Modes of Interest Intermediation and Models of Societal Change in Western Europe", *Comparative Political Studies*, Vol. 10, April.

Schmitter, P. C. (1979), "Still the Century of Corporatism?", in: P. C. Schmitter and G. Lehmbruch (eds.), *Trends Towards Corporatist Intermediation*, Beverly Hills – London: Sage.

Schmitter, P. C. (1983), "Neo-corporatism, Consensus, Governability, and Democracy in the Management of Crisis in Contemporary Advanced Industrial-Capitalist Societies", unpublished manuscript, Florence: European University Institute.

Soskice, D. (1991), "The Institutional Infrastructure for International Competitiveness: A Comparative Analysis of the U. K. and Germany", in: A. B. Atkinson and R. Brunetta (eds.), *The Economies of the New Europe*, London: Macmillan.

Soskice, D. (1999), "Divergent Production Regimes: Coordinated and Uncoordinated Market Economies in the 1980s and 1990s", in: H. Kitschelt *et al.* (eds.), *Continuity and Change in Contemporary Capitalism*, Cambridge: Cambridge University Press, p. 101-134.

Soskice, D. (2000), "Macroeconomic Analysis and the Political Economy of Unemployment", in: T. Iversen, J. Pontussen and D. Soskice (eds.), *Unions, Employers, and Central Banks*, Cambridge: Cambridge University Press, p. 38-74.

Streeck, W. (1997), "Beneficial Constraints: On the Limits of Rational Voluntarism", in: J. R. Holllingsworth and R. Boyer (eds.), *Contemporary Capitalism. The Embeddedness of Institutions*, Cambridge: Cambridge University Press, p. 197-219.

Streeck, W. and P. C. Schmitter (eds.) (1985), *Private Interest Government: Beyond Market and State*, Beverly Hills, Calif.: Sage.

Streeck, W. and P. C. Schmitter (1999), *The Organization of Business Interests. Studying the Associative Action of Business in Advanced Industrial Societies*, MPIfG Discussion Paper, Cologne: Max Planck Institute for the Study of Societies (MPIfG).

Swank, D. (2001), "Political Institutions and Welfare State Restructuring: The Impact of Institutions on Social Policy Change in Developed Democracies", in: P. Pierson (ed.), *The New Politics of the Welfare State*, Oxford: Oxford University Press.

Thelen, K. A. (1999), "Historical Institutionalism in Comparative Politics", *Annual Review of Political Science*, Vol. 2, p. 369-404.

Traxler, F. and B. Kittel (2000), "The Bargaining System and Economic Performance. A Comparison of 18 OECD Countries", *Comparative Political Studies*, Vol. 33, p. 1154-1190.

Traxler, F., S. Blaschke and B. Kittel (2001), *National Labour Relations in Internationalized Markets: A Comparative Study of Institutions, Change and Performance*, Oxford: Oxford University Press.

Vandenbroucke, F. (2002), Foreword, "Sustainable social justice and 'open coordination' in Europe", in: G. Esping-Andersen (ed.), *Why We Need a New Welfare State*, Oxford: Oxford University Press, p. viii-xxiv.

Visser, J. and A. Hemerijck (1997), *"A Dutch Miracle" Job Growth, Welfare Reform and Corporatism in the Netherlands*, Amsterdam: Amsterdam University Press.

Wallerstein, M. (1999), "Wage-Setting Institutions and Pay Inequality in Advanced Industrial Societies", *American Journal of Political Science*, Vol. 43, p. 649-80.

Weir, M. (1992), *Politics and Jobs*, Ithaca NY: Cornell University Press.

Wilensky, H. L. (2002), *Rich Democracies: Political Economy, Public Policy, and Performance*, Berkeley: University of California Press.

Zeitlin, J. (2003), "Introduction: Governing Work and Welfare in a New Economy: European and American Experiments", in: J. Zeitlin and D. M. Trubek (ed.), *Governing Work and Welfare in a New Economy*, Oxford: Oxford University Press, p. 1-30.

Zeitlin, J. and D. M. Trubek (eds.) (2003), *Governing Work and Welfare in the New Economy. European and American Experiments*, Oxford: Oxford University Press.

CHAPTER 2

Thoughts on France's Industrial Relations System

From Strike Action to Representative Democracy?

Claude DIDRY

Introduction

The notion of an "industrial relations system" is often linked with what one might call a "negotiation network", in which union organisations are said to play a central role in negotiating agreements with employers' representatives. In this classical view of industrial relations, this "negotiation network" is distinct from the legal sphere since it would appear to be a source of "self-regulation" independent of government and hence the legislature. The union, as a collective organisation, negotiates rules with the employers and plays a role in applying them via the threat of action against individuals who do not comply. The question of unions' "representativeness", often raised in France in discussion of the "decline of unionism", presupposes just such a model. Here, the decline of unionism and the unions' loss of representativeness are linked to the fall in union membership levels, thus calling into question their ability to represent employees' interests.[1]

The most radical question here is whether France in fact has a system of industrial relations. I would like to demonstrate here that this question only arises because the notion of a system of industrial relations is taken in the prescriptive sense of a corporate or "neo-corporate" framework for the negotiation of working conditions that does not apply in France.[2] Unlike in countries such as the United Kingdom, unions in

1 Among the wide range of publications on the crisis of unionism and of union representativeness in France, cf. Tixier, 1992 and Ray, 2004.

2 I understand neo-corporatism as the action of interest groups representing employees on the one hand and employers on the other, organised on a large (usually national) scale, to deal via collective negotiation with questions such as that of reducing wage costs in the fight against inflation. For a retrospective explanation of a model that had its heyday at national level in the 1970s, cf. Streeck and Schmitter, 1999: 137-180.

France "can rarely be likened to workforce cartels" (Jobert and Saglio, 2004: 79-93, 81) and are distinguished both by their political and denominational pluralism and by their smaller size. Their function is not simply that of social pacification through the signature of agreements, where the pursuit of consensus renders it impossible to distinguish between demands arising from the union's need for recognition from the other party and those arising from genuine efforts to defend of employees' interests. In France, a union is a legal person according to the law on the "syndicat professionnel" passed in 1884, and as such has the task of assisting workers in their "struggle for law" (as in the title of von Jehring, 1979). It is thus appropriate to include not only unions' ability to resolve conflicts by the signature of agreements, but also their function of raising difficulties "realistically".[3] It was thus that in the insurrection of May'68 unions directed employees' demands towards political discussion, separating social conflict from the anti-institutional rut driven by student radicalism.

Returning to the viewpoint of the actors themselves, to come closer to the practitioner's perspective (as suggested by John T. Dunlop in the introduction to his seminal work, *Industrial Relations Systems*, 1993), it becomes possible to go beyond the paradoxical liberalism of the corporate model and to envisage national law's capacity to structure industrial relations (including as an initial approximation laws, legally valid contracts and court rulings) particularly – but not exclusively –[4] in a country such as France. To illustrate this proposal, and by way of introduction, I would like to reproduce the comments made on the social progress of the Front Populaire by an important French unionist, Ambroise Croizat. As Secretary General of the CGT metalworkers' federation,[5] he wrote the following in the federation's journal in July 1936:

> Everyone must know his rights and act to ensure they are respected. Any contravention of social laws, any violation of contract clauses or of agreements reached must lead to intervention by a delegate or delegates. Should this be insufficient, there is the union and there are the industrial tribunals.

3 For Lewis Coser, 1956, "realistic conflict" is characterised by its function of social integration and is thus distinct from "unrealistic conflict" based on sentimental impulses that aim to overturn the whole social order.

4 This question probably arises for most societies subject to the rule of law, where relations between individuals tend to avoid reciprocal physical or violent coercion and are instead referred to (mainly civil) legal bodies as *cases*.

5 Croisat was also a member of parliament, the rapporteur on the law adjusting legislation on collective labour agreements in June 1936, a negotiator involved in many industries in the Paris region, and the future Minister of Labour after the liberation with the introduction of works councils and the social security system in his portfolio.

Furthermore, joint committees shall be set up in each *département* to examine any conflicts that may arise and to seek solutions to them.[6]

Including in this crucial period for labour law, collective agreements were not seen as forms of collective discipline to be imposed by the unions both on employers and on individual workers by the threat of action. They were seen as a part of the "web of rules"[7] that established the rights of each worker, that is of individuals who had signed an employment contract with an employer. The outcome of collective bargaining was an addition to an eminently legal institution that is crucial in labour law: the employment contract. What is at stake here is not a challenge to individual labour rights from "collective" labour law,[8] these are rights that workers have, rights that can be asserted in a specific legal arena, the industrial tribunal, and which define the contractual framework within which industrial relations are couched in a capitalist society.[9] What is at stake here is a balance of power within which employees act in concert so that a real relationship can be forged between individuals: the employer and the employee. The employer's management power is balanced by the worker's capability power, which is exercised collectively via bodies representing employees and individually via the right to leave one's post and to take the employer to an industrial tribunal. This power to resist and demand discussion of employers' orders is based on knowledge of the work and supported by a crucial legal instrument: the employment contract.[10]

---

6 "Il faut que chacun connaisse ses droits et agisse pour les faire respecter. Toute infraction aux lois sociales, toute violation des clauses du contrat ou des accords conclus doivent [*sic*] nécessiter l'intervention du ou des délégués. Si celui-ci ne suffit pas, il y a le syndicat et aussi les conseils de prud'hommes. Il sera, en outre, constitué dans chaque département des commissions paritaires qui auront pour mission d'examiner les conflits pouvant surgir et de rechercher une solution" ("La valeur des Lois sociales et des avantages acquis", *L'Union des métaux*, June-July 1936).

7 "The actors in a given context establish rules for the work place and the work community, including those governing the contacts among the actors in an industrial system. This network or *web of rules* consists of procedures for establishing rules, the substantive rules, and the procedures for deciding their application to particular situations" (Dunlop, 1993: 51, italics by CD).

8 On the transition from individual labour rights to collective rights, cf. Gurvitch, 1932, who takes labour rights as one of the manifestations of legal pluralism challenging the presence of the state in the workings of the law.

9 In Weber's view, capitalism can be caracterised by the "rational organisation of free labour" (see Weber, 2002). The rational dimension is attached to legal frameworks and the liberty in question is based more specifically on the contractual framework.

10 On the employment contract as a recognition and a limitation of the employer's managerial power, *inter alia* in the room he has for manoeuvre in drawing it up, before coming to a "modification" of the contract, cf. Waquet, 1999: 383-394.

Labour law is necessary so that industrial relations can legitimately be based on a contract that deals with a specific matter: the exchange of work for pay. It establishes the worker's liberty outside of work and, to some extent, within work itself. Without the worker's liberty, no contract is possible. This law, which is understood to be the basis for freedom of work, is a voluntary legislative act by the state to create rights that are not part of natural law, the rights of the worker as an individual who is capable of deciding on his or her professional future. Without the state's involvement, forms of community organisation fill the void. The community may be egalitarian, as is the case with cooperatives and mutual benefit funds. It may be hierarchical with management exercising absolute control of workers. Hence, at Le Creusot, under the iron rule of Émile Cheysson, the programme for management put forward by Frédéric Le Play was implacably realised and "the whole town was born of the factory and received its mark, whilst the master's domination of the worker extended to every sphere of private life" (Segrestin, 1996: 15).[11]

As a frame of reference that is ultimately defined by the legislature, the employment contract brings a crucial state dimension to industrial relations, *inter alia* by providing the possibility of referring a case for public authorities, in the form of a judge, to examine and resolve disputes.

What are the consequences of this? What do we learn from having identified the presence of labour law and hence of the state in the very heart of industrial relations even on the most individual level? My argument is that this situation, which may be specific to France,[12] forces us to define the references of industrial relations sociology in France. Following on from the work of legal specialists such as Paul Durand and sociologists and philosophers such as Georges Gurvitch, this sociology has for a long time been viewed as synonymous with "social law", that is an investigation of social and (most commonly) economic causality with the aim of explaining the legal conditions applicable to industrial relations. But on the contrary, to examine the causal reach law has on the evolution of industrial relations, in other words to escape the

---

11 "La ville tout entière naît de l'usine et en reçoit sa marque, tandis que la domination morale du maître sur l'ouvrier s'étend à toutes les sphères de la vie privée" (Segrestin, 1996).

12 But that is also undoubtedly due to a point of view in which the institutional aspects of the labour movement have been erased from the social history of the various countries, including Great Britain, where the complexity of common law has sidelined legal factors still further. For a comparison of the social histories of France and Great Britain that takes account of the important difference between the legal systems of the two countries, cf. Olzak and Wrigley, 1997: 237-254.

"economism" that dominates social law, it seems to me to be necessary to look at the sociology of industrial relations as a sociology of labour law. The sociology of labour law is an attempt to identify the law's contributions, both in giving representation to workers and in shaping industrial relations: it thus links up with sociology as understood by Durkheim and Weber.[13] The aim, then, is to enrich a body of research that, both in sociology and in history, has tried to break away from practices and social movements in order to examine the scope of these legal references both in explicit collective action situations and in normal work situations. It is difficult, for example, to discuss strike action without raising the question of what a salaried employee's legal position is:[14] this means looking beyond the focus on repressive law that takes the Le Chapelier law as a compulsory topic in French social history whilst ignoring the "revolution" introduced by the adoption of a civil code. Today, the slight drop in strike actions recorded since the 1980s is a major consideration for the French industrial relations system,[15] one which calls for a new look at the role of the legislature in the double institutionalisation of the actors and of the rules they produce. This drop in the number of strikes recorded also calls for an examination of the way public record institutions operate, above all those of the *Inspection du Travail*, whose staff, their numbers having been reduced, prefer to concentrate on dealing with workers' problems rather than on collective conflicts, especially in cases of redundancies made for economic reasons.[16]

To give this institutional dimension the attention it deserves, I shall take France's industrial relations system as a non-linear process that

---

13 A "Weberian" programme of research into law is based upon the causal reach of the law (Weber, 1979). On the role of law in the creation of non-community professional groups presented by Émile Durkheim (1893), cf. Didry, 2000: 513-538.

14 The works by Perrot, 1974 and Sirot, 2002, confine themselves to a varied collection of practices in the case of Perrot and caricatured historicism in the case of Sirot. The reader will search in vain for any illumination of the notion of strike action itself, since the institutional dimensions are ignored.

15 As is witnessed by the trend in the number of man-days not worked because of strike action, noted by Jobert and Saglio, 2004: 85, within the limitations of this indicator in taking account, *inter alia*, of disputes in defence of jobs, where strike action is a weapon used sparingly by workers in order not to precipitate the undesirable outcome of redundancy.

16 For Sophie Camard, who, as a political science researcher has observed the administration's practices in quantifying strikes, "Strike statistics are the rhythm section in the orchestra of 'farewells to the working class' [...] Strikes in the private sector are thus seen as a move against redundancy programmes, whereas the majority of disputes are still over the traditional issues of working time and salary negotiations" (Camard 2004: 23).

stems from the fundamental framework of the employment contract, and which aims at a form of collective representation that allies collective negotiation by the unions with the consultation of bodies elected by the staff. To demonstrate the importance of the legal structure of France's industrial relations system, I will first look at the development of the legal framework for collective negotiation at the beginning of the 20th century, then secondly at the mobilisation of this framework in the 1930s. Thirdly and finally, I will look at the historic compromise of the job security agreement of 1969 and its impact on an institution whose role in industrial relations in France has been underestimated, the works council.

Collective Bargaining in France at the Beginning of the 20th Century

The emergence of "collective regulation" in industrial relations is generally thought to have occurred in the course of the 1930s. That is, at least, the view espoused by proponents of "regulation theory" (Boyer, 1990). The developments in law and in convention that the strong collective movements of this era gave rise to or at least accelerated were certainly important, but if we are to grasp the dynamics at play it will first be necessary to examine the initial legal frameworks that were taken as their reference (as in Moutet, 1996). These can then be given their proper place among the many forms that rationalisation took at the time.

A law on collective labour agreements was in fact finally adopted in 1919 after a gestation period that had lasted approximately twenty years. Given this long gestation, which was part of the rare ferment of intellectual activity that is aroused when a political regime places legislative power at its centre, we can conclude that the collective dimension to industrial relations was not born simultaneously with the spread of factory work. It was one of the aspects of industrial relations that, in employment and capitalism, went hand in hand with the recognition that individual relations that were previously in the control of the corporation would now be contractually shaped.[17]

There had always been a collective dimension to industrial relations: it had taken new legal forms to keep up with a changing institutional

---

17 On the problems raised simultaneously by the shaping of industrial relations in industrial districts and the implementation of collective contracts regulating working conditions, cf. Didry, 1994: 183-211. This article presents the fundamental debates of the *Société d'Études Législatives* that I unearthed in 1990 at the beginning of my doctoral work.

environment. The largely legal problems that led to the drafting of a law on collective labour agreements emerged in a broad social context that included increased openness to the legal questions that arose for the actors of the era in their social activities and particularly in the world of labour. In order to grasp what was at stake, it is necessary to avoid the concept of market regulation as spontaneous social order being opposed to administrative, state, semi-state or collective regulation, and to think instead of a continuous process of evolution based on the civil code, which, for a capitalist society, was the fundamental legal corpus.

Strike Action as the Paradoxical Legacy of the Revolution

Regulation of industrial relations did not come from nowhere; it cannot be reduced to a period of anomie made good by the emergence of labour rights at the beginning of the 20th century. The revolution and the civil code are the foundations for industrial relations rules in common contract law, leading to specific recourse to the civil code in industrial tribunals.

From this standpoint, the main change introduced by the revolution was the recognition of the worker's right to leave work, called the *droit de désertion* by Alain Cottereau. This right is a departure from the Letters Patent legislation of 12 September 1781, the notorious *Lettres patentes pour entretenir la subordination parmi les ouvriers dans les pays manufacturiers* that were introduced after the Turgot reforms and were the basis for employers' ability to act via the criminal courts against the departure of their workers (Cottereau, 2002: 1536). After the tightening of masters' domination at the end of the Ancien Régime, the right to leave work was a legacy of the revolution, and one which remained unchallenged in the state of emergency created by the war and the terror. It consisted of the freedom unilaterally to dissolve the contract for the provision of services or of work as a realisation of the principle forbidding perpetual employment. During the period leading up to the adoption of the civil code in 1804, the issue was, according to Cottereau, to move the legal characteristics of labour relations linked to domestic service towards the characteristics of labour relations that applied to the highly qualified workers who would gather on the *Place de Grève* to offer their services at a fixed price. Hence, rather than perceiving employment as an extension of domestic service to the sphere of industrial work,[18] it was necessary to see the opposite, that of an enduring world of work in which workers would have real room for manoeuvre in determining the way they worked, as would be described later, in the Second Empire, in Denis Poulot's *Le sublime* (1980).

---

[18] As would be suggested by industrial complexes like Le Creusot in France.

The second transformation was less spectacular than the first, but it was very important in directing the legacy of the revolution and placing it in a framework that was to some extent corporate, with the introduction of commercial courts and industrial tribunals with the power to adjudicate in disputes arising from the performance of employment contracts. These bodies (along with the *justice de paix*) had to refer to the civil code in hearing cases and making their rulings. In this respect they tended to favour customary practice in the execution of contracts, in line with Article 1135 of the code. They were also part of a jurisdictional system that allowed the possibility of appeal. Their creation was accompanied by an unheard-of "judiciarisation" of French society, where the number of cases overall and the number of cases being heard in appeal courts both grew.

The overall outcome of these two initiatives was a type of collective regulation of working conditions that led to the effects of the Le Chapelier law being reread. The right to leave work could in fact be exercised by a group, meaning that workers had the means of breaking off relations with employers who did not provide an acceptable wage. The situation remained compatible with forms of *chômage de dignité*, as in the printing industry, where the union reimbursed workers unable to work at a rate equal to or greater than the minimum union rate.[19] The Le Chapelier law thus coexisted with the right to leave work and in the 19th century only really applied, with extremely varying and greatly overrated severity, to situations of disturbance, according to Alain Cottereau (2002). Overall, collective standards were able to approach what from the end of the 19th century began to be called strike action,[20] standards that renewed and established the customary practices that served as references in disputes adjudicated in industrial tribunals.

The Problems[21]

A general reappraisal of the employment contract covering the issues of strikes, conciliation, arbitration and union rates was the response to two major problems that arose at the end of the 19th century:

---

19 For a look at the vitality of workers' organisations in the 19th century, cf. Office du Travail, 1899-1904.

20 In French, the word for a strike, *grève*, comes from the place called *Place de Grève*, where workers would offer their services at a set price, i.e. with reference to established professional rates. It is significant that this word is more commonly used than "concertation", which harks back to the repressive language of the Le Chapelier law.

21 For a more in depth presentation of these problems and their resolution by a republican regime, cf. Didry, 2002.

1. Collective regulation by means of established practice allowed by the industrial tribunals had become unsatisfactory due to the increase in the numbers of appeals and employers' appeals. Rulings from industrial tribunals that favoured customary practice (often determined on the basis of end-of-strike agreements) were often challenged on the grounds that stipulations contained in individual contracts should take precedence. The problem became increasingly acute when the law of December 1890 opened the way for damages to be sought where open-ended service provision contracts were broken off abruptly. Faced with a contract explicitly stipulating renunciation of the right to terminate after a notice period, the parties and the judge found themselves unprepared to face the question of damages arising from its suddenly being broken off The problem grew with the adoption in December 1892 of a conciliation and arbitration procedure for collective disputes to be heard by justices of the peace (*juges de paix*), since the question of the legal value of what were then called statements of conciliation and mediating (*procès-verbaux de conciliation et d'arbitrage*) was at the centre of disputes raised by workers and their representatives.

2. The recognition of a right to unionise (introduced by the law of 1844) opened the way for the formation of legal persons who, by having this status, were able to enter into contracts. It was then a question of establishing whether the end-of-strike collective rate could be considered to be a contract, and whether, in the frequent cases where unions had no part in drawing it up, they could ensure it was applied to individual employment contracts, for example by virtue of their role as defenders of the interests of the profession. A ruling by the court of cassation in 1893 in the case of the weavers of Chauffailles settled the question by establishing that the employees concerned were free to renounce the collective rate for their individual contract and that defence of the interests of the profession was not an interest that could be applied in law, which depleted unions' influence.

Two twin problems thus arose at the end of the 19th century: the question of who was bound by a joint agreement, and the question of what rights unions had to bring cases in law.

The Law as a Compromise between Several Registers of Argument

The two problems went side by side in legislative debates, but they could not be resolved by a single law setting union legislation in order. Draft laws to reform unions as institutions that aimed to establish an obligation for employees in a union to abide by collective agreements signed by their union[22] were opposed by liberal criticism, damning in the political environment of the chamber at that time, based on defending freedom of work. Ultimately, it was the debates aiming to develop a draft law on the "employment contract" that gave rise to a satisfactory legal architecture for the question of collective labour agreements. This draft law was initiated from 1904 by a scholarly society of lawyers, the Société d'Études Législatives, as part of an overhaul of the civil code on the occasion of its centenary. It was fuelled by debates conducted in other organisations, in particular the Conseil Supérieur du Travail, which had undertaken an examination of the notice period in 1903, and the Commission de codification des lois ouvrières et de prévoyance sociale established by the socialist Alexandre Millerand at the end of his tenure at the Ministry of Industry in 1901. It was also based on the basic draft submitted by Alexandre Millerand and Pierre Waldeck-Rousseau (who was at that time chairman of the council) in 1900 (see extensively Didry, 2002). These two men proposed that a system of labour councils be organised, starting with the Conseil Supérieur du Travail at national level and working down via regional councils (*conseils départementaux*) to the level of factory councils.[23]

The provisions applying to collective labour agreements in the draft submitted by the Société d'Études Législatives were not agreed upon until the debates concluded in 1907-1908, and they represented a compromise between three lines of argument that I propose to take as being registers testing the institution being created, and which came out of the various debates held in parallel in several different places.[24]

Register No. 1: The key register in the creation of this new institution built itself around a new notion, that of a *groupement* (group). This was defined as a body of individuals linked to negotiators who represented them on the basis of a mandate, whether implicitly given or explicitly in writing. The *groupement* was envisaged in discussions as a first step towards what it was hoped could be agreed on in the chamber, the labour councils promoted by Alexandre Millerand, which were held

---

22 Reform of the unions was one of the main thrusts of social Catholicism, an extension of the *Rerum Novarum* Encyclical. Abbé Lemire's draft of 1891, which aimed to introduce into the law on unions a provision on the obligatory nature of collective contracts, is an illustration of this.

23 On these issues, cf Didry, 2002. On Millerand and the labour councils, see Rousselier, 1992.

24 These debates were held in three main fora: the Société d'Études Législatives, the Chamber of Deputies, and the Association Nationale pour la Protection Légale des Travailleurs. Echoes of these debates can also be found in the Assemblies of Freemasons of the Grand East of France and, in the church, the *Semaines Sociales* assiduously attended by a crucial lawyer of the period, Raoul Jay.

to be the desired outcome in the attempt to give structure to strike action. C. Perreau set out the types of group that would participate in negotiating collective labour agreements. The first type was the strike committee. The second type was the factory council "which, although it is not organic, would have a more apparent air of stability and permanence". "It is a group accepted by the employer, which submits workers' grievances to him every month" (*Bulletin de la Société d'Études législatives* (BEL), 1907: 535). For Perreau, these two types of group were crucial to the effective drawing-up of collective labour agreements, since they referred back to the requirements for conciliation and arbitration introduced by the law of 27 December 1892.[25] Collective labour negotiations were thus by their nature given an elective dimension, both through the way they were instituted by delegates mandated by their colleagues in a general assembly during a strike and through the permanent representatives who prefigured shop stewards and works councils.[26]

Register No. 2: A move to defend unions as the bodies who should represent workers in collective labour negotiations was reflected in comments by lawyers on the trades unions' right to go to court. The intention was, in spite of the Chauffailles ruling of 1893, to find proof in existing case law of the existence of a union's *interest* in ensuring the execution of collective labour contracts. The legal principle used by lawyers such as Marcel Planiol (1903) to justify such an interest was the provision in favour of a third party (*stipulation pour autrui*) existing in the field of life insurance. This holds that in a collective labour agreement, the union acts on behalf of a third party to the contract, the workers: the contract opens two rights to go to court, one for the workers directly affected by a breach of the contract, another for the union as a party to the contract.

Register No. 3: Liberal resistance[27] linked to the ideal of an entirely rational individualistic law, both in the activities of individuals and in the organisation of rules, led to the introduction of a cooling-off period of eight days for individuals who might be affected by a collective agreement either because of their membership of a union or because they had participated in a strike or a lock-out.

---

25 For Perreau, rejection of the arbitration and conciliation provided for in the law of 27 December 1892 would have led to the destruction of all collective agreements in France at the time (BEL, 1907, p. 535).

26 Having the role, *inter alia*, of ensuring the law and the conventions were applied.

27 Whose principal promoters were Paul Cauwès, then president of the Société d'Études Législatives, and Clément Colson. Both were economists.

By 1919, the regulatory experience of the Great War had settled nothing. The senate ultimately gave its backing to the draft adopted by the chamber in 1913, probably, given the liberals' domination of that body, out of a wish for damage limitation in the face of drafts to extend collective labour agreements by means of prefectoral orders that took their cues from the way the war economy had been managed under Albert Thomas' Ministry of Armament. But at the same time it was regulation invoked at macroeconomic level by the main trade union confederation CGT (Confédération Générale du Travail) and the Conseil National Économique and a form of elected representation for workers that were recognised in the legal wording. The law of 1919 on collective agreements created a link between two different experiences of collective labour negotiation: on the one hand, conciliation and arbitration via a *groupement* giving a mandate to negotiators; on the other hand the union as a specific organ of negotiation, and above all as executor of the agreement, *inter alia* via court action against recalcitrant employers.

In the social turmoil that marked the end of World War I and in that of the major strikes of 1919, collective labour agreements became a familiar legal instrument for the economic actors of the time, with a number of regional agreements being signed in the metals sector on the basis of the example of the Parisian metals industry.

The crisis of the 1930s changed that situation: rationalisation became a weapon employers could use in effectively blackmailing people to work. Employers went on the offensive against collective labour agreements that they considered to be damaging because of their inflexibility over pay. In this context, national confederations returned to a more pragmatic and demanding conception of collective labour agreements. Departing, at least for a time, from the grand project of macroeconomic regulation of workers' incomes, union organisations began to use the collective labour agreement as a lever to mobilise workers both at the level of individual businesses and nationwide against employers' rationalising offensives.[28]

[28] Cf. *inter alia* Aimée Moutet's analysis of the strikes against the rationalisation of the metals industry of the Stéphanoise region of France from 1934, which were part of a dynamic that was probably fuelled by the unity of political action between socialists, communists and radicals, which led to the Front Populaire's victory in the Saint-Étienne local elections of 1934 (Moutet, 1996).

The Recognition of Twin Representation Channels in 1936

An issue of *Le Métallurgiste* (published by the Fédération Unitaire des Métaux)[29] dated 1934 in many ways illustrates the impact that the Front Populaire's strikes were to have on France's industrial relations system. In the left-hand column is an article entitled "*Imposons les contrats collectifs*" (Let us impose collective contracts), written by B. Frachon; in the right-hand column is an article called "*Le comité d'usine*" (The Factory Committee), written by A. Croizat. The Front Populaire moved labour law forwards in response to this two-pronged expectation: on one hand it gave recognition to the principle that collective labour agreements could be extended by means of the law of 24 June that was drawn up in the midst of the wave of strikes that followed the election of a Front Populaire majority to the chamber; on the other hand, it also ushered in elected representatives for workers through the recognition of delegates in the Matignon agreement of 7 June, which became a provision that had to be applied if sectoral agreements were to be subject to an extension order from the Ministry of Labour.

The Collective Labour Agreements as an Expression of the Differences between Professions in the Face of Rationalisation[30]

After World War I, collective labour agreements were seen as a means of sharing out the productivity gains achieved via rationalisation. This is particularly apparent in the activities of the Conseil National Économique and in the approach of economomic planning and control adopted by the CGT. But the concept of rationalisation remained vague and was understood in many different ways. It was a concept that stemmed from employers' ideologies and referred to different means of reinforcing management power, as Aimée Moutet (1996) has shown (Moutet, 1996).

In the 1930s, the collective labour agreement came under attack from employers claiming rationalisation and wanting to be able to exert more downward pressure on wages. Rationalisation cannot be seen simply as a means of achieving productivity gains: in a recession, it is a lever for axing jobs and increases employers' scope to introduce wage reductions. Union strategies reflected the effects it had:

---

29 A federation that was affiliated to the CGTU (Confédération Générale du Travail Unitaire) and was under the direct (but secret) control of the Central Committee of the French Communist Party.

30 The analyses presented here are from Didry, Machu and Margairaz, 2000.

– the socialist CGT fell back on a pragmatic approach, seeing in the collective labour agreement a means of resistance to employers' rationalisation offensives.

– the Christian CFTC (Confédération Française des Travailleurs Chrétiens) sought to affirm unionism as representing employees, breaking away from mixed unionism aimed at uniting employers and employees in one Christian brotherhood.

– the communist CGTU (Confédération Générale du Travail Unitaire), and particularly the metalworkers' federation Fédération Unitaire des Métaux, saw in the collective labour agreement a possible means of bringing workers together in a strategy of "rank and file unity" via efforts at sustainable mobilisation.[31]

The result was a spate of sit-down strikes, starting with initial attempts in 1934 and 1935, culminating in the negotiation of sectoral agreements which vary to this day from one sector to another. The collective labour agreement as altered by the law of 1936 is thus a reflection of the differences between different systems of industrial relations at sector and company level, and also between different "worlds of production" (in the sense used by Salais and Storper, 1993). The law of 1936 in fact created a new category of collective labour agreement, ones which could be extended to the whole workforce by ministerial decree after an examination procedure intended to establish the sectoral nature of the agreement[32] and the credentials of the signatory organisations as representative of the workforce. It opened the way to a form of negotiation that began at the level of factories occupied by workers and moved up to regional levels, driven simultaneously by the unions and by the *Inspection du Travail*. Analysis of a corpus of the first hundred collective labour agreements published by decree in the *Journal Officiel* in 1937 has yielded the overview in table 1: A plurality of themes reflects the simultaneous existence of a plurality of forms of action and a plurality of economic situations. This means that explanation of the Front Populaire's victory and the developments that followed it cannot be reduced simply to the dynamics resulting from the spread of scientific organisation of labour in the homogeneous form of "fordism".[33] Work-

31 Bertrand Badie (1972) shows that this strategy led militants to leave aside the practice of "heroic" strike action leading to the strikers and especially ringleaders losing their jobs. The focus for these militants then moved to discussion with other workers in order to draw up platforms of demands and publish factory newssheets on a regular basis.

32 That is, having a scope beyond that of the company itself.

33 The aim here is to challenge this model, whose simplifications lead to an economics-based view that is reductive of historical and sociological processes.

ing on the basis of a corpus of the first hundred sectoral agreements to be extended, I produced three large tables giving an outline of the much greater diversity of cases of social struggle and economic situations that existed in France at the time.[34]

Model No. 1: The Corporative Tradition

Issues relating to conciliation and to the adjustment of the purchasing power of wages recur in most of the agreements. They play a more significant role in agreements dealing with the sectors with the strongest traditions of collective negotiation: this stems from the brevity of these conventions, particularly in their presentation of the professions and qualifications involved, which refer back to more local agreements. In the centre of this body is the national collective agreement for the printing industry, which has the role of a framework document in the negotiation of agreements to establish minimum acceptable wages for each city, based on cost of living indices.

Model No. 2: "Workers' Control"

A second model, whose most developed example is the metals industry agreement for the Saint-Étienne region, is based on making explicit the qualifications workers must have, introducing a form of workers' control (in the sense used by Dehove, 1937) at the level of individual businesses. The definition of workers' qualifications was undoubtedly of little real weight and remained limited to the three broad categories of skilled worker, semi-skilled worker and unskilled labourer. But it bears witness to a deeper activity of *analysis* of the way work was organised, based on professional knowledge that made it difficult, if not impossible, for employers to exercise total control of the way production was organised. It is also based on a very significant body of prior union work at individual business level, which had created platforms of demands. Collective labour agreements thus became a fulcrum for disputing internal classifications of workers in businesses, which management had tried to draw up unilaterally, by questioning the ways in which these classifications related to the three main categories of worker. Collective Labour Agreements (CLAs) carried with them an initial challenge to employers' authority, which was to be developed with the formation of bodies to represent staff at different levels: at business level with works councils, but also at sectoral level with the constitution in Saint-Étienne of a joint committee.[35]

---

34 By lexical examination of the corpus using *Alceste* computer software.

35 On this joint committee in the years 1937-1939, cf. Zancarini-Fournel, 1998: 178-192.

Table 1: CLAs: The Three Models of Mobilisation

Action model	*Register of conventions presented in the corpus*	*Negotiation conditions*	*Nature of product*	*Conception of work*	*Economic horizon*
Corporative tradition	Adjustment of wage purchasing power to cost of living	Start of negotiations in autumn 1936, after the first wave of strikes	Stabilised	Specialisation	Continuity of activity
Workers' control	Skills' classification as critical of rationalisation (class 5 in the analysis)	Leading role in the strategy of sit-in strikes	Constant innovation of the product	Individual specialisation understood as incorporated know-how	Develop-ment by training
Productivism	Yields as a basis for wage levels (class 6)	Follow-my-leader role in strike strategy	Standardi-sed mass products	Keep one's job	Reduction of work-force, mechanisa-tion of work

This model was based on knowledge of the work built on the workers' skills that had been defined at sectoral level. It embodied the limits of rationalisation based exclusively on the authority of the employer: workers' action was based on the difficulties this type of rationalisation faced in sectors where the product was constantly evolving, particularly in responding to public procurement orders with very high levels of technical specification, as in the manufacture of arms. This model of workers' control was capable of spreading, at least at regional level, into agreements concerning non-production workers, technicians and supervisors (*Employés, Techniciens et Agents de Maîtrise*), to the extent that it continued the examination at employee level of the skills needed to occupy a given post.

Model No. 3: Productivism

A third model, strongly linked to the textiles industry, sought to link wages with output. Here, workers themselves see the work as the manufacture of goods whose value has in a sense already been determined and for which it is therefore possible, even before production begins, to evaluate a worker's theoretical yield. Negotiations aimed to reconcile wage rises, a drop in unit production costs and a stable cost of living at national level.

From Factory Committees to Works Councils

A strategy was developed in the struggles of 1934-1935 that was at the heart of the Front Populaire strikes and caused unprecedented concern among employers: sit-in strikes. But beyond sit-ins, a form of elective representation was established that picked up the programme of Belle Époque socialism. In the Front Populaire strikes, one of the key goals of Unitarian and Christian unionists in their attempt to diverge from the legacy of mixed unionism was the formation of an elected representation for the *whole* of the workforce at factory level. Recognition of the workforce's delegates was a step forward in elective representation for workers. However, this institution ran into particularly ferocious opposition from employers, as can be seen in the mass dismissals that staff delegates suffered from 1937 onward. The role of staff delegates (along with the question of wage readjustment in line with the rising cost of living) was thus one of the main sources of disputes to be subject to the compulsory conciliation and arbitration procedure for labour disputes introduced as of 31 December 1936.

The recognition of works councils after the liberation, first via a decree in February 1945, then a law in 1946, to some extent completed the programme set by the unionists of the 1930s. The precise role of this body was not clearly defined, but undoubtedly tended to focus on social works. They were weakened after the split of 1947 with the divide in politics and the unions caused by the Cold War in France, relegating communist organisations to a "tribunitian" role.[36] However, this introduction of elective representation was nonetheless a major advance in the formation of a French industrial relations system. In the first place, it opened a space for representatives of the workforce, elected mainly in representative union organisations, to question employers' authority. And furthermore it completes what are known as the workforce elections (*élections professionnelles*) that allow the representativeness of union organisations to be established. Beyond unionisation as such, unions also compete for workers' votes in the election of representatives to workforce representation bodies and to seats on industrial tribunals.

[36] On this period and for a reading based on the pre-eminence of the political question in explaining the events following the war and the strength gained by works councils through the way social work was managed, cf. Le Crom, 2003.

Restructuring and the Works Council: The French Compromise of the 1960s[37]

In the post-war years, the industrial relations system encountered recurring policies relating to income, which limited the social partners' room for manoeuvre in negotiating wages. At the same time, the European construction begun with the Treaty of Rome was one of the central thrusts of Gaullist policy in the 1960s. The choice made at the time was essentially to integrate the French economy into Europe, whilst creating "national champions" that would bring together production forces in a given sector around a national business, the aim being to eliminate the redundancy known from the *cinquième plan* (Fifth Plan) of 1965 onwards as "*double emploi*". Industrial and financial concentration were thus accompanied by large-scale operations that began to be known as "restructuring" and were characterised by redundancies and site closures. It was against this background that works councils once again became active after the period of lethargy that had followed the enthusiasm of the immediate post-war years. The agreement on job security signed in 1969 was thus an important step, since it concluded a process of legislation and dialogue that had lasted throughout the decade and been accelerated by the events of May and June 1968. As with the Wassenaar Agreement,[38] its institutional scope remained vague. It was nonetheless periodically renegotiated when major reforms were introduced affecting economic redundancy[39] in order to attain a national consensus via the social partners. It also operated as a kind of ideas' box for new legislation, yielding for example the notion of "redundancy programmes" in a law of 1989.[40] The social partners' influence in

37 The analyses presented here are based on Didry and Aucouturier, 1997.

38 Cf. *inter alia* Doreen Arnoldus, "The Wassenaar Agreement (1982), the Timing of a Social Pact", chapter 7 in this volume.

39 In 1974, a few months before the 1975 reform that introduced the "administrative autorisation of dismissal" (*autorisation administrative de licenciement*), the social partners negotiated the first amendment to the agreement of 1969. In 1986, they negotiated a second amendment, after the removal of the *autorisation administrative de licenciement* and before the vote on 31 December on the new system of dismissal for economic reasons (*nouveau regime du licenciement économique*). At the time of writing, the government has opened an inter-professional discussion with the social partners over amendments to the legislation following the suspension of the *Loi de Modernisation Sociale* in January 2003. The particularly controversial nature of the question in a situation where delocalisation processes are on the rise leads one to believe, however, that collective negotiation will for now result in stalemate and that a political initiative will be the only way to resolve the issue.

40 Some authors suggest that "inter-professional agreements whose content is repeated in laws demonstrate a new mechanism for the co-production of standards by state authorities and actors in the world of work, which can be called a *negotiated law*"

industrial restructuring was indeed erased for a time with the prerogatives given to the *inspection du travail* by the "administrative authorisation of dismissal" (*autorisation administrative de licenciement*) introduced in 1975 and abolished in 1986. However, over the last thirty years the works council's role has ultimately been boosted by the functions of information and consultation that it has been accorded. This evolution suggests that the features of the French system of industrial relations have become more clearly defined, with economic and social expertise within workforce representation bodies such as works councils gaining increased recognition.

The Liberal Structuralism of the 1960-1970s

The notion of structure is often linked to a current in philosophy, structuralism, which in economics has mainly appeared in schools of thought inspired by Marxism. However, this notion has influenced many ideas outside of the most left-leaning spheres of economics and is to be found, *inter alia*, in the analyses of Jacques Rueff dating from the end of the 1950s.

In this context, the notion refers to an approach that I propose to call one of "liberal planning and control", of which Jacques Rueff is the most accomplished proponent. For Rueff,

> [...] social structures are the product of individual behaviours, the product of natural and legal persons, and the product of the groups they make up and of states themselves. These behaviours represent individuals' reactions to their circumstances. They are "a certain manner of treating the world, of being in the world or of existing".[41]

For Rueff, structures are linked to the behaviours of individuals and are therefore flexible. The Common Market thus represented an upheaval of all behaviours, that is, the *social structures* that resisted it.[42]

("Les accords interprofessionnels, dont le contenu est repris par des lois, mettent en évidence un mécanisme original de co-production de normes par les pouvoirs publics et les acteurs du monde du travail qualifié de *loi négociée*) (Jobert and Saglio, 2004: 85).

41 "Les structures sociales sont le produit des comportements individuels, celui des personnes physiques aussi bien que des personnes morales, celui des groupements qu'elles constituent aussi bien que celui des États. Ces comportements traduisent la réaction des individus aux circonstances qui les entourent. Ils sont 'une certaine manière de traiter le monde, d'être au monde ou d'exister'" (Rueff, 1979, 168) (First published in 1957). The quote inside the citation refers to Merleau-Ponty, 1942.

42 He wrote in 1957-1958: "It is not unimaginable that the removal of direct and indirect protection measures, under whose shelter *existing economic structures* took shape, should cause difficult or even painful transitions ("Il n'est pas imaginable que la suppression des mesures de protection directes et indirectes, à l'abri desquelles se

For this, new rules were needed (a Treaty), and new institutions to ensure the rules were applied. Rueff saw the market as a structuring institutional entity that would require changes in the existing national structures. Rueff thus saw the EEC Treaty as opening states up to new forms of policy in respect of full employment that aimed to maximise social wellbeing within a single country by raising barriers to the optimal location of production activities (Rueff, 1979: 333).

In France, Rueff's analysis marked the start of a period of large-scale restructuring in the mining and metals industries from the beginning of the 1960s onwards. The restructuring of large companies aimed to eliminate "redundancy" at national level in order to increase national economic competitiveness based around "national champions". This restructuring was thus the result of an industrial policy that was presented as an unquestionable priority and was at the centre of the Fifth Plan from 1965 onwards. It had a social component based on two important social rights: unemployment benefit, with the "UNEDIC agreement"[43] of 1958 (which was made obligatory by the government in 1959), and retirement rules allowing "interim pensions" financed by the National Employment Fund (Fonds National pour l'Emploi) set up in 1963. It was in this context that works councils' rights to be consulted and receive information became more precisely defined, with, *inter alia*, a law passed in 1966 and a concern for the increased involvement of staff representative bodies affirmed by the general multi-industry agreement of 1969.

A book written by a worker-priest (Combe, 1969) allows us to understand restructuring from the viewpoint of those most directly involved, workers and management. The book in fact tells of the closure, in 1964, of the establishment where the author was working. This operation was preceded by an important change in the management of the business, which was bought from the family that had founded it by a merchant bank, and with the arrival of a CEO from the world of banking, who had been educated at the École Nationale d'Administration. This new CEO pursued a policy of mass acquisitions of businesses. His vocabulary was dominated by terms of "structures", leading to the notions of "restructuring" and "organisation". These two terms were often linked to the idea of simplification: "As you can see, this entire structure we have created is intended to simplify the way "Paris" and

---

sont dessinées les *structures économiques existantes*, n'entraîne pas des adaptations difficiles, voire douloureuses") (Rueff, 1979, 344).

[43] UNEDIC: Union nationale interprofessionnelle pour l'emploi dans l'industrie et le commerce, the Employment Office.

the executive board operate, by creating clear responsibilities. We know who is responsible for what in each sector" (Combe, 1969: 188).

The "economic reason" for redundancies here takes the form of a constraint arising from change beyond the individuals concerned: the economic climate means that "the operation is irreversible". But the CEO agrees to "make solving the resulting human problem a priority" (Combe, 1969: 236) in responding to these economic constraints. Management representatives insist on the importance of "reclassification" in responding to the "human problems" resulting from restructuring. The director of the site closed as part of the 1964 restructuring thus declares: "I regret this shock. I am sorry for the staff. If we resolve the reclassification well, the trauma will soon disappear". Reporting on the operation the day after the company has made 500 staff redundant, management writes in a communiqué that "Staff have been reclassified without difficulty [...] The operation is complete: on the social level it has been achieved in an exemplary way, without conflict and without difficulty, in spite of involving several hundred persons" (261). The "reclassifications" involve forty-nine "old workers" being taken on by the National Employment Funds. The works council is then called on to debate the "accompanying" measures to be applied alongside restructuring that is already presented as a fait accompli: for Maurice Combe, this new role is an "alibi" for the policy decisions on restructuring. This alibi role was redoubled by the results of the reclassification projects, which according to Combe (who confronted the management's plans with results that at the time were being regularly published in the newspaper *Le Monde*) fell far short of the ambitions professed by management during consultations with the works council.

Beyond the social criticism of a man of convictions, Combe's book allows us to see the way the vocabulary of restructuring was formed and propagated, with terms such as "interim pensions", "reclassification", and "accompanying measures". The problem of employment and unemployment began to appear from the end of the 1950s (with the signature of the UNEDIC agreement on unemployment benefit by the social partners and its extension by the government in 1959) and took on a new intensity after a decade of restructuring and industrial policy. By the end of the 1960s, the question of economic redundancies had become a matter of public debate and a real part of the political agenda that was continually being driven by the Pompidou government, which wanted to institute social accompanying measures for redundancies resulting from its industrial policy.

The Grenelle Agreements and Job Security: The Invisible Handshake?

Alongside social accompanying measures for restructuring, one of the most important aspects of the Pompidou government's social policy was the policy of keeping wages under control in order to limit inflation. This policy led to a freeze on wage negotiations under the control, *inter alia*, of the employers' association Conseil National du Patronat Français (CNPF), which relayed government policy to its members (cf. Machu, 2004). The Grenelle agreements concluded on 27 May 1968, which framed concessions made by employers and the government, were a significant remedy, since they led to a near-30 per cent rise in the SMIG (minimum guaranteed interprofessional wage) and laid out the basis for monthly payment of wages.

The Grenelle agreement and the movement of May 1968 also led to the interprofessional agreement on job security (*accord interprofessionnel sur la sécurité de l'emploi*) of 10 February 1969, which introduced the broad procedural rules for collective redundancies. This agreement attracted a broad consensus, since it was signed by the CNPF and all the representative unions, *inter alia* the CFDT and the CGT. It enshrined union recognition of employers' right to make adjustments to the workforce, in return for the creation of a procedure allowing solutions to be sought for employees made redundant. It was based around two points: (1) A definition of the role of joint committees for employment set up on differing geographic levels for each profession. These committees were given an arbitration role in case of serious problems within the works council.[44] (2) Consultation of the works council, which is the framework linking the various legal regimes for redundancies that have followed since. This section was in continuity with the order of 22 February 1945 on job placement control and the law of 18 June 1966, which made it obligatory to consult the works council if redundancies were to be made. It set out the periods between the consultation meeting with the works council and the management decision to make redundancies, and the conditions under which qualified workers could be "downgraded" and thus avoid redundancy.

The combination of the Grenelle agreement in May 1968 and the agreement on job security that followed it closely in 1969 seems to me to outline what some economists have presented as being an "invisible handshake" between employers and employees. For Olivier Garnier, for

[44] These committees, combined with the procedures for consultation of the works councils, are in some ways reminiscent of the structure of the *conseils du travail* proposed, in his own time, by Alexandre Millerand.

example, transactions between employers and employees are a manifestation of a particular kind of market where the price remains intangible, in which the transactions bring a degree of predictability to employees' wages whilst they for their part seem to concede to the employer the right to adjust staffing levels in order to keep the business as profitable as possible (Garnier, 1986). In these circumstances the term "market" seems relatively ill-suited for application to labour, since supply and demand are not measured or adjusted via flexibility in the price of the goods. This economic model does, however, take acceptable account of one of the characteristics of employment, freedom of work in the form of both parties' right unilaterally to break off the employment contract. The social partners have recognised employers as having this right as part of the "politique contractuelle" (Machu, 2004) pursued in France since the Pompidou government. For employers, it was protected by new guarantees with the introduction of the "administrative authorisation of dismissal" (*autorisation administrative de licenciement*) in 1975. Authorised redundancy effectively became immune to attack from employees and their representatives, since the basis for both the administrative decision and the employer's decision had simultaneously to be challenged.[45] Under the Fabius government (from 1984 to 1986), this administrative authorisation system allowed the state to carry out large-scale restructuring in nationalised companies, reaching the record level for economic redundancies of 600,000 in 1986.

The Role of Works Councils in Economic Decision-Making: The Law Opens a New Field of Negotiation

The removal of the *autorisation administrative de licenciement* in 1986 opened a new period, in which guarantees to employees and the right to high-quality information and consultation became priorities for the legislature. Provisions that had been at the drawing-board stage in the agreement on job security in 1969 now progressively became part of the legal language, and the procedural rules for collective redundancies were progressively fleshed out in Book III of the *Code du Travail*. These provisions were thus late in coming, and were in fact subsequent to a European directive adopted in 1975, which set out a procedure for informing and consulting employees' representatives in cases of collective redundancies.

---

45 Authorisation was obtained in most cases (a figure of above 80 per cent has been spoken of), and this was reinforced by the way authorisation was conducted: by way of derogation from the principles of administrative law, the absence of a response from the administration within one month of the employer's notifying the *Inspection du Travail* of the proposed redundancies could in itself be taken as authorisation.

Since the law of 31 December 1986, works councils have tended to become more combative, since they are now better supported by employment law. From this point onwards, the requirement for employers to provide accompanying measures where redundancies are planned was supplemented by provisions in the Auroux law of 1984 that give the works council recourse to an independent economic expert paid for by the employer. A number of legal actions resulted from this, between 1986 and 1989, in which works councils and their experts attempted to establish time periods that would allow a consistent economic evaluation of the situation to be produced. This power to go to court was relaunched in 1993, with a law stipulating that redundancy programmes must contain reclassification measures, and that without these the redundancy procedure as a whole was null and void. The legislature thus played an important role in granting or denying access to the courts to employees and their representatives, and in challenging the unilateral nature of the decision to effect redundancies.

The movement that began to form from the second half of the 1980s thus turns out to be more complex than is implied by a model such as the "invisible handshake" (Garnier, 1986). The law defines a regime for "redundancies for economic reasons", which confirms the employer's right to make workers redundant in order to increase the profitability of the business. It thus provides a new instrument for human resource management. This instrument reached optimum effectiveness with the law of 1989 limiting the period within which the works council's expert could act to three weeks, defusing the controversy introduced by the law of 1986. This 1989 law thus opened the way for large-scale redundancies in the early 1990s, in a climate where the fight against overstaffing became a key signal to attract shareholders. However, the boom in collective redundancies in 1992 shook the left's majority in the *Assemblée Nationale* (Parliament). In January 1993, as a result of joint moves by socialist and communist parliamentary groups, parliament adopted a law setting out an obligation for redundancy programmes to include reclassification measures on penalty of nullity. By opening the way for works councils to call for a redundancy procedure to be nullified in a *tribunal de grande instance* (district court), this reform led to new case law on collective redundancies.

From the annulment of the champagne company LMVH's redundancy procedure by the *tribunal de grande instance* in Chalons sur Marne in 1993 up to that of the redundancies among workers at La Samaritaine by the *cour de cassation* (supreme court, final court of appeals) in January 1997, the law opened new channels of contention for works councils. The number of appeals to the courts based on this law remained limited, but it nonetheless fuelled case law that encouraged works councils to be combative in consultation procedures. It provided staff representatives with the means to challenge the good faith in which economic information is supplied by management, to exert downward pressure on the numbers of employees made redundant, to try to avoid compulsory redundancies, and to improve compensation for employees who lose their jobs (Didry, 1998) Without challenging the unilateral nature of job cuts, the legal regime for economic redundancies created the necessary conditions for discussion of and, if necessary, a challenge to employers' decisions on questions of employment.

In an ambiguous way, the development of *accords de méthode* encouraged by the Minister of Labour after the suspension of the Law on Social Modernisation (*Loi de Modernisation Sociale*)[46] is a further manifestation of the influence of law on collective negotiation.[47] The challenge here was to provide an improved consultation procedure, with funding for economic experts and legal advisors and more works council meetings, with as a counterpart to this the certainty for the employer of realising his goals at the end of the specified period. Agreements such as this would have been worthless without case law on redundancy programmes, since employers would not have been incentivised by the assurance that the redundancies envisaged would be achieved.

The method agreements were fuelled by the prevailing legal situation, but they nonetheless hid the deeper nature of "negotiation" that resulted from the legislative action of 1993. "Negotiation" cannot be reduced to reciprocal concessions aiming at any cost to reach an agreement between employers and employees on questions where the two parties' interests are fundamentally at odds. It is not opposed to conflict and to the contradiction of interests as expressed in the employment contract. On the contrary, it corresponds to the options that legal resources offer for employees and their representatives to influence the

[46] The suspension of some articles of the *Loi de Modernisation Sociale* is the first part of the law of 3 January 2003 "to relaunch collective negotiation of economic redundancies".

[47] "Article 2 of the law (of 3 January 2003 'to relaunch collective negotiation of economic redundancies') allows for the conclusion at company level of a collective agreement on the consultation procedures for staff representatives on the proposed economic redundancy of more than ten employees within the same 30-day period" ("L'article 2 de la loi (du 3 janvier 2003 'portant relance de la négociation collective en matière de licenciements économiques') prévoit la possibilité de conclure au niveau de l'entreprise un accord collectif portant sur les modalités de consultation des représentants du personnel sur les projets de licenciement pour motif économique de plus de dix salariés dans une même période de trente jours" (*Circulaire de la Délégation Générale à l'Emploi et à la Formation Professionnelle du 26 février 2003 relative à la mise en œuvre de la loi n° 2003-6 du 3 janvier 2003 portant relance de la négociation collective en matière de licenciements économiques*).

employer's economic decisions. Seen in this way, the capacities for discussion of collective redundancies that the legislation gives to staff representative bodies have in fact allowed them to move beyond simple bargaining on the conditions under which employees made redundant will leave work, and to question the soundness of the economic information being used to justify the redundancies envisaged.[48]

Conclusion

In France, the state's role in industrial relations goes beyond that of arbiter between pre-existing social forces, the role often assigned to it in neo-corporatist analyses. As legislator, it has the exclusive power to set the compulsory basis on which industrial relations are presented as "contractual" because of each party's right unilaterally to terminate the agreement. The worker hence has two channels of action open to him or her in defending interests that are distinct from and often contradictory to those of the employer: strike action and resignation on one hand, and legal action, *inter alia* in industrial tribunals, on the other. This is also the reason why, since the law of 1892 on conciliation and arbitration, strikes are organised as a form of democratic expression on the part of all workers. Before the unions became social forces on the national level, it was therefore up to the legislator to put in place the conditions that would allow workers to express themselves democratically, leading to the recognition, in parallel with the formation of large confederations, to the recognition of staff representative bodies.

Within this framework, with public policy involvement at every stage, unions have, step by step, found a role that is distinct from that of the British trades unions to which they are often likened. Far from dictating working conditions by the exercise of a monopoly that the legislature refuses to grant them, their energies are often directed towards the defence of benefits already obtained via strike action. A union is a collective body, whose existence is based on a law passed in 1884, and which exercises influence through its right to go to court in order to enforce end-of-strike agreements. The legal definition of collective labour agreements of 1919 clarified unions' ability to conclude agreements with employers and then, from 1936 onwards, raised the problem of representativeness, that is the union's ability to conclude agreements that could then be applied by state representatives to the all affected employees. In parallel with this process of assimilating unions as "social partners" capable of concluding agreements on working conditions, the

[48] This was the reason behind the cancellation of the redundancy procedure at Neyrpic (now Alstom Power Hydro) in Grenoble in 1996.

recognition of staff representative bodies led union organisations to engage in the pluralist electoral competition on which a part of their representativeness is based. Collective negotiation should be seen in a broad sense, as should any challenge to the unilateral decision-making powers of employers. Understood in this broad sense, it is based on legal foundations that go back to the legacy of the revolution, which leads to the understanding that to "reinstitutionalise collective negotiation in France" today is in itself a recognition of the fundamental role played by the state.

References

Badie, Bertrand (1972), "Les grèves du Front Populaire aux usines Renault", in: Patrick Fridenson (ed.), *Le monde de l'automobile*, Spec. Issue *Le mouvement social*, 81, p. 69-109.

Boyer, Robert (1990), *The regulation school, a critical introduction*, New York: Columbia University Press.

Camard, Sophie (2004), "Statistiques: des chiffres et des luttes", *Vacarmes*, Vol. 26, p. 21-23.

Combe, Maurice (1969), *L'alibi, vingt ans d'un comité d'entreprise*, Paris: Gallimard.

Coser, Lewis (1956), *The Function of Social Conflict*, London: Routledge & K. Paul.

Cottereau, Alain (2002), "Droit et bon droit, un droit des ouvriers instauré puis évincé par le droit du travail", *Annales HSS*, Vol. 57, 6, p. 1521-1561.

Dehove, Gérard (1937), *Le contrôle ouvrier en France, l'élaboration de sa notion, ses conceptions*, Paris: Librairie du Recueil Sirey.

Didry, Claude (1994), "Le chômage entre conciliation et contrat de travail", in: R. Salais, N. Whiteside and M. Mansfield (eds.), *Aux sources du chômage, une comparaison interdisciplinaire France-Grande-Bretagne*, Paris: Éditions Belin, p. 183-211.

Didry, Claude (1998), "Les comités d'entreprise face aux licenciements collectifs, trois registres d'argumentation", *Revue Française de Sociologie*, Vol. 3, p. 495-534.

Didry, Claude (2000), "La réforme des groupements professionnels comme expression de la conception durkheimienne de l'Etat", *Revue Française de Sociologie*, Vol. 41-3, p. 513-538.

Didry, Claude (2002), *Naissance de la convention collective, débats juridiques et luttes sociales en France au début du XXe siècle*, Paris: Éditions de l'École des Hautes Études en Sciences Sociales.

Didry, Claude and Anne-Lise Aucouturier (1997), *Des politiques de l'emploi à la pluralité des formes juridiques de la relation de travail, analyse socio-économique de deux expériences: l'aide aux chômeurs créateurs d'entreprise et le rôle du comité d'entreprise dans le contrôle des plans sociaux*, Rapport pour le Commissariat Général du Plan.

Didry, Claude, Laure Machu and Michel Margairaz (2000), *Action publique et convention collective sous le Front Populaire: une parenthèse républicaine dans les années 1930*, rapport pour le Ministère de l'Emploi.

Dunlop, John T. (1993 – revised edition), *Industrial Relations Systems*, Boston: Harvard Business Press.

Durkheim, Émile (1902 [1893]), *De la division du travail social*, Paris: Fernand Alcan.

Garnier, Olivier (1986), "La théorie néo-classique face au contrat de travail: de la 'main invisible' à la 'poignée de main invisible'", in: Robert Salais and Laurent Thévenot, *Le travail, marchés, règles et conventions*, Paris: INSEE Economica, p. 295-312.

Gurvitch, Georges (1932), *Le temps présent et l'idée du droit social*, Paris: Vrin.

Jehring, Rudolf von (1979 [1915]), *The Struggle for law*, Westport Ct.: Hyperion Press.

Jobert, Annette and Jean Saglio (2004), "Réinstitutionnaliser la négociation collective en France", *Travail et Emploi*, Vol. 100, p. 79-93.

Le Crom, Jean-Pierre (2003), *L'introuvable démocratie salariale, le droit de la représentation du personnel dans l'entreprise (1890-2002)*, Paris: Syllepse.

Machu, Laure (2004), "La négociation collective et la politique contractuelle", in: Alain Beltran and Gilles Le Beguec (eds.), *Action et pensée sociales chez Georges Pompidou*, Paris: PUF.

Merleau-Ponty, Maurice (1942), *La structure du comportement* (Bibliothèque de Philosophie contemporaine), Paris: PUF.

Moutet, Aimée (1996), *Les logiques de l'entreprise, la rationalisation dans l'industrie française de l'entre-deux-guerres*, Paris: Éditions de l'EHESS.

Office du Travail (1899-1904), *Les associations professionnelles ouvrières*, 4 volumes, Paris: Imprimerie Nationale.

Olzak, Norbert and Chris Wrigley (1997), "Les contraintes de la loi", in: Jean-Louis Robert, Friedhelm Boll and Antoine Prost, *L'invention des syndicalismes, le syndicalisme en Europe occidentale à la fin du XIXe siècle*, Paris: Publications de la Sorbonne, p. 237-254.

Perrot, Michèle (1974), *Les ouvriers en grève*, 2 tomes, Paris-La Haye: Mouton.

Poulot, Denis (1980), *Le sublime ou le travailleur comme il en est en 1870, et ce qu'il peut en être*, Paris: Maspéro.

Ray, Jean-Emmanuel (2004), *Droit du travail, droit vivant*, Paris: Belin.

Rousselier, Nicolas (1992), "Alexandre Millerand et la question de l'arbitrage des conflits du travail", in: Jean Luciani (ed.), *Histoire de l'Office du Travail*, Paris: Syros, p. 103-118.

Rueff, Jacques (1979 [1957]), "Institutions et marché commun dans le Traité de la Communauté Européenne du Charbon et de l'Acier", in: *Œuvres complètes*, tome III, volume 1, Paris: Plon.

Rueff, Jacques (1979 [1957]), "Le projet de communauté économique européenne et la nécessité d'un marché institutionnel", in: *Œuvres complètes*, tome III, volume 1, Paris: Plon.

Salais, Robert and Michaël Storper (1993), *Les mondes de production*, Paris: Éditions de l'École des Hautes Études en Sciences Sociales.

Segrestin, Denis (1996), *Sociologie de l'entreprise*, Paris: Armand Colin.

Sirot, Stéphane (2002), *La grève en France, XIXème-XXème siècles, une histoire sociale*, Paris: Odile Jacob.

Streeck, Wolfgang and Philippe C. Schmitter (1999), "Du corporatisme national au pluralisme transnational", in: E. Gabaglio and R. Hoffmann, *La CES: un processus en évolution*, Bruxelles: Institut Syndical Européen, p. 137-180.

Tixier, Pierre-Eric (1992), *Mutation ou déclin du syndical, le cas de la CFDT*, Paris: PUF.

Waquet, Philippe (1999), "Le renouveau du contrat de travail", *Revue de Jurisprudence Sociale*, Vol. 5, p. 383-394.

Weber, Max (2002), *The Protestant Ethic and the Spirit of Capitalism*, Los Angeles: Roxbury.

Weber, Max (1979), *Critique of Stammler*, New York: Free Press.

Zancarini-Fournel, Michelle (1998), "Collective agreements in France in the 30's: products, territories, scales: the Saint Etienne example", in: Noel Whiteside and Robert Salais (ed.), *Governance, Industry and Labour Markets in Britain and France*, London – New York: Routledge, p. 178-192.

CHAPTER 3

Fixed by Law

The Significance of the Legislation on Collective Labour Agreements in Belgium and the Netherlands (1945-1980)

Gregory VERCAUTEREN

As small capitalist countries bordering the North Sea, Belgium and the Netherlands have a number of important characteristics in common. Both countries have an open economy with only a small internal market. They are highly dependent on exports and consequently devote a great deal of attention to the competitive position of their respective industries. The last hundred years has seen the creation of a very extensive welfare state, together with a social climate in which problems are discussed in joint consultations and where labour relations are strongly institutionalised (Mok, 1985: 4-17; van Ruysseveldt and Visser: 1996, 205-207). The Collective Labour Agreements (CLAs) play a major role within this system. Approximately 75 per cent and 90 per cent of Dutch and Belgian employees respectively come under the scope of a CLA in one way or another (van Ruysseveldt, 2002: 332). The areas regulated by these agreements are wide-ranging, from primary working conditions to matters including job opportunity, quality of work, training and preventing absences through illness. In this way, the CLA forms the basis for an important part of social regulation in general and work-related regulation in particular (Brug and Peer, 1993: 12)

The game rules for CLA negotiations are set out in the CLA legislation. In both countries, it consists of a private and a public law section. The private law provisions designate the parties that will be given access to collective bargaining, the rights and obligations of CLA parties and the formal requirements that must be met by a CLA. The provision for a Generally Binding Declaration (GBD) (*algemeen bindend verklaring* – AVV) amounts to a statutory right entitling the government to intervene in CLA negotiations. It gives the Minister the right to make agreements, reached in collective bargaining, binding for all companies that fall under the scope of a CLA. In these cases, a CLA can be imposed compulsory on firms that took no part in the negotiations. By these provisions, the CLA legislation aims to regulate relations between the employer and employee organisations. Therefore, adjusting legislation marks an important step in the development of the consultative economy in Belgium and the Netherlands.

Despite the similarities, the two countries differ greatly in the way they interpret CLA law. While Dutch law locks up collective bargaining in a strict legal straitjacket, Belgian legislation stands out by its liberal character. Even the history of the appearance of the first CLA laws is different. Collective bargaining in the Netherlands is anchored in the CLA Act of 1927. The legislation was tightened up again by the GBD Act of 1937. Legal provisions for CLA negotiations were very late to appear in Belgium. Though the CLAs could be declared generally binding from 1945 onwards, they were only given a legal statute in 1968.

How are these differences to be accounted for? In order to answer this question, we will assume that CLA legislation cannot be regarded as a free-standing reality in a vacuum but as contingent upon power relations within society. The institutionalisation of labour relations is generally defined in terms of exchanges and power relations between employers (or employer organisations), employees (or employee organisations), and the state (Gevers, 1981: 71) In addition to this 'contest for power', there is also the play for ideas. Labour relations can also be related to a dynamic process of fluctuating positions and social relations between parties for defining situations and problems, by which they establish their own positions, set up objectives, create coalitions, or simply refuse to cooperate. In this respect, the institutionalisation of labour relations can be interpreted as a process of 'puzzling' and 'powering'. Puzzling points at the process of identifying problems and possible solutions; powering means the struggle for political support needed to safeguard the acceptance of these solutions (Heclo, 1974; Hall, 1993; Hemerijck and Visser, 1997).

This chapter investigates how these processes of puzzling and powering have manifested themselves in both countries in the interpretation of the CLA legislation. Our aim is to reveal the parties whose aspirations are ultimately best served by the interpretation of CLA legislation as it has unfolded in both countries. This is by no means an unimportant topic, given that the legislative objectives involved are not solely concerned with the outcomes of processes of puzzling and powering within the society. The underlying objectives of the respective legislations consolidate these processes to a significant extent.

A Tentative Start (19th century-1918)

During the last quarter of the 19th century, a number of important changes in the system of labour relations took place in Belgium and the Netherlands, mirroring developments elsewhere in Western Europe (Crouch, 1993: 67-124). Working class numbers expanded under the pressure of structural changes in the capitalist system. This resulted in a quantitative and qualitative growth of the trade unions in both Belgium and the Netherlands. The workers movement gradually abandoned the traditional trade unionism from which it had originated and expanded its scope to cover industry as a whole.

The ideological fragmentation of society, which took hold in both countries during this period, placed its stamp on the growing workers movement (Gerard, 1991: 114-171; Mahoux, 1997: 13-32; Slomp and van Mierlo, 1984; Windmuller and de Galan, 1970). The Socialist Party in Belgium took the initiative to set up the SK (Syndicale Kommissie – Syndical Commission) in 1896. Also in existence at the end of the 19th century were a number of independent Christian workers associations. These attempted to centralise themselves during the 1900s. The process resulted in the launch of the ACV (Algemeen Christelijk Vakverbond – Confederation of Christian Trade Unions) in 1912. In the Netherlands, the Vaderlandsche Werkmansvereeniging (National Workingmen's Association) was set up in 1871. This Protestant organisation, which took its inspiration from antirevolutionary social ideals, evolved in 1877 into the Protestant Christian association Patrimonium and via the Christelijk Arbeidssecretariaat (Protestant Worker's Secretariat) (1900) ultimately into the CNV (Christelijk Nationaal Vakverbond – Protestant Trade Union Federation) in 1909. The Catholic population was also in the process of setting up its workers associations around this time. In the same year that the CNV was founded came the formation of the Bureau voor de Roomsch-Katholieke Vakorganisatie (Bureau for Roman Catholic Trade Unions). As a companion piece to the socialist movement, the NAS (Nationaal Arbeidssecretariaat – National Labour Secretariat) was established in 1893. This organisation was the first national association of workers affiliated to the Revolutionaire Socialistische Partij (Revolutionary Socialist Party). The more moderate NVV (Nederlandsch Verbond van Vakvereenigingen – Dutch Federation of Trade Unions) was set up in 1905 alongside it, operating as a deliberate counterweight to the steadily increasing syndicalising tendency exhibited by the NAS.

The employers had their own ideological divisions, although this was less manifest. The Christian employers were the only ones to organise themselves into separate associations. In the Netherlands, there had been various attempts by Catholic employers to organise themselves from the end of the 19th century onwards. The ARKW (Algemene Rooms Katholieke Werkgeversvereniging – General Association of Roman Catholic Employers) was eventually set up in 1915 (Bruggeman and Camijn, 1999: 45-53). In Belgium, separate Catholic employer associations were only established after World War I. All these organisations wanted to propagate Catholic social teaching among employers. In addition, Boaz, a Protestant employer organisation, had been in existence in the Netherlands since 1892. Most influential in both countries were the 'neutral' employer organisations. In Belgium, this was the CCTI (Comité Central du Travail Industriel – Central Committee for Industrial Work), set up in 1895 and reorganised in 1913 to become the CCI (Comité Central Industriel – Central Industrial Committee). Its counterpart in the Netherlands, the VNW (Vereniging voor Nederlandse Werkgevers – Association of Dutch Employers) had been set up in 1899. Both of these organisations projected themselves as the representative body for the entire industry and firmly maintained classical liberal principles.

Within the labour relations system the CLA made a relatively late entrance in both Belgium and the Netherlands compared to Germany and the United Kingdom (Mineur, 1936: 27). One of the first striking factors relates to the attitude of the unions and the employer organisations towards collective bargaining. Workers unions in both Belgium and the Netherlands fully subscribed to the effectiveness of the CLA, albeit with slight differences of emphasis between the socialist and confessional unions. The confessional unions gave an ideological interpretation to collective bargaining, contrasting it with the class conflict espoused by socialism. The only parties still severely doubtful of the CLA were the Dutch and Belgian employers' associations, the VNW and the CCI. In line with their liberal ideas, these organisations regarded bargaining with the unions as an infringement of employer authority. The employers preferred to make wage and working conditions arrangements through individual agreements between employer and worker (Brion, 1995: 52; Bruggeman and Camijn, 1999: 139).

Employer unwillingness to conclude CLAs needs to be related to the lack of actual trade union power. The regulation of wages and labour working conditions by means of CLAs presupposes the existence of well-developed trade unions. Unions in both countries were involved in a battle for their right to exist. For instance, the freedom to set up a union and to join a union was not guaranteed by the state. The coalition ban, which had been in force since the beginning of the 19th century, was a powerful brake on the evolution of the union movement. This coalition ban forbade any 'conspiracy' in order to achieve wage increases (Chlepner, 1972: 19-22).

In the Netherlands, the situation only changed during the last few decades of the 19th century. The coalition ban was repealed in 1872. By the 1890s, a start was also made on social legislation. The idea gradually gained ground among the liberal citizenry that the legislator should venture more into the social field and protect the worker (Windmuller and de Galan, 1970: 16). The period of unquestioned belief in *laissez-faire* solutions had come to an end. A number of draft bills, designed to pave the way towards the regulation of individual contracts of employment, were toiled over from 1900 onwards. A bill was adopted and the Act finally passed in 1907. It also acknowledged the existence of the CLA and defined it as a series of arrangements between one or more employers (associations) agreed with one or more workers (associations) with legal status. The legal validity of the CLA, which now took precedence over the individual contract of employment, became an established fact under the new Act (Vijn, 1993: 97).

This legal recognition largely accounts for the fact that the instrument was used with increasing frequency in the Netherlands subsequent to 1909. However, employer mistrust continued to be an important barrier against any real breakthrough of the CLA. This situation changed just before World War I (1914-1918), a war in which the Netherlands was protected by its neutrality. In 1913, a long-running strike in the cigar industry was finally brought to an end by a victory for the union and a CLA. Many employees saw this conflict as a sign that resistance to collective labour agreements was a risky business and one only few, well-established employers could afford to take. Collective bargaining increased rapidly from that time onwards. In particular during the war years, many CLAs were concluded. There was a drastic rise in the cost of living, while business profitability soared, except for during the period 1916-1917. The opportunity seemed to be there for wage rises and the unions were the means par excellence to achieve this (Windmuller and de Galan, 1970: 47) As a consequence, union membership rose sharply and, by the end of the war in 1918, use of the CLA had become quite widespread throughout the Netherlands, in particular in the domestic industries.

The state's distrust of the workers movement remained high in Belgium. Liberal opinion dominated social relationships for longer and upper- and middle class liberals failed to reach out to the working classes (Strikwerda, 1997: 222). While the coalition ban was repealed in 1867, in its place came an article from the Criminal Code (Article 310) that protected the freedom of labour. In practice, it meant that it was almost impossible to organise a strike and bring it to a proper conclusion. This significantly hampered the development of Belgian trade unionism. Despite heavy industrialisation, Belgium had a much smaller percentage of union members before 1914 than countries with similar levels of industrialisation, such as Great Britain and Germany and even less-industrialised countries like the Netherlands (Crouch, 1993: 115-118). Given that the efficient representation of interests is closely allied to the recognition of trade unions, it is no surprise that in Belgium, nothing in the way of legal instruments for the regulation of collective bargaining ensued.

The Differences Continue (1918-1927)

In Belgium, World War I and its aftermath allowed the trade unions to finally emerge as major participants in politics. Like elsewhere in Europe, the country experienced a strong shift to the left. The new social consciousness had raised membership of the trade unions to unprecedented heights, allowing them to present themselves as a valuable discussion partner.[1] Furthermore, the Belgian government changed its attitude towards the union movement. Conservative distrust of the workers movement had in fact fallen sharply. By its patriotism during the war years, the socialist party had provided convincing evidence that it accepted capitalist society. As a result, it could now be included in government. However, the party made its participation in government conditional on the state granting universal suffrage and scrapping Article 310 from the Criminal Code. Both of these requirements were met in 1921. Freedom of association has been protected in the criminal code since that time (Chlepner, 1957: 19-22). Trade unions in Belgium were constituted on the basis of this Freedom of Association Act and by Article 20 of the Constitution. They refused to possess legal status, despite being offered the opportunity by the Professional Organisations Act and the Non-Profit-Making Associations Act (June 27, 1921). As such, they were *de facto* associations, operating outside the normal legal system.

The Freedom of Association Act removed a significant impediment to the use of the strike weapon. Spurred on by steadily growing membership numbers, the unions supported their demands by means of sector-by-sector strikes. This wave of strikes continued until 1921 (Neuville, 1981: 64-97). The government, for whom reconstruction of the country was a priority, now stimulated the conclusion of CLAs.

[1] Especially socialist union membership skyrocketed from 127,000 in 1913 to 689,000 in 1921. The ACV remained a long way behind its socialist counterpart (Pasture and Mampuys, 1990: 19).

With this in mind, it created an institutional framework for collective bargaining: the joint commissions. These commissions were originally advisory committees that had been given the task of studying the issue of reducing working hours. In practice, they functioned as consultative bodies in which CLAs were hammered out (Antonopoulo, 1926: 27-34). While it was true that joint commissions constituted a framework that allowed the conclusion of CLAs, the opportunity of doing so was not always used in the 1920s, mainly because of the persistent resistance of the employers (Luyten, 1996a: 34-42). Under these circumstances, Belgium lacked a social basis for a debate on legal regulation of the CLAs.

In the Netherlands, where the CLA made steadily increasing inroads during the 1920s (Harmsen and Reinalda, 1975: 426), a wide scale debate on industrial organisation took place. The Dutch government, which was similarly confronted by revolutionary threats and social disquiet, had proposed to give CLAs a wider legal framework in 1918. After all, the increase in the numbers of CLAs had by then highlighted the limitations of their legal status (Molenaar, 1957: 360). Moreover, the government was considering the option of declaring CLAs generally binding. In doing so, it was attempting to prevent a situation whereby non-affiliated employers could have lower wage bills, meaning that job opportunities for employees of affiliated employers could be endangered (Vijn, 1993: 98). The Dutch government's plans brought especially the VNW into fierce agitation. This organisation regarded them as an illicit government intervention in the production process. The VNW also feared that making the CLA binding would lead to higher operational costs, since the working conditions set out in the CLA would be likely to rise far above the minimum (Schrover, 1991: 17).

The CLA bill submitted to Parliament by the Minister of Social Affairs in September 1926 eventually accommodated the complaints of the VNW (Bruggeman and Carijn, 1999: 185). The decision was taken for a private law regulation only, which would set out the rights and obligations of the CLA parties. An example was the peace clause, which obliged the union to refrain from any campaign to change the agreed working conditions for the duration of the CLA. This meant that, in the event of a strike, the union concerned could be brought before the courts. Other provisions in the bill also strengthened the position of the employers in CLA negotiations. The signature of a single union for instance was sufficient in order to conclude a valid CLA. An employer (or association of employers) was thereby relieved from any compulsion to reach agreement with all unions in a particular sector. They could reach an accord with the most compliant union. The bill also left aside the option of making the CLA generally binding.

The Corporatism Debate in the 1930s

Those who supported making CLAs generally binding naturally greeted the CLA-Act with little enthusiasm. They accordingly continued to urge a public law regulation of the CLA throughout the 1930s (Molenaar, 1957: 363). Similarly, in Belgium a broad social debate started up on the question of a statute to govern the CLA and the GBD. Not because more CLAs were being concluded – on the contrary – but due to the profound economic crisis that set in at the beginning of the 1930s. This crisis deeply affected the economic, social and political fabric of the society. Liberal doctrines, which until that time had formed the basis of all political and economic regulation, were now being severely criticised. In the light of experiences gained in the 1920s, the debate in the two countries resulted in different outcomes. In the Netherlands CLA legislation was brought to a conclusion by the passing of the GBD Act in 1937. Belgium in contrast was unable to take the issue further than a legislative proposal in 1938 that was never debated in parliament.

Discussions on a statute for the CLA took place within a framework of debate on corporatism in both countries. The debate revolved around the structure and administration of the economic order under public law. This kind of corporate structuring, also called industrial organisation, was based on the Christian ideal (shared by Protestants and Catholics) of class partnership. As early as in the 1920s, a number of advocates prepared to argue in favour of a legal statute for CLAs as an important precondition for a corporate structuring of society. In both countries the debate was spurred on when the Pope commended industrial organisation as a solution to social upheaval in his encyclical Quadragesimo anno (1931). In particular, confessional employer and employee organisations argued for a statute for CLAs and for legal personality for unions so that industrial peace would be sanctioned by civil law (Crijns, 1974: 92-97 and 247-289; Kwanten, 1984: 337-347; Mampuys, 1984: 395-418).

Corporatism did not find an easy acceptance among socialist unions in either of the two countries. The Dutch socialist union NVV came out in support of the generally binding declaration, but mainly for pragmatic reasons. The union had been integrating itself into the capitalist system for some time and the stance it adopted connected well with the collective bargaining strategy that had by then become dominant. A similar attitude was found among Belgian socialists. Mainly the large union federations, such as those belonging to the metal workers and the miners, saw industrial organisation as a continuation of the consultative tradition. However, in contrast to its Christian counterpart the ACV, the SK was unwilling to see the absolute right to strike compromised under any circumstances. While it chose consultation above conflict, the strike weapon had to be maintained without restriction so that it could be used as a vital means of pressure or in support of collective bargaining (Luyten, 1996a: 130-146).

The bill tabled by the Belgian government in 1938 took into account the wishes of the socialists to a significant extent. The CLA statute and the legal statute for professional associations were drafted very flexibly (Luyten, 1996a: 170). Despite this, the bill never received a parliamentary debate. To explain why the CLA legislation was successfully completed in the Netherlands but not in Belgium, we must turn our attention to the attitude adopted by the CCI and the VNW. These organisations developed clearly different views with regard to collective bargaining and the respective roles of the government and the union movement.

By the middle of the 1930s, the VNW had abandoned its obstinate resistance to the GBD. Discussion was given a boost following the promulgation of the Act relating to the binding or non-binding nature of corporate agreements (1935). Agreements on price controls, production quotas and market allocations had spread quickly during the Depression. These were binding only for companies that had affiliated themselves to the cartels. In order to avoid the possibility that independent entrepreneurs might undermine the efficiency of these agreements, the employers urged the introduction of an Act that would make it possible for the government to render corporate agreements binding for companies within industrial sectors that had not signed the agreements (Windmuller and de Galan, 1970: 71).Given that the principle of government intervention in the market was accepted in employer circles by virtue of this proposed Act, an important barrier against declaring CLAs universally binding had now been removed. The VNW abandoned its principle of objection to government intervention as far as working conditions were concerned. It stated that declaring a particular CLA binding or non-binding was a complex matter and one that involved advantages as well as disadvantages. It was true that the disadvantages outweighed the advantages, but the procedure was no longer characterised as unacceptable, as had been maintained during the 1920s (Bruggeman en Carijn, 1999: 186-187).

In Belgium, the CCI had adopted a different attitude. Nonetheless, a similar Cartels Act was promulgated in 1935. The CCI continued to abide by its liberal principles and saw no reason to accept the intervention of the government in other areas of social and economic life. When the government consulted the unions and employer associations regarding the question of an industrial organisation bill, the CCI raised the most fundamental objections. The organisation was not prepared to create a structural framework for collective bargaining that would lead to a general improvement in wages and working conditions. Such a framework would be too rigid. For the same reason, the CCI was opposed to the option of making CLAs generally binding (Luyten, 1993: 326-327).This opposition made any legal framework for a CLA Act impossible.

How are we to explain the diverging attitudes of Belgian and Dutch employers? To a significant extent, economic factors lie at the basis of this divergence (van Thijn, 1979: 159-187; Luyten, 1993: 334-335). Opposition to the CLA in Belgium, just as in the Netherlands, was greatest among export orientated industry sectors due to the fact that the issue raised fears for the competitive positions of companies in these sectors. Other sectors, which produced for the internal market, such as the food industry, were much less recalcitrant towards collective bargaining. The CCI was dominated by employer organisations drawn from the heavy export industries (structural engineering, steel and mining) and the Société Générale, Belgium's largest holding company, which had financial interests in these sectors. However, the VNW was also dominated by employer organisations drawn from export-orientated industries that opposed the CLA legislation for the same reason. But the Belgian exports' structure was not entirely the same as that of the Netherlands. Exports in Belgium were focused on goods for which demand on the world market was stable or in recession. Unlike the Netherlands, it was incumbent on Belgian industry not to try and compete on the basis of ever-increasing specialisation of goods with a high added value, but rather on the basis of low prices and wages. This explains why the CCI was exceptionally distrustful towards further expansion of collective bargaining. It was afraid that this would involve an increase in wage costs, which it regarded as a threat to the country's competitive position (Luyten, 1996a: 331; van Gerwen, 2000: 24-27).

However, the differing attitudes of the CCI and the VNW cannot sufficiently be accounted for solely on the basis of the underlying economic structure. Ideological considerations also need to be considered. The CCI, and the Société Générale in particular, held firmly to their economic liberalism. The attitude of these organisations tightened even more when Belgium, like France, was inundated by a wave of strikes in 1936 (Luyten, 1993: 334-335). The cards were laid out differently in the Netherlands. There, the VNW had recognised the unions as a valuable discussion partner over the course of the interwar years. This had been part of a gradual process starting in the 1900s, in which the government had never felt the need to exert any special pressure. The Acts of 1907 and 1927 had paved an important road towards the acceptance of the CLA. It was true that there had been a decline in the number of CLAs during the 1930s and that the country had been troubled by a number of strikes. But there had never been a general strike, as in Belgium. The relation between workers and entrepreneurs in the Netherlands during the interwar years was in other words much less characterised by conflict than in Belgium. This allowed consultation arrangements to develop in a much more rectilinear fashion (Harmsen and Reinalda, 1975: 186-187; Houtman en Schimmel, 1993: 135). The GBD Act thereby became the result of a gradual evolution that had started thirty years earlier.

The Dutch Legislation in Practice (1937-1980)

Once the VNW had abandoned its opposition, the Dutch government announced a bill that would make the GBD possible in 1936. The Act passed without much difficulty in 1937. It simultaneously opened up the possibility of making CLAs not binding in cases in which the government thought this necessary in the public interest (Konig, 1987: 108). The option of declaring agreements non-binding created a legal instrument that gave the government great power to intervene in collective bargaining. In this way, the legislator created what was to be an important precedent for Dutch wages following World War II (Windmuller and de Galan, 1970: 73).

Clandestine negotiations took place during the nazi-regime, resulting in an informal agreement that gave the social parties an extended voice in national socio-economic consultation and the government a supporting role. The Dutch government, however, decided otherwise and pressed for extensive control over wages and prices. Since the Netherlands emerged from the war in a state of total collapse, the government undertook vigorous action to rapid reconstruction. The Board of Government Mediators (College van Rijksbemiddelaars) was consequently set up by the Extraordinary Decree on Labour Relations (Buitengewoon Besluit Arbeidsverhoudingen, 1945). The Board listed among its powers the authority to approve or reject the provisions of a CLA or to declare it either binding or non-binding on the sector concerned. Although the employer and employee organisations could establish wages and employment conditions through CLAs, they where subject to the Board of Government Mediators review procedure, which always involved a decision as to whether they conformed to previously established governmental norms. While establishing these norms, the government was prepared to be guided by economic facts that were accepted as guidelines for negotiations by all parties. In this manner, CLA consultations in the Netherlands took place on the basis of more or less economic model-orientated negotiations (Geul, Slomp and van Snippenburg,

1986: 5-13). After 1945 the Dutch economy was centrally managed and labour conflicts were kept under tight regulation. The centralised wage bargaining system strengthened the position of the unions and especially of the national confederations. This explains why they were cooperating with a system aimed at controlling the increase in wages. In this way, the Dutch trade unions opted for a leading role in national socio-economic consultation, at the expense of developing an active trade unions presence on the shop floor (van Zanden, 1998: 81; Mok, 1985: 4-17). They became generally accepted as social partners who were held responsible for economic development and the growth of employment. The word strike even disappeared from the vocabulary of the unions.

Though the Extraordinary Decree on Labour Relations was intended as a temporary measure, it systematically continued to operate until the early 1960s. Through the rigorous compression of wages, the Netherlands became a low cost zone, occupying a favourable position in world markets. The determination for greater differentiation in wage levels nevertheless increased during the 1950s. A second Special Decree on Industrial Relations was approved in 1963. It removed the establishment of wage policy goals from the influence of the government and delegated it to the social partners. The employer and employee organisations were to commit themselves to defending the nationally agreed maximums for permissible wage adjustments to their membership. This decree was already superseded by the 1970 Wage Bargaining Act. It made the contracting parties no longer subject to a binding central standard and dissolved the Board of Government Mediators. The act once again accorded significant power to the government. Henceforth, collective agreements must be registered at the Ministry of Social Affairs and Employment. If national interests dictate it, the minister can order a temporary suspension of a new agreement. This happened regularly until 1981, but has not occurred since (Visser, 2001: 302; van Bottenburg, 1995: 135-159; van Hulst, 1984: 205-206.)

The Road to the CLA Act in Belgium (1940-1968)

In Belgium, the debate on a legal framework for the CLA had by no means died down after 1938. Consultation was suspended in Belgium, as in the Netherlands, during World War II, yet several proposals were still being worked out clandestinely, intended to shape the structure of consultations after the war. Particularly from the autumn of 1941, when a German victory was no longer self-evident, some of the employer organisations entered into negotiations with the pre-war, mainly socialist, union leaders in order to prepare the ground for post-war labour relations. These discussions led to the signing of the Draft Agreement for Social Solidarity (Ontwerp van overeenkomst tot sociale solidariteit) in 1944. This Social Pact is the most well-known – though certainly not the only – blueprint for the post-war system of labour relations in Belgium. It prescribed, among other things, that the joint commissions should be established as a general rule. There was no question of a strike ban (Luyten and Vanthemsche, 1995; Pasture, 1993: 695-714).

From the time of Liberation (1944) onwards, endless discussions were held between senior leaders of the union movement, the employers, and the government on the institutionalisation of labour relations The Royal Decree of 9 June 1945, which gave the joint commissions a legal statute, was an important step along this road. This RD also devoted a number of its articles to CLAs that were concluded in the joint commissions. Firstly, only recognised unions would be allowed to conclude CLAs in the joint commissions. By this measure the traditional unions intended to keep the radical employee organisations, which had surfaced in the wake of the war, outside the negotiations. Secondly, based on the decree, the Belgian government could make a collective agreement, concluded within a joint committee, generally binding (Vercauteren, 2007; Luyten, 1995: 55-88; Keulemans, 1989: 189-223).

Given the intense industrial pacification emphasis in the bill itself, the government had requested a smooth passage through the house. In order to persuade the CCI and the socialist trade union to get on board, the decree was introduced accordingly as nothing more than a temporary solution. As a result, it was far from complete. The issue of sanctioning the industrial peace obligation for instance, still provided for under the Social Pact, was neatly evaded by giving legal force only to CLAs declared to be generally binding. This gap resulted in a number of practical difficulties as the joint commissions became an important platform for the regulation of wages and labour conditions in the 1950s. In particular, the issue of a statute for CLAs not being declared generally binding formed a breeding ground for polemics among jurists. Despite successive Ministers of Labour recognising the problem, it was never resolved (Horion, 1954: 814; Lagasse, 1959: 41).

There are two reasons for the failure to complete CLA legislation in Belgium. Firstly, it was opposed by the ABVV (Algemeen Belgisch Vakverbond – General Belgian Trade Union Federation), which was created in 1945 out of a merger of the prewar SK and new, largely communist trade union committees that had arisen in some industries during the Occupation (see in particular Hemmerijckx, 2003). The main problem for this union was that the issue of the CLA's statute was closely bound up with the legal status of professional associations and the associated responsibilities. In the CLA negotiations, it wished to see the achievement of policy results mainly dependent on the union's counterforce they were able to raise. It was true that negotiation was the dominant strategy of the unions, but the strike weapon had to remain intact in order to be deployed as a final form of insurance. The Belgian unions had now become powerful enough to enforce compliance with CLAs in their own right. After all, they had doubled their combined membership within the first post-war decade, increasing unionisation from a quarter to just below half of the workforce (Visser and Ebbinghaus, 2000: 121). The strong position of trade unionism in Belgium is traditionally attributed to a number of factors. First, they owed their growth largely to their extensive service provision, especially to the unemployment insurance that they provided to their affiliates. As – in contrast to their Dutch colleagues – they continued to pay out the benefits, the introduction of general mandatory unemployment insurances after World War II boosted their membership rates. This certainly benefited the confederational structures, but different from the Netherlands the weight of trade union power remained in the hands of the sectoral trade union federations, while the unions could also hold and even strengthen a strong position in the companies, at the workplace. That offered them greater opportunities to provide services, whereby service and the promotion of both individual and collective interests went hand in hand. Finally, the close relationship with the socialist and the progressive wing of the Christian democrat party gave the unions also direct influence on policy-making. The Ministry of Labour maintained especially strong ties with the trade unions. The close relationship between unions and their political allies accounts for the fact that the Belgian governments did not really insist on a statute for the CLAs (Pasture, 1996: 93; van Ruysseveldt and Visser, 1996: 232). A second reason was that the VBN (Verbond der Belgische Nijverheid – Federation of Belgian Industry), which became the successor to the CCI in 1946, continued to maintain its social conservatism for a long time. Only in the mid-1950s did it fully accept the reality of union power. The reason for this turnaround lay in the shift in power relationships that had occurred within the VBN. Following a reorganisation of the coal mining sector, which had been initiated by the European Community for Coal and Steel, the economic weight of this industry had declined and the conservative mining federation had therefore become less influential within the VBN (Luyten, 1996b: 164, 170). Cooperation with the unions became the starting point in the social politics of employers. The VBN no longer pressed for a system of labour relations with strict sanctions to guarantee compliance with social peace, but it was content with a flexible codification of labour relations for reasons of feasibility. What mattered at the end of the day was that good relations should be maintained with the unions.

The employers appeared to have found the ideal means for this purpose by the end of the 1950s in the guise of social planning. Under the social planning agreements, a number of social advantages were distributed over a period of time agreed in advance and spread out over different levels of consultation (central, industrial sector, and individual company). For the duration of the agreements, usually one or two years, the unions would agree not to make any new demands or organise or support any strikes (Bleeckx, 1970). The first centrally organised social planning agreement, concluded at the initiative of the VBN on 11 May 1960 ran until the end of 1962 but was thwarted by wide scale strikes during the winter of 1960-1961. These were directed against the government's plans to reduce public spending and were of a particularly angry nature. The VBN ultimately declared itself prepared to continue with the agreement, subject to certain conditions. For example, the government would need to work out a statute for the CLA and provide a legal anchor for the right to strike, in close cooperation with the social partners.[2]

The Minister of Labour gave in to the VBN's complaints, after severe pressure from the conservative wing of his own Christian democratic party. However, in order not to offend the ABVV, the provisions on the CLAs were given only minimal interpretation. The bill restricted itself to specifying a number of formal conditions that CLAs would need to fulfil. The sanction for compliance with the industrial peace obligation remained limited to a particular guarantee. There were no strike-related provisions. The bill mainly provided a number of institutional mechanisms that strengthened the position of the unions in CLA negotiations. In this way, the representational monopoly that was formulated in the 1945 decree was upheld. Moreover, in contrast to his Dutch colleague, the Belgian employer, was denied any legal option to escape from the conditions of a sector CLA; he no longer had any options at all if the CLA was declared generally binding. For that reason, even the senior leaders of the ABVV could accept the bill.[3] This is how the CLAs finally received a legal statute by the Act of 5 December 1968.

Conclusion

We commenced this chapter by stating that there are significant differences between the CLA legislation in Belgium and in the Netherlands. Processes of puzzling and powering explain this difference. The

---

2 Archives VBN. Board of Management. Report of 11.4.1961.

3 Cf. the discussion in the National Committee of the socialist textile worker's trade union, Archives TACB-Eeklo. National committee. Minutes of 19.4.1967 (AMSAB, Ghent).

existing legislation on individual contracts of employment in the Netherlands created a favourable climate in which the CLA could evolve. Employer resistance to collective bargaining, the GBD and the CLA also broke down more rapidly. This allowed the legislation to be gradually expanded. By contrast, the recognition of collective bargaining procedures in Belgium was much more difficult. Employers remained aloof to collective bargaining into the 1950s. After this time opposition mainly came from the socialist trade union, which opposed the legal encapsulation of CLA consultations. Under these circumstances, the scope of Belgian legislation on the CLA was rather restricted. The Act primarily created a number of institutional mechanisms that ensured a strong position for the Belgian unions in CLA negotiations. In this way, CLA legislation in Belgium became an additional source of power for the Belgian union movement. By contrast, the legislation in the Netherlands leaned in favour of the employer organisations. After World War II, it forced the unions into an economic straitjacket and brought them under the control of the state.

The differing scope of the CLA legislation in Belgium and the Netherlands exposes a more fundamental difference between collective bargaining in Belgium and the Netherlands. In the Netherlands, the consensus shared by the government, the employers and the unions was that wages might be too high in relation to the general interest, which was regarded as being the country's competitive position. The unions were therefore prepared to accept the obligations, as well as the rights, that came with CLA bargaining. For its part, in its contacts with the social partners, the government was prepared to be guided by established economic facts that were accepted as guidelines for negotiations by all parties. This explains why the government obtained the means to pry open CLAs that it considered in conflict with the general interest, defined in terms of the competitive position of the country. In other words, collective bargaining in the Netherlands primarily took into account economic criteria and was consequently hammered out principally in the forges of the employers. In Belgium, by contrast, the government did not have the freedom of movement to intervene in collective bargaining after World War II. Negotiations were mainly borne by a powerful and well-developed union movement that displayed considerable opportunism with regard to the use of the legislation. It demanded that the legislator would strengthen its monopoly position in collective bargaining but shied away from any submission that would make it tributary to the jurisprudence. Much more than was the case in the Netherlands, the Belgian unions opted for class interests instead of any 'general interest' and they were powerful enough in their own right to force through such class interests in collective bargaining. In doing so, they used all the power they were able to exert in order to achieve results that served their agendas at the times that appeared most favourable. Any legal tying up of the collective bargaining process and the responsibilities that this would entail, could not be other than disadvantageous to them in this power game.

Literature

Antonopoulo, H. (1926), *Les commissions paritaires d'industrie en Belgique*, Brussels: Imprimerie scientifique et littéraire.

Bleeckx, F. (1970), "La programmation sociale: analyse critique et projection sur l'avenir", Unpublished PhD, Sociology, UCL, Louvain-la-Neuve.

Brion, R. (1995), *100 jaar actie voor de onderneming, 1895-1995*, Tielt: Lannoo.

Brug, L. and H. Peer (1993), *Collectief geregeld. Uit de geschiedenis van de cao*, Amsterdam: Stichting FNV Pers.

Bruggeman, J. and A. Camijn (1999), *Ondernemers verbonden. 100 jaar centrale ondernemersorganisaties in Nederland*, Wormer: Imerc.

Bundervoet, J. (1973), "Het doorstromingsprobleem in de hedendaagse vakbeweging: kritische literatuurstudie en verkenningen in de Belgische vakbonden", Unpublished PhD, Sociology, KU Leuven.

Chlepner, B. (1957), *Cent ans d'histoire sociale en Belgique*, Brussels: ULB.

Crijns, H. (1990), *Tussen arbeid en kapitaal: een eeuw katholiek en protestants sociaal denken*, Aalsmeer: Luyten.

Crouch, C. (1993), *Industrial Relations and European State Traditions*, Oxford: Clarendon.

Fourier, E. (1986), "La Commission du Travail et l'amorce de la législation sociale", in: E. Fourier and D. Pector (eds.), *1886. La révolte des damnés de la terre! Le soulèvement ouvrier de mars 1886 dans le pays de Liège et de Charleroi*, Charleroi: Le Progrès.

Gerard, E. (1991), "Ontplooiing van de christelijke arbeidersbeweging (1904-1921)", in: E. Gerard (ed.), *De Christelijke Arbeidsbeweging in België, 1891-1991*, Leuven: Universitaire Pers, p. 114-171.

Geul, H., H. Slomp and L. B. Van Snippenburg (1986), "Vakbondskracht en vakbondsinvloed in Nederland en België", in: *Tijdschrift voor Arbeidsvraagstukken*, Vol. 2, No. 2, p. 5-13.

Gevers, P. (1981), "Relatieve weerbaarheid, veel pragmatisme, toenemende interdependentie. De arbeidsverhoudingen in België", in: *Arbeidsverhoudingen in Europa. Coöperatie – coalitie – conflict*, Alphen aan de Rijn: Samson.

Hall, P. (1993), "Policy Paradigms, Social Learning and the State. The Case of Economic Policy Making in Britain", in: *Comparitive Politics*, Vol. 25, p. 275-296.

Harmsen, G. and B. Reinalda (1975), *Voor de bevrijding van de arbeid. Beknopte geschiedenis van de Nederlandse vakbeweging*, Nijmegen: Socialistiese Uitgeverij.

Heclo, H. (1974), *Modern Social Politics in Britain and Sweden: from Relief to Income Maintenance*, New Haven: Yale University.

Hemerijck, A. and J. Visser (1997), *A Dutch Miracle: Job Growth, Welfare Reform and Corporatism in the Netherlands*, Amsterdam: Amsterdam University Press.

Hemmerijckx, R. (2003), *Van verzet tot Koude Oorlog, 1940-1949: machtsstrijd om het ABVV*, Brussel: VUB press.

Horion, P. (1954), "La force obligatoire des accords collectifs de travail", in: *Revue d'histoire de sociologie*, Brussels, Vol. 27, 801-816.

Houtman, A. and H. Schimmel (1993), "De CAO nader beschouwd: waarnemingen van de algmeene werkgevers-vereniging", in: L. Brug and H. Peer (eds.), *Collectief geregeld. Uit de geschiedenis van de CAO*, Amsterdam: Stichting FNV Pers.

Keulemans, D. (1989), "De institutionalisering van het sociaal-economisch overleg. De wet van 20 september 1948 'houdende organisatie van het bedrijfsleven", in: E. Witte (ed.), *Tussen restauratie en vernieuwing. Aspecten van de Belgische naoorlogse politiek (1944-1950)*, Brussels: VUB Press, p. 189-223.

Konig, F. (1987), *Het systeem van het collectieve arbeidsvoorwaardenrecht*, Deventer: Kluwer.

Lagasse, A. (1959), "La valeur des décisions des commissions paritaires non approuvés par arrêté royal", in: *Revue du Droit social*, Vol. 30, p. 41-49.

Luyten, D. (1993), "Ontstaansvoorwaarden voor het corporatisme", in: *Tijdschrift voor Sociale Geschiedenis*, Vol. 19, No. 3, 52-74.

Luyten, D. (1995), "De dialectiek van het overleg. Collectieve arbeidsverhoudingen, 1944-1952", in: D. Luyten and G. Vanthemsche (eds.), *Het sociaal pact van 1944: oorsprong, betekenis en gevolgen*, Brussels: VUB Press.

Luyten, D. (1996a), *Ideologisch debat en politieke strijd over het corporatisme tijdens het interbellum in België*, Brussels: Koninklijke academie voor wetenschappen, letteren en schone kunsten van België.

Luyten, D. (1996b), *Sociaal-economisch overleg sedert 1918*, Brussels: VUB press.

Luyten, D. and G. Vanthemsche (eds.) (1995), *Het sociaal pact van 1944: oorsprong, betekenis en gevolgen*, Brussels: VUB press.

Magts, M. (2001), "De Wet van 10 maart 1900 op de arbeidsovereenkomst: de honderdjarige evolutie vóór en na", in: M. Stroobant and O. Vanachter (eds.), *Honderd jaar arbeidsovereenkomstenwet*, Antwerpen: Intersentia.

Mahoux, J.-P. (1997), "Voorgeschiedenis van de Syndicale Kommissie 1885-1898", in: L. Peiren and J.-J. Messiaen (eds.), *Een eeuw solidariteit 1898-1998*, Ghent: Ludion.

Mineur, J. (1936), *La réglementation conventionnelle des salaires en Belgique*, Gembloux: Duculot.

Mok, A.-L. (1985), "Arbeidsverhoudingen in Nederland en België. Een oefening in differentiële sociologie", in: *Tijdschrift voor Arbeidsvraagstukken*, Vol. 1, No. 1, p. 4-17.

Molenaar, A.-N. (1957), *Arbeidsrecht*, Zwolle: Tjeenk Willink.

Neuville, J. (1981), *L'évolution des relations industrielles.* Tome II: *La lutte ouvrière pour la maîtrise du temps*, Brussels: Vie ouvrière.

Pasture, P. (1992), *Kerk, politiek en sociale actie. De unieke positie van de christelijke arbeidersbeweging in België*, Leuven/Apeldoorn: Garant.

Pasture, P. (1996), "Belgium: Pragmatism in Pluralism", in: P. Pasture, J. Verberckmoes, and H. De Witte (eds.), *The Lost Pespective. Trade Unions Between Ideology and Social Action in the New Europe*, Vol. 1: *Ideological Persistence in National Traditions*, Aldershot: Avebury, p. 91-135.

Pasture, P. and J. Mampuys (1990), *In de ban het getal, Ledenanalyse van het ACV (1900-1990)*, Leuven: KUL. Hoger instituut voor de arbeid.

Rhijn, A.A. van (1969), "Uit de geschiedenis der CAO", in: *Sociaal Maandblad* Arbeid, Vol. 24, p. 87-89.

Rigaux, M. and T. Van Peijpe (1994), *Knelpunten in Nederlands en Belgisch CAO-recht*, Alphen aan de Rijn: Samsom.

Rutjens, R. (1993), "Wonderbaar werkend geneesmiddel. De CAO in het katholiek sociaal denken voor de Tweede Wereldoorlog", in: L. Brug and H. Peer (eds.), *Collectief geregeld. Uit de geschiedenis van de cao*, Amsterdam: Stichting FNV Pers.

Ruysseveldt, J. van (2002), "CAO-onderhandelingen in België en Nederland: kleine verschillen, grote gevolgen", in: *Tijdschrift voor Arbeidsvraagstukken*, Vol. 18, No. 4, p. 321-334.

Ruysseveldt, J. van and J. Visser (1996), "Weak Corporatisms Going Different Ways? Industrial Relations in the Netherlands and Belgium", in: J. Van Ruysseveldt and J. Visser (eds.), *Industrial Relations in Europe*, Heerlen: Open University.

Schrover, M. (1991), *Het vette, het zoete en het wederzijdse profijt. Arbeidsverhoudingen in de margarine-industrie en in de cacao- en chocoladeindustrie in Nederland 1870-1960*, Hilversum: Verloren.

Slomp, H. and T. Van Mierlo (1984), *Arbeidsverhoudingen in België*, Antwerp-Utrecht: Spectrum.

Strikwerda, C. (1997), *A House Divided. Catholics, Socialists and Flemish Nationalists in Nineteenth-Century Belgium*, Lanham: Rowman and Littlefield.

Stuurman, S. (1992), *Wacht op onze daden, het liberalisme en de vernieuwing van de Nederlandse staat*, Amsterdam: Bakker.

Thijn, T. van (1979), "Bijdrage tot de wetenschappelijke studie van de vakbondsgeschiedenis", in: P.A.M. Geurts and F.A.M. Messing (eds.), *Theoretische en methodologische aspecten van de economische en sociale geschiedenis*, Vol. 2, The Hague: Nijhoff.

Toren, van den J.-P. (1991), *Van loonslaaf tot bedrijfsgenoot. 100 jaar christelijk sociaal denken, medezeggenschap en sociale zekerheid*, Kampen: Kok.

Vercauteren, G. (2007), *In naam van de sociale vooruitgang. De rol van de overheid in het sociale overleg in België (1944-1981)*, Leuven: ACCO.

Vijn, M. (1993), "De CAO, sociaal beschouwd", in: L. Brug and H. Peer (eds.), *Collectief geregeld. Uit de geschiedenis van de cao*, Amsterdam: Stichting FNV Pers.

Visser, J. (2001), "The Netherlands: The Return of Responsive Corporatism", in: A. Ferner and R. Hyman (eds.), *Changing Industrial Relations in Europe*, Oxford: Blackwell.

Visser, J. and E. Ebbinghaus (2000), *Trade Unions in Western Europe since 1945*, London: Macmillan.

Werkman, P. (1993), "'Een voorbehoedmiddel voor openlijken strijd'. Het CNV en de collectieve arbeidsovereenkomst voor de Tweede Wereldoorlog", in: L. Brug and H. Peer (eds.), *Collectief geregeld. Uit de geschiedenis van de cao*, Amsterdam: Stichting FNV Pers.

Wilde, B. de (1995), "De collectieve arbeidsverhoudingen", in: D. Luyten and G. Vanthemsche (ed.), *Het sociaal pact van 1944: oorsprong, betekenis en gevolgen*, Brussels: VUB Press, p. 39-54.

Windmuller, J.P. (1969), *Labor Relations in the Netherlands*, Ithaca (N.Y.): Cornell University Press.

Windmuller, J.P. and C. de Galan (1970), *Arbeidsverhoudingen in Nederland*, Antwerp-Utrecht: Spectrum.

Zanden, J.-L. van (1998), *The economic history of the Netherlands 1914-1995: a small open economy in the Long 20th century*, London: Routledge.

Zanden, J.-L. van and R. Griffits (1989), *Economische geschiedenis van Nederland in de 20ste eeuw*, Utrecht: Spectrum.

CHAPTER 4

The Dynamics of Consultative Arrangements in 20th Century Europe

The Case of Austria (1945-2000)

Peter BERGER

Only a few institutions of post-1945 Austrian origin have captured the interest of an international scientific community. In a wider sense, the Austrian School of Economics featuring prominent names such as Friedrich von Hayek or Ludwig von Mises can be considered one of them. But both Mises and Hayek were born before 1900, and in spite of their important contributions to economic and social analysis after World War II they were products of the intellectual sphere of the inter-war period rather than of a later time. In addition, they acquired world-wide renown not as residents of Austria but as expatriates in the US, Britain and Germany (Vaughn, 1994; Hennecke, 2000). Present-day Austria cannot reasonably claim parentage of economic liberalism of the Mises-Hayek brand, and politicians in Vienna never followed a course considered appropriate by "Austrian economics".[1]

In contrast, Austrian neo-corporatism (or social partnership, as some prefer to call it) is a genuinely native product of the Alpine Republic. It did not exist as a fully fledged system of consultative arrangements before 1957 though some of its institutional and mental prerequisites date back to the early 20th or even the 19th century. As Andrei Markovits pointed out, several aspects of it were considered special in a European or even global context, and quickly became subjects of international scholarly attention. For Austria's modern history social partnership was seminal inasmuch as it helped forging a positive national identity after the traumatic experiences of the collapse of the Habsburg Empire,

1 According to John K. Galbraith, their decision not to do so was most beneficial to their country. The socialist statesman, Bruno Kreisky, remembered Galbraith saying that while liberal economists abounded in Austria's intellectual circles (in the 1920s and 1930s), the country found itself in permanent economic crisis. Only when the Austrian school firmly established itself overseas, but lacked a noteworthy following in Austria proper, the stage was prepared for the Second Republic's post-1945 economic miracle (Kreisky, 1986: 168).

interwar socio-political tensions, and seven years of national socialist rule following the *Anschluss* of 1938. If one can speak of a West German Deutschmark patriotism or "constitutional patriotism" emerging in the wake of the Federal Republic's foundation in 1949, it is equally legitimate to call the patriotic consensus of post-1945 Austrians a consensus owed to *Sozialpartnerschaft* – and neutrality during the Cold War (Markovits, 1996: 6).

Ever since its invention in the 1950s, Austria's neo-corporatist model enjoyed overwhelming popular support (Pelinka, 1998). For a brief while after 1989, optimists even believed in its capacity to function as a paragon for social and economic reform in Eastern Europe's emerging democracies. But lately, the combined impact on Austria of economic globalisation and an increasingly confrontational political climate raised doubts among experts and the general public alike as to what the future of social partnership would bring. In February 2000, a new Austrian government composed of the Catholic, centrist People's Party and the right-wing Freedom Party of Jörg Haider replaced the previous coalition of Catholics and social democrats. Regime change was quickly followed by partial abandonment by the government of time honoured consultative practices involving peak organisations of capital and labour. As a result, Austria experienced a wave of strikes unparalleled since fall 1950, when communist-inspired worker unrest threatened to derail post-war economic recovery (Jelavich, 2003: 261-262). In 2003, people went to the streets to protest proposed amendments of the retirement regulations system and the national pension scheme, plans to modify the structure of Austria's state owned railroads, and wage cuts affecting the pilots of Austrian Airlines – the national carrier of which the state is a minority shareholder. In the face of mounting social tension, the president of Austria's Trade Union Federation, Fritz Verzetnitsch, admitted to the press that Austrian social partnership needed to adapt to new challenges if it wished to recapture a significant amount of its former political influence (Kattinger, 2003: 19).

In this chapter, I shall try to analyse recent developments in Austrian neo-corporatism based on literature of Austrian and American origin.[2] Such a venture is impossible, however, without a brief initial discussion of the roots of corporatist institutions in the 19th and early 20th centuries. Following this excursion into the history of Habsburg Austria and the First Republic, I will sketch the institutional framework and modes of action of Austria's *Sozialpartnerschaft* as they evolved from the 1950s

2 Among the publications utilised to this end the most important are Bischof and Pelinka, 1995; Pelinka, Plasser, and Meixner, 2000; Dachs, Gerlich, *et al.*, 1992; Prisching, 1996; Gerlich, Grande, and Müller, 1985.

to the present. An attempt at juxtaposing the positive and negative contributions of neo-corporatism to Austria's post-1945 economic and social development will be made before we arrive at our tentative answer to the question: does Austro-Corporatism have a perspective, and if yes, will it be significantly different from its past?

The Heritage of History

In Austria, attempts at forming pressure groups for the promotion of business-related interests date back as far as the early 19th century. Already before industrialisation began on a massive scale in parts of the Habsburg Empire, "craft associations" sprang into existence in Bohemia (1829), Lower Austria (1835), and Inner Austria/ Styria (1837) (Fischer, 1978: 7 ff.).[3] The Styrian association enjoyed special protection of a Habsburg prince, Archduke John, who in 1848 – on behalf of the liberal Frankfurt-based German National Assembly – briefly acted as Germany's vice regent (*Reichsverweser*). Following the abortive revolution of 1848-9, a triumphant absolutist regime in Vienna under the young heir to the imperial throne, Francis Joseph I, authorised the creation of *chambers of trade*. Under a law issued in 1868 these chambers were given the right to deliver expert opinions to the government on all matters falling into their purview, and to send a number of elected deputies to the provincial diets (Sandgruber, 1995: 237). The trade chambers were also, if only irregularly, involved in the work of advisory bodies like the Customs and Trade Conference (Zoll- und Handelskonferenz) charged with economic policy formation under the Austro-Hungarian "compromise" regime of 1867 (Paulinyi, 1973: 571-572). The compromise or *Ausgleich*, as it was called in German, came only one year after Habsburg's catastrophic military defeat in a brief war against Prussia. It represented a joint effort of both the Viennese Court and the Magyar landed nobility to counter the twin challenge of Slavic nationalist aspirations and liberal democratic ideas (Jászi, 1971). The compromise in fact carved up the Habsburg Empire between ethnic Germans (who were to dominate its western half mainly at the expense of the Czechs), and Magyars, who were given a free hand in the East to deal with "their" Croat, Serb, Slovak, and Romanian minorities. Economically, the two "halves" of Austria-Hungary after 1867 functioned as separate entities. However, they were bound to maintain a currency and customs union whose clauses had to be renegotiated once in ten years by parliamentary "delegations", drawing heavily on the expertise

3 For a discussion of early industrial growth within the Habsburg Empire see Rudolph, 1975.

of the aforementioned Customs and Trade Commission. Also, the Commission assisted in fixing the quotas, i.e. the proportion to be set regarding the financing of a few remaining joint Austro-Hungarian concerns, among which the imperial army and navy were the most important (Beller, 1996: 96).

By 1900, most industries and trades in the Austrian lands possessed their lobbying organisations. It became common for the state bureaucracy to seek cooperation with organised business, although the dominant attitude of the bureaucrats still mirrored the maxim of Austria's notorious enlightened despot, Joseph II (1780-1790), to "rule for the people", but without much popular participation. Whenever such participation occurred, it did so within a framework of more than 50 bipartite expert committees and advisory boards (Tálos, 1985: 44).

Paramount importance for the development of Austrian corporatist culture must be attributed to the rise of modern mass parties which predated the introduction of universal male suffrage in 1907. Social democrats, Christian socials, and German nationalists all owed their popular support to social change connected with industrialisation in the western Habsburg lands. Each of these mass movements met with suspicion on the part of the Court, the Catholic high clergy, and the liberal *haute bourgeoisie*. Francis Joseph went as far as to delay for two years the appointment of Karl Lueger, the charismatic leader of Austrian Christian socialism, to the post of mayor of Vienna – despite a resounding victory of Lueger's party at the municipal elections of 1895. While the social democrats were the party of the industrial proletariat, and German nationalists appealed mainly to an urban middle class of professionals and civil servants, the Christian socials set out as a "ragbag of clerical, radical, and anti-Semitic elements" (Beller, 1996: 141) among Viennese artisans, shopkeepers, and petty bourgeois. Outside the capital, they drew support mainly from the lower ranks of the Catholic clergy, and from the small peasantry. In 1907, they merged with the Catholic Conservatives, a party appealing to wealthier farmers and large urban business. But despite their gradual movement to the political centre, and their growing respectability and administrative brinkmanship, Christian socials continued to criticise the liberal capitalist order as well as Marxist notions of class struggle. Under the influence of Catholic social thinkers such as Silesian-born Karl von Vogelsang (1818-1890), they professed belief in a society characterised by "a just balance of legitimate interests" (Tálos and Kittel, 1996: 26). Idealising the corporatist social and political order of a medieval past, they recommended organisation of the society into "estates" which were to include all practitioners of the same profession, irrespective of whether they owned means of production or not. Within and between such "estates"

(*Berufsstände*) a peaceful trade-off of interests would then take place. This concept exerted some influence on Austrian politics up to the 1930s when chancellors Dollfuss and Schuschnigg, backed by the Catholic high clergy, professed to reform society in accordance with the teachings of two Papal encyclicals, *Rerum novarum* and *Quadragesimo anno* (van Kersbergen, 1995: 33-34). In actual fact, Austria's semi-fascist dictatorship of 1934-1938 belied the anti-authoritarian spirit of Catholic corporatism. Failure to reduce social tensions precipitated the downfall of the regime. But popular support in Austria for ideologies of class-transcending harmony – religious or secular – survived World War II, and helped in the creation of a new social partnership after 1945 (Tálos, 1992: 391).

Transposing a famous phrase of the American economic historian, Alexander Gerschenkron, one could say that World War I and the early interwar years in Austria saw "a spurt towards government-mediated cooperation between business and labour that failed" (Gerschenkron, 1977). The military effort of 1914-1918 required peace at the economic front and a pliable workers' movement. In the early stages of the War, Austria's imperial government relied on strict discipline to extract maximum performance of an increasingly strained industrial workforce. But when in 1917 labour unrest reached a critical level, labour and business representatives were jointly given a say in the management of the Austrian war economy (Hanisch, 1994: 207-208). For example, wages and working conditions in the military-industrial complex became subject to tripartite regulation by Grievance Committees, or *Beschwerdekommissionen*. The Habsburg Empire's ultimate defeat, followed by the transfer of authority in Vienna and the Western Alpine provinces to a republican government led by social democrats, set the stage for more comprehensive arrangements between labour, business and the state. Like in other European countries, willingness of the propertied classes to co-operate temporarily with organised labour stemmed from a widespread fear of bolshevism.[4] Containing the bolshevist threat seemed impossible without the participation of moderate left-wing forces (such as the Austrian social democrats) in the daily management of the state's affairs. Austrian post-1918 social partnership amounted to more than practical anti-communism, however. It also resulted from the country's weak economic position. Common efforts of business and labour were a prerequisite to overcome the initial dramatic

4 For a brief discussion of Austrian interwar anti-communism see Fraberger and Stiefel, 2000: 57-8. Collaboration in Western European states of (moderate) democratic socialists and bourgeois forces, resulting from the common perception of a communist threat, is dealt with in Maier, 1975.

shortage of foodstuffs, energy, and capital; to combat the adverse effects on foreign trade of "economic nationalism" in East Central Europe; to reconvert hundreds of thousands of soldiers into gainfully employed civilians; and to control the impact of inflation on domestic income distribution. For all these purposes, tripartite committees and sub-committees of workers, employers, and delegates of the government were created (Tálos, 1995: 376-378). In most cases, the state took the initiative in setting up these committees, but sometimes they were based on voluntary decisions to co-operate. As a rule, corporatist agencies of the First Republic had a short lifespan – either because the purpose for which they had been established ceased to be relevant, or due to shifts in the general socio-political climate which over the years made business less inclined to negotiate over workers' demands. Some of the First Republic's prominent tripartite commissions lasted only a year or two. Cases in point were the Industrial District Commissions (*Industrielle Bezirkskommissionen*) of 1918-1919, created to deal with the problem of post-war mass unemployment; or the Industrial Conference (*Industriekonferenz*) of 1919, whose job it was to prevent a fall in workers' real wages by linking them to the inflation rate. This became obsolete after inflation was halted in fall 1922 with the aid of foreign loans. Another mixed committee established in March 1919 to advise the government on the issue of "socialisation" – i.e. the transfer of strategic industrial sectors from private hands into joint property of the state, the workers, and consumers' associations – ceased to be operative after the electoral defeat of the social democrats in October 1920 and the subsequent formation of a right-of-the-centre coalition of bourgeois and peasant parties (Kindley, 1996: 54).

Among the factors accounting for the quick demise of consultative arrangements during the First Austrian Republic, the absence of a basic consensus on the general direction of economic and social policy stands out. Such a consensus could not be achieved for two reasons: excessive pressure group pluralism and political polarisation. Despite some visible progress between 1920 and 1933 in creating peak organisations of labour, agriculture, and the trades,[5] the field of interest group lobbying remained highly fragmented. In the trade sector alone, more than 300 lobbying associations (apart from the Chambers of Trade with their

[5] In 1920, Chambers of Labour (designed as counterparts to the older Trade Chambers) were established by law. Between 1919 and 1921, interest representation of mid-size industry was centralised in the hands of a Federation of Austrian Industries (Hauptverband der Industrie Österreichs). Provincial Chambers of Agriculture and a Presidents' Conference of Agricultural Associations came into existence in the early 1920s, as well (Sandgruber, 1995: 351-352; Marko, 1992: 436).

regional and sectoral branches) catered to the needs of their clientele. Most of them had close links to one or the other political party of the bourgeois-peasant camp. Similarly, white and blue collar workers were represented by separate craft and industrial unions of varying political creed: social democratic/ communist,[6] Catholic, or pan-German. In the 1930s, Austria's largest industrial enterprise, the Österreichisch-Alpine Montangesellschaft Steelworks, even ran a yellow trade union of its own. To achieve compromises within the camps of business and labour between various party-affiliated sub-groups – not to speak of class transcending co-operation – met with enormous difficulties, given the conflict oriented nature of Austrian democracy at the time of the First Republic. As the political scientist Anton Pelinka aptly put it, the average Austrian's loyalty to one of the country's political subcultures (*Lager*) reflecting religious, class, and ethnic cleavages tended to be stronger than feelings of shared responsibility for the common weal (Pelinka, 1998: 109-110). Under such circumstances, a tripartite-corporatist approach to economic and social policy matters remained limited to exceptional periods of Austrian interwar history: 1919-20, when elections resulted in a stalemate between the bourgeois and socialist camps,[7] and when the communist threat left Catholics and social democrats no choice but to co-operate; 1930, when the consequences of the economic slump began to be felt in Austria, and the government convened a short-lived tripartite Economic Conference (*Wirtschaftskonferenz*) to develop strategies against the crisis; and 1934-1938, when Austro-Fascism claimed to have found a formula for social harmony – which, however, denied "Marxists" of all shades a voice in policy formation and politics.

Under the Dollfuss-Schuschnigg regime, new efforts were made towards concentration and centralisation of interest organisations – but at the expense of converting the latter into instruments of the "corporate state". In 1934, a monopolistic Trade Union Federation (TUF) came to replace the competing party-affiliated labour unions of the democratic period. The TUF comprised five sections, one for each major area of employment (industry and mining, crafts, finance, trade and transportation, professions). Ex-social democrats and communists were more or less effectively barred from top functions in the TUF-hierarchy, the

---

6 Social democrats and communists united under the umbrella of the Free Trade Union Movement (Österreichischer Gewerkschaftsbund ÖGB) in Austria, but the communists saw themselves mainly as a "revolutionary opposition force" within this alliance (Weber-Felber, 1995: 319-338).

7 The leading theorist of Austrian social democracy, Otto Bauer, called these years a "period of balanced power of the social classes" (*Gleichgewicht der Klassenkräfte*) (Bauer, 1976: 743 ff.).

exclusive right of appointment to such functions resting with the minister of Social Affairs.[8] Shortly before the *Anschluss*, the Schuschnigg government launched a new peak association of employers, the Federal Trade Chamber (*Bundeshandelskammer*) (Butschek, 1996: 84-8) Critics of this move from within the government camp argued that chambers representing the interests of business constituted a remnant of the pluralist, liberal order, and that they ought to be replaced by supra-partisan "estates" as quickly as possible. The advent of nazi rule put an end to controversies over the chamber system, but not to the Austrian chamber organisation, which the Germans incorporated into their own network of *Gauwirtschaftskammern*. While employers' associations as such fit into the national socialists' picture of a corporatist economy, this was of course not the case with trade unions or chambers of labour. The *Anschluss* delivered the death knell to Austria's Trade Union Federation. Its financial assets were transferred to the German *Arbeitsfront* (DAF). State control of the process of wage and price formation, and of labour relations in general, became complete under the Nazi regime. During the short period between Hitler's conquest of Austria and the outbreak of World War II (March 1938 – September 1939), the Third Reich's labour law and social insurance regulations were put into effect on Austrian soil. As a consequence, many Austrians enjoyed a marked improvement of their living standard – which, among other factors like the disfranchisement of the Jews, contributed to their initial enthusiasm for the "new order" (Bukey, 2000).

The Golden Age of Austrian Neo-Corporatism (1947-1970)

The second Austrian Republic, created in 1945 by the common will of the victorious allied powers, was to the same extent as its interwar predecessor a state dominated by political parties. But these parties had changed considerably since 1933. People's Party (ÖVP) and socialists (SPÖ) were equally anxious to de-emphasise their ideological roots – which in the case of the former involved emancipation from the Catholic Church, while the socialists deliberately chose not to renew official ties to their pre-war leadership-in-exile.[9] In the absence of "fundamentalists" both of the right and the non-communist left (which unfortunately amounted to a loss of brilliant minds as well), and fully conscious of the fact that internal peace increased the chances for lifting the four-

---

8 The Trade Union Federation came to be dominated by Catholic trade unionists, but shortly before the end of Austrian independence former social democrats were able to exert some influence on the shop level (Senft, 2002: 172-192).

9 Otto Bauer, who spent five years as an emigrant first in Czechoslovakia and later in Paris, did not live long enough to witness the resurrection of independent Austria.

power occupation of Austria, the new party elites adopted consociationalism as the basic pattern of domestic politics. As Arend Lijphart and others have taught us, consociational democracy means continued fragmentation of society, combined with co-operation across existing cleavage lines of the top echelons of all political camps (Lijphart, 1977). In Austria, such co-operation was facilitated by the shared belief of everyone except a tiny minority of communists that – within the framework of a mixed economy comprising a significant nationalised sector – efforts should be directed primarily at generating growth. Even if this involved sacrifices on the part of both labour and capital, medium-term payoffs for the nation as a whole were expected to be higher than the rewards of open clashes over the distribution of a stagnating (or shrinking) GDP (Seidel, 1996: 95).[10]

The new culture of compromise found its initial expression in five agreements on wages and prices concluded between 1947 and 1951. Their purpose was to ascertain that post-war economic reconstruction, based on rising production and productivity, would not be endangered by unchecked inflation (Tálos, 1985: 62).[11] There were four official parties to the wage-price deals: the Austrian Trade Union Federation (Österreichischer Gewerkschaftsbund – ÖGB); the Federal Chamber of Business (Bundeswirtschaftskammer – BWK); the Federal Chamber of Labour (Bundesarbeitskammer – BAK); and the umbrella organisation of Austrian farming called "The Presidents' Conference of Agricultural Chambers" (Präsidentenkonferenz der Landwirtschaftskammern – PKLK). All four were new creations of the Second Austrian Republic although the chambers of agriculture and business, as well as the Trade Union Federation, inherited some traits of their internal organisation either from the Austro-fascist or national socialist regimes (Böhmer, 1999: 3). And all four can be seen as expressions of a strong will on the part of the country's elites not to repeat mistakes of the past. In contrast to the plethora of pressure groups that existed during most of the inter-war period, the "big four" after 1945 were highly centralised bodies. With the sole exception of the trade unions, they were built on the principle of compulsory membership.[12] They operated as representa-

[10] The history of the 1930s taught Austrians the lesson that unrestrained conflict between labour and business can lead to disaster. However, as Knut Borchart convincingly argued, interwar developments were characterised by a high degree of inevitability (Borchardt, 1982: *passim*).

[11] The Western occupation powers made sure that cooperation building in the economic arena would be matched by the consensual politics of the grand coalition. Cf. Bischof and Kofler, 2004: *passim*.

[12] To be accurate, one should speak of the "big five". The Association of Austrian Industrialists (Vereinigung Österreichischer Industrieller – VÖI) plays an important

tional monopolies or near-monopolies for labour (ÖGB/ Federal Chamber of Labour), business (BWK), and the farming sector (Chambers of Agriculture). And they gained considerable political clout from their close ties with political parties, the parliament, and the government. We will return to this issue later.

The Composition of Austrian Governments, **Proporz,** *and the Strength of Social Democracy*

Uniquely among western-style liberal democracies, post-1945 Austria has seen two decades of uninterrupted joint government of the country's largest political parties, Catholics and socialists. Co-operation between the "black" and "red" camps resulted from the double necessity to heal the wounds remaining from Austria's interwar history, and to cope with the challenges of economic reconstruction and four-power occupation. Moreover, there was considerable US pressure for a durable consociational democracy (Jelavich, 2003: 252 ff.). To overcome deep-seated mutual distrust of the partners in government, a complicated scheme of proportional distribution of power was devised to extend beyond the limited sphere of cabinet posts. It came to be applied in most of the state administration, the nationalised sector of the economy, and the realm of public education. When in 1966 the grand coalition gave way to a single-party government under an ÖVP-chancellor, Austria's *Proporz* system continued unabated. It then survived thirteen years of socialist government under Bruno Kreisky and his successor, Fred Sinowatz. One can plausibly argue – as Andrei Markovits does – that the combined effect of twenty years of grand coalition, and of continuing "proportionalism" as a form of political culture, must have been conducive to the flourishing of social partnership (Markovits, 1996: 14). Implicitly, this means to acknowledge the crucial role of Austrian social democracy in sustaining neo-corporatism. Socialist dominance of the Trade Union Federation and the Chambers of Labour, accompanied by the party's strong influence both in the management of nationalised industries and in the guidance of social affairs, militated against a free market-approach to interest regulation. The Austrian case seems to underscore the thesis, that in countries with a stable pattern of socialist participation in government, policy styles tend to be cooperative and concerted rather than confrontational (or market-inspired) (Korpi, 1983).

---

part in representing the interests of large firms, which are not always in line with those of small and medium-size business. Membership of the VÖI is voluntary (Heinisch, 2000: 17).

Formalised "Vertical" vs. *Informal "Horizontal" Participation of Interest Associations in the Process of Policy Making*

In modern Austria, organised interests participate in economic and social policy formulation and implementation in different ways. "Vertical participation" indicates a procedure in which interest associations of business, farming and labour are either required by law to deliver expert opinions to state legislators on questions affecting their respective clientele; or act as consultants to the government administration in permanent or *ad hoc* advisory boards/ commissions (*Beiräte*). As we have seen, Austria's Chambers of Trade already in the 1860s enjoyed the right to comment on draft laws. The same prerogative was granted to labour's and agriculture's interest organisations during the First Republic (but not under the Austro-fascist regime of 1934-1938). Establishing advisory boards to various cabinet departments has been regular practice in Austria since the days of Habsburg rule. In contrast to the transparency and formal character of "vertical" participation, "horizontal" participation – i.e. inter-associational bargaining under state mediation – developed in an atmosphere of almost complete informality. Neither the Parity Commission of 1957 nor its sub-committees had a basis in Austrian constitutional law. There are good reasons to assume that their practical success – as well as that of other institutions of social partnership of a later date, such as the Economic Policy Forum (*Wirtschaftspolitische Aussprache*) and the High-Level Contact Group (*Verbändekomitee*)[13] – depended on the readiness of all parties involved to dispense with formal regulations. Rare instances when one social partner pleaded for a higher degree of formality of consultative arrangements (as in 1951, when the Trade Union Federation favoured the legal establishment of an Economic Directorate) ended in failure.

The Personal Factor

One of the keys to understanding the efficiency of Austrian social partnership probably lies in the German word *Personalunion*, and the distinctly Austrian practice of *Ämterkumulierung* (accumulation of offices). In his recent discussion of this phenomenon, Reinhard Heinisch speaks of three intersecting institutional frameworks dealing with potential socio-economic conflict in Austria: "(i) the state institu-

[13] The Economic Policy Forum was brought to life in the mid-1960s by the Federal Chancellery as an expert body to discuss economic policies. Among its 50-70 members were the President and Vice-President of Austria's Central bank, the heads of several economic research institutes, and high-ranking civil servants. The High Level Contact Group (created in 1967) served as a tripartite brain trust to the ministry of finance.

tions and administrative bureaucracy; (ii) the institutions of Austro-Corporatism, and, as the overarching bracket, (iii) the two major political parties and their affiliated networks" (Heinisch, 2000: 19 ff.). Since the earliest days of the second Austrian Republic, these frameworks have shown the tendency to intersect on a personal level, in the sense that representatives of the peak interest associations occupied functions in parliament, as well as in government. Depending on their political affiliation, they also exercised a right based on custom to hold positions of influence in the party hierarchies of ÖVP and SPÖ. Following an unwritten rule, the cabinet minister in charge of social affairs used to be a high-ranking member of the Trade Union Federation's (preponderant) socialist wing. Similarly, functionaries of the ÖVP-dominated Farmers' Chamber were preferred candidates for the post of Minister of Agriculture (Nick and Pelinka, 1993: 96). Two conservative Federal Chancellors, Julius Raab in the 1950s, and the incumbent, Wolfgang Schüssel, began their careers as president and secretary general of the Business Chamber, respectively. The chiefs of the "big four" (ÖGB, BWK, BAK, PK) always held seats in parliament. Anton Benya, long-time president of the ÖGB, even acted as speaker of the house. Heinisch tells us that as late as 1999 32 per cent of the socialist deputies were directly or indirectly tied to the trade unions or the Federal Chamber of Labour (Heinisch, 2000: 20). A similar percentage of conservative MPs can be assumed to have had close ties to interest associations of business and farming. Such personal linkages, though seriously violating Montesquieu's principle of separation of legislative and executive powers, no doubt contributed to Austria's internal peace and political stability – by imbuing political life with the spirit of consociationalism.

The Rise of the Techno-Corporatist Paradigm[14]

Economic and social historians agree today that the early 1960s in Austria constituted a watershed between "ideology-driven" and "technocratic" styles in politics. Growing emphasis on scientific (i.e. mainly economic and statistical) expertise came as a reaction to the poor performance of the Austrian economy resulting from non-participation in the EEC of the Rome treaties.[15] Austria's government, parliament, and the political parties – in their efforts at defending solid economic growth rates, full employment, and monetary stability – learnt to rely on the advice of interest group-related brain trusts like the "Advisory Council

[14] The term "techno-corporatism" is from Hanisch, 1994: 442.

[15] EFTA membership proved to be a poor substitute: cf. Sandgruber, 1995: 481-482.

for Economic and Social Questions",[16] or the Institutes of Economic Research (*Wirtschaftsforschungsinstitut* – WIFO), and Higher Studies (*Institut für Höhere Studien* – IHS). This happened to an extent which caused critics to chastise the illegitimate arrogation of government functions by the social partners. It is important to note, though, that the emergence of Austrian techno-corporatism coincided with a global trend towards economic fine-tuning; and that it proved useful in formulating a strategy by which Austria survived the consecutive oil-price shocks of 1973 and 1979 without too much damage.[17]

The Tide Turns (1970-2000)

At the beginning of the period commonly referred to as "Kreisky-Era" (1970-1983), Austrian social partnership looked back on almost two decades of rich experience under the grand coalition regime, and on four years of conservative single-party rule. The advent to power of democratic socialism in 1970 held the potential of continued de-emphasising of market forces, and of intensified neo-corporatism. On the other hand, the possibility of direct collusion between a leftist government and the Trade Union Federation/ Chamber of Labour-axis appeared as a threat to the conventional practice of tripartite social bargaining and joint macro-economic management by all social partners. But in the end chancellor Bruno Kreisky, like his conservative predecessor Josef Klaus, refrained from impairing the fundamentals of Austrian tripartism. It has been argued that in pursuance of his "activist" macro-economic policies (commonly referred to as Austro-Keynesianism), Kreisky depended on a functioning liaison of business and labour. Indeed, the social partners by means of their concerted income policy succeeded in keeping the wage-price structure intact and thus contributed to the government's efforts at simultaneously fighting inflation and unemployment. An important feature of Austrian macro-economic management during the 1970s and 1980s, the peg of the national currency (*Schilling*) to the *Deutschmark*, relied on the Trade Union Federation's determined stance to practice wage restraint. It has

16 In Hans Seidel's words, the Advisory Council "was based on the technocratic idea of an economic policy guided by scientific research and advanced economic models" (Seidel, 1996: 98). Both the ÖVP's and SPÖ's party programs of the 1960s were influenced by the same conviction that macro-management of the economy in accordance with scientific principles was possible and necessary.

17 This is not to say that Austrian economic policies during the critical period of the 1970s were formulated in the main by the Advisory Council. Equally important policy-formulating agencies were the ministry of finance and the directorate of the Central Bank, sometimes complemented by the Federal Chancellery's Economic Policy Forum (see below).

drawn critical comments, however, that Austrian social partnership persistently ignored considerable discrepancies between wage-levels in various sectors of business, as well as gender-related wage differentials.

As the period of socialist majority rule in Austria drew to its close, signs of a crisis of neo-corporatism became visible. The economic correspondent in Austria of Switzerland's *Neue Zürcher Zeitung*, Matthäus Kattinger, has pointed to the fact that there was no sudden loss of influence of the social partners, but rather a gradual decline in their importance (Kattinger, 2003: 19). It lasted throughout the 1980s, and resulted in a thoroughgoing reorganisation of neo-corporatist structures and processes in 1992 (Karlhofer, 1996: 124-125). An agreement signed by the heads of Austria's peak interest associations on November 23 of that year redefined the scope of consultative policies. Forthwith, promotion of the competitive strength of Austria's economy, active participation in the process of European integration, and defence of a healthy natural environment would explicitly fall within the social partners' purview. Structural reforms mainly affected the Parity Commission (to which the finance minister was admitted as a new, if non-voting, member),[18] and the Advisory Board for Economic and Social Questions (which came to include a permanent working group for environmental issues). A new sub-committee of the Parity Commission was created to perform the double task of monitoring integration of Austria into the EU, and devising strategies how to cope with the economic consequences of the fall of the iron curtain.

Literature dealing with the waning strength of social partnership abounded in the decade after 1985 (Prominent examples are Gerlich, Grande and 1985; Prisching, 1996; Unger, 1999). While political scientists correctly diagnosed an ongoing strong penchant of Austrians to rely on co-operation, concertation and consensus, they acknowledged that Austrian neo-corporatism was under pressure to adapt to changing national and global environments. On a national level, at least seven factors – economic and political – contributed to the "winds of change":

- Lower rates of growth of GDP, and a rise in unemployment
- Limitations to public spending due to high budget deficits
- Increasingly critical condition of the nationalised sector of industry

18 All other cabinet members holding a seat in the Parity Commission, including the head of government, waived their voting rights as early as 1966. After that date, the Parity Commission was referred to by political science as the "autonomous" section of social partnership.

- The lagging behind of investment into R&D, and an undue emphasis in production and exports on basic commodities, as opposed to sophisticated ("high-tech") final products
- Decomposition of formerly homogenous social environments ("de-pillarisation"), and, consequently, changes in voting patterns – i.e. shifting of voter loyalty away from ÖVP and SPÖ, to the advantage of new parties such as the "Greens"
- Decline of legitimacy of the chambers and their principle of obligatory membership, as a result of waste of membership fees by – or fraudulent actions of – top functionaries. In 1994, following disclosure of exorbitant salaries paid to a labour chamber official, voters' turnout at chamber-wide elections dropped to 30 per cent
- Sizeable electoral gains of the Freedom Party (FPÖ) under Jörg Haider, heir to Austria's pan-Germanic tradition, and self-styled mouthpiece of all Austrians excluded from the benefits of the *Proporz*-system – that unique power-sharing cartel devised by "Reds" and "Blacks", and identified earlier as one of the elements sustaining the business-labour consensus.[19]

Among the global developments which in the 1980s and 1990s posed a major challenge to Austrian neo-corporatism, analysts have emphasised: (i) the fatal blow delivered to the Keynesian concept of economic macro-steering by believers in unrestrained market capitalism; (ii) progressive deregulation of national economies, and privatisation of publicly owned industries and services; (iii) the consequent loss of importance of centralised national governance, accompanied by an enhanced role in the management of industrial relations of the sectoral and corporate level; (iv) the partial transfer of political decision-making powers from the nation-state to supranational bodies such as the European Commission, the European Council, etc.

Under the double impact of national and global change, social partnership ceased to be a force that decisively shaped Austrian politics. Instead, representatives of capital and labour accused each other of devoting too much time and energy to the defence of untenable, and mutually exclusive, standpoints on practical policies. On the side of labour's associations, the Trade Union Federation as well as most of its affiliated individual unions had to cope with a persistent loss of members. Overall membership was 1,498 million in 1997, down from

---

19 A minority of libertarians within the Freedom Party opposed *Proporz* because it ran counter to their principles, and not as populists who wished to maximise votes. In 1993, the "libertarian wing" left the FPÖ to found a new party, the Liberal Forum (LIF). For a discussion of both pan-Germanic and libertarian roots of the FPÖ, see Riedlsperger, 1989. On Haider and his iconoclasm, see Höbelt, 2003.

1, 653 million in 1987 (Karlhofer, 2000: 385). Incapability of simultaneously defending the particular – and often diverging – interests of blue and white collar workers, of employees in the private sector and civil servants, etc. contributed to the trade unions' difficulties. At the same time, the chambers of labour came under attack from the Freedom Party for charging excessive membership fees to their (non-voluntary) clientele, and using them in a fraudulent way. The renewed grand coalition-government of SPÖ and ÖVP – in power since 1986 – thereupon ordered both the Federal Chamber of Labour and the Federal Chamber of Business to hold ballots on the future of compulsory membership. In 1995 and 1996, respectively, these ballots produced reassuring majorities in favour of the status quo (Karlhofer, 2000: 383) – without, however, resolving the problem of weak intra-organisational democracy within the "mini-kingdoms" of BAK and BWK.[20]

A major shift in relative strength has occurred over the past years from the Federal Chamber of Business to the Association of Austrian Industrialists (VÖI), representing large-scale private enterprise. This development was triggered by a multiplicity of factors, such as partial privatisation of Austria's state-owned industries; the transition from communism to capitalism in regions of East-Central Europe adjacent to Austria; progressive European integration; and the rising share in Austria's economy of foreign direct investment and transnational firms. Traditionally, the Association of Industrialists – which is not directly involved in the procedure of Austrian collective bargaining – shows a more decidedly pro-market (and anti-regulationist) profile than the business chamber. It is compelled to do so, as any deviation from the liberal philosophy favoured by its member firms would result in their choice of the exit option. The rise to opinion leadership within the employers' camp of the industrial lobby can be seen as a telling symptom of Austria's new "corporatism in transformation". Important changes were also reflected in the lower intensity of co-operation between social partnership agencies such as the Advisory Council for Economic and Social Questions, and the government. Between 1964 and 1992, the Council submitted to the cabinet 67 expert studies; a number that has been reduced to 11 in the period 1993-2001, and to nil in the past two years, 2002 and 2003 (Kattinger 2003: 19).

20 The paternalistic style of leadership practiced in both the major Austrian Chambers is illustrated by the near-mythical reverence enjoyed during their periods in office by past presidents Anton Benya (ÖGB), and Rudolf Sallinger (BWK) (Knoll and Mayer 1976: 109).

Peace between Business and Labour – At Any Price?

In the concluding section of this paper I will return to an assessment of the potential of neo-corporatism to overcome its present crisis, and to remain an influential factor in Austrian politics. But first, an attempt shall be made at evaluating the neo-corporatist impact on Austria's economic and social development, from the end of the post-war reconstruction era (1955) to the present. Georg Winckler has left no doubt that social partnership – despite its undeniable contribution to a stunning post-war growth performance of the Austrian economy[21] – was a costly exercise in many respects. The brunt of the cost was borne by consumers who were forced to live through long periods with no downward flexibility of prices, a low degree of competition, and limited access to imported products. Other occasional "victims" of neo-corporatist overregulation, according to Winckler, were people in retirement; individuals and groups lacking a strong lobby within either the chambers of labour or business (such as professional workers and artists); the jobless; and the state.[22] Looking back on more than 45 years of activity of the Parity Commission's Subcommittee for Price Regulation, one cannot deny that social partnership promoted unofficial cartelisation in Austrian industry – as the American occupation personnel strongly suggested already in the early 1950s.[23] Under the Parity Commission's aegis, prices tended to rise uniformly over entire sectors of industrial production, instead of leaving individual firms the freedom to develop their own (competitive) pricing strategies. Winckler argues, however, that tolerated unofficial cartelisation in the 1960s and 1970s helped insulate Austria from the potentially damaging volatility of international markets for energy and basic commodities. In addition, it protected industry as a whole from the mounting pressure exercised by a powerful group of buyers, the international trade chains; and it held

21 The Austrian economy in three consecutive stages of growth since 1950 performed better than most OEEC economies. Annual rates of increase of *per capita* GDP were 4.9 per cent between 1950 and 1973, 3 per cent between 1973 and 1979, and 2.1 per cent between 1979 and 1990. Dutch GDP, in comparison, grew at an annual rate of 3.7 per cent (1950-1973), 1.7 per cent (1973-1979), and 1.2 per cent (1979-1990). One must keep in mind, however, that Austria "benefited" from an initial state of economic backwardness, characterised, *inter alia*, by a sizeable reservoir of unused rural labour (Berger, 1993: 120-121).

22 An example for significant costs incurred by the state in support of the social partners can be found in the soaring budget deficits and exploding public debt of 1975 ff. During these years of crisis, organised labour had to be compensated by publicly financed employment programs for its previous willingness to accept lower wages. Cf. Winckler, 1985: 309.

23 In this context, the history of the "Johnstone Report" of 1951 is particularly enlightening. Cf. Seidel, 2000: 278-279.

major advantages for consumers as well, by reducing their need to invest in speculative stock-keeping. Today, the issue of set prices in Austria has almost no practical relevance anymore. While in the late 1970s about 50 per cent of industry's selling prices, and approximately 20 per cent of all Austrian consumer prices were subject to approval by the Parity Commission, these ratios have since been reduced very significantly – owing to the strong presence in Austria of imported goods, and to lower inflation rates worldwide (Tálos, 1992: 404).

With respect to wage management, the Parity Commission's role consisted (and still consists) in giving its consent to the launching of each annual round of collective bargaining – after having received from the Trade Union Federation an estimate of the order of magnitude of wage increases aimed at by its individual member unions. The fact that agreement between single unions on their respective wage demands has to precede submission of an integrated benchmark proposal to the Parity Commission's subcommittee for wages contributed to the maintenance of extraordinary wage-discipline in Austria – and thus to a significant comparative sales-advantage of Austrian export trades. The remarkable inclination of Austrian white and blue collar workers to settle with comparatively modest wages (and wage-hikes) is explained in literature as a consequence of employment risks being assumed not by the employed person, but by (i) the firms, and (ii) the state. In return for trade-union support in keeping the brake on labour costs, Austrian industry from the late 1950s to the 1970s more or less guaranteed the maintenance of full employment on the company level. During the period of Austro-Keynesianism, which was characterised by a series of external shocks to Austria's economy, the state intervened with activist macro-economic policies to support national employment, that is, to help crisis-ridden industries avoid massive layoffs of personnel (mainly in the nationalised steel and chemical sectors). Against those who stressed the harmful long-term impact on economic modernisation of Austria's tripartite arrangement to safeguard job security at all cost,[24] advocates of neo-corporatism pointed at an undoubtedly impressive record of social harmony in Austria. Peaceful industrial relations were upheld way into the 1980s. Between 1980 and 1987, strikes caused the Austrian economy to loose an annual average of no more than two workdays per 1000 employees – compared to 162 lost days in the USA, 35 in West Germany, 191 in Sweden, and 719 in Greece (Tálos, 1992: 404).

24 Austro-Keynesianism is sometimes reproached with having unduly delayed what the Austrian economist, Joseph A. Schumpeter, termed "creative destruction", i.e. the modernising force of aggressive capitalism. Cf. Kattinger, 2003: 19.

Outside the restricted realm of wage-price bargaining, time-honoured Austrian habits of reaching consensus within the framework of social partnership, no matter at what cost, have recently drawn critical voices by political scientists and journalists alike. In the Viennese daily paper, *Der Standard*, Conrad Seidl attacked what he called "a decades old tradition" of Austrian neo-corporatism to reconcile opposing standpoints by avoiding final decisions on important, but controversial, legislative matters. In Seidl's opinion, Austrian economic and social policies after 1945 largely consisted in building heaps of unsolved problems, equal in height to the mountains of files in Austria's state administration waiting for scrutiny by slow-working civil servants (Seidl, 2003: 32). Given the impressive array of laws passed between 1960 and 1986 by the Austrian parliament, and drafted under active participation of the three big chambers and the Trade Union Federation, such hyper-critical views seem unwarranted.[25] But Seidl is certainly right in noting that, in some recent instances, failure to reach unanimity between labour and business on one hand, social partners and the government on the other, delayed progress in legislative reforms – and that therefore it seems justified to question the sacrosanctity of the principle of tripartite consensus-building, both on ideological and on cost grounds.

Conclusion

This is exactly what the new Austrian government, composed of Conservatives (ÖVP) and the national-populist Freedom Party (FPÖ), has done since assuming power in February, 2000. Determined to replace consociationalism with a new policy style introduced as "competitive democracy" (Sperl, 2000: 152), the ÖVP-FPÖ coalition benefited from Austria's EU membership in a double way. Upon entering the European Union, important economic policy issues (agriculture, currency management, competitive policies) became matters of decision by "Brussels". Thus, Austria's model of social partnership automatically suffered a substantial loss of authority. In addition, EU instances usually communicate with national governments rather than with peak organisations of labour and business in member countries – let alone with informal bodies such as the Austrian Parity Commission for Wages and Prices. This, too, strengthened the position of Austria's government as opposed to the social partners, and gave it a pretext to exclude not peak interest associations as such, but mainly those under socialist influence

[25] An overview of the subject matters of important Austrian economic and social legislation is given in Tálos, 1992: 394.

(the Federal Chamber of Labour and the Trade Union Federation) from the process of drafting important economic and social reforms. Participation of the Austrian chambers in all sorts of advisory councils, commissions, and mixed committees – whether established by law or not – continues to this day. The Viennese Chamber of Labour alone sends its delegates to 209 of these bodies (Karlhofer and Tálos, 2000: 392). But its practical influence in the making of laws (as that of the trade unions in the field of industrial relations)[26] is waning. The same can not be said of the Association of Austrian Industrialists. It is regularly consulted by the government on key issues such as budget consolidation, attraction of foreign direct investment, and the creation of a business-friendly tax environment.

Must we expect, then, a "slow fading away" of classical social partnership in Austria? This is a plausible assumption, given that tripartite consultative arrangements of the kind seen in Austria over the past decades are undermined not only by European integration, but also by the increased economic leverage of transnational companies that are more or less independent of labour's support in advancing their interests. Moreover, there are no signs of an imminent reversal of that global trend, favouring a "particularised" safeguarding of group interests over interest mediation by monopolistic "dinosaurs" like Austria's chambers and the Trade Union Federation.

Defying the pessimistic outlook, some scholars, however, still see a future for Austrian neo-corporatism; although they admit that the myth of the social partners' infallible problem solving capacity is bound to die. 21st century corporatism in Austria, according to those who believe in its survival, will exercise influence mainly in key areas where it commands special competence, that is, in the fields of industrial relations, economic policy, and social policy. It will become international, in the sense that Austria's peak interest associations contribute to "the optimal representation and coordination of Austrian interests in future EU activities" (Karlhofer, 1996: 130). Already today, Austria's mission in Brussels runs a staff composed of government officials as well as functionaries of the main interest associations. On the national level, social partners can be expected to add valuable expertise to the discussion of key policy issues such as regulation of access to the health care system, pension reform, and the control of labour migration. "New

26 Here, transposition of the negotiating process for premium payments, working times, etc. to the level of the individual company militated against the continued dominance of a centralised body like Austria's Trade Union Federation. Recently, the Trade Union Federation was compelled to restrict its part in Austrian politics to defending its clientèle against net losses of income, a worsening of labour conditions, and painful cuts into the welfare system.

social partnership" will probably pay tribute to the increased difficulty of mediating specialised group interests, and refrain from rigid centralisation of wage bargaining and related activities. Consequently, the Austrian public may have to accommodate to a tougher social climate, in which even strikes – like those recently staged by railroad workers and pilots – occupy their normal place as expressions of a civilised culture of conflict. Austrian democracy (it must be hoped) will face the challenge and continue to flourish, as a newspaper commentator has recently put it, *streitlustig und doch friedlich* – contentiously, but mindful of peace.

References

Bauer, Otto (1976), "Die österreichische Revolution", *Werkausgabe*, Vol. 2, Vienna: Europaverlag, p. 489-866.

Beller, Steven (1996), *Francis Joseph*, New York-London: Longman.

Berger, Peter (1993), "Berührungspunkte und Gegensätze. Anmerkungen zum wirtschaftlichen Wandel in Österreich und den Niederlanden, 1918-1990", in: Jeroen B. van Heerde (ed.), *Österreich-Niederlande. Beziehungen in Politik, Wirtschaft und Kultur*, Horn-Vienna: Verlag Berger, p. 109-125.

Bischof, Günter (1995), "'Austria looks to the West'. Kommunistische Putschgefahr, geheime Wiederbewaffnung und Westorientierung am Anfang der fünfziger Jahre", in: Thomas Albrich *et al* (eds.), *Österreich in den Fünfzigern* (Innsbrucker Forschungen zur Zeitgeschichte 11), Innsbruck: Studienverlag, p. 183-210.

Bischof, Günter and Martin Kofler (2004), "Austria's Postwar Occupation, the Marshall Plan, and Secret Rearmament as 'Westernizing Agents' 1945-1968", in: Günter Bischof and Anton Pelinka (eds.), *The Americanization/Westerization of Austria* (Contemporary Austrian Studies 12), New Brunswick NJ: Transaction, p. 199-225.

Bischof, Günter and Anton Pelinka (eds.) (1995), *Austro-Corporatism: Past, Present, Future* (Contemporary Austrian Studies 4), New Brunswick NJ: Transaction.

Böhmer, Peter (1999), *Wer konnte, griff zu. "Arisierte" Güter und NS-Vermögen im Krauland-Ministerium (1945-1949)*, Vienna-Cologne-Weimar: Böhlau.

Borchardt, Knut (1982), *Wachstum. Krisen, Handlungsspielräume der Wirtschaftspolitik. Studien zur Wirtschaftsgeschichte des 19. und 20. Jahrhunderts*, Göttingen: Vandenhoeck & Ruprecht, p. 165-182.

Bukey, Evan Burr (2000), *Hitler's Austria. Popular Sentiment in the Nazi Era 1938-1945*, London: Chapel Hill NC.

Butschek, Felix (1996), *Vom Konflikt zur Konsensorientierung – die Kammer für Arbeiter und Angestellte und die österreichische Wirtschaftspolitik 1920 – 1995*, Vienna: ÖGB.

Dachs, Herbert *et al.* (eds.) (1992), *Handbuch des politischen Systems Österreichs*, Vienna: Manz, 1992.

Fischer, Peter G. (1978), "Freie und genossenschaftliche Interessenvertretungen der gewerblichen Wirtschaft in Österreich vom Vormärz bis zum 'Ständestaat'", *Zur Geschichte der Handelskammerorganisation, Schriftenreihe der Bundeskammer der gewerblichen Wirtschaft*, Vol. 37, Vienna: BWK, p. 7-29.

Fraberger, Ingrid and Dieter Stiefel (2000), "'Enemy Images': The Meaning of 'Anti-Communism' and its Importance for the Political and Economic Reconstruction in Austria after 1945", in: Günter Bischof, Anton Pelinka, and Dieter Stiefel (eds.), *The Marshall Plan in Austria* (Contemporary Austrian Studies 8), New Brunswick NJ: Transaction, p. 56-97.

Gerlich, Peter, Edgar Grande, and Wolfgang C. Müller (eds.) (1985), *Sozialpartnerschaft in der Krise. Leistungen und Grenzen des Neo-Korporatismus in Österreich*, Vienna-Graz-Cologne: Böhlau.

Gerschenkron, Alexander (1977), *An Economic Spurt that Failed. Four Lectures in Austrian History*, Princeton, NJ: Princeton University Press.

Hanisch, Ernst (1994), *Der lange Schatten des Staates. Österreichische Gesellschaftsgeschichte im 20. Jahrhundert*, Vienna: Ueberreuter.

Heinisch, Reinhard (2000), *Populism, Proporz, Pariah. Austrian Political Change, its Causes and Repercussions*, New York: Nova Science Publishers.

Hennecke, Hans Jörg (2000), *Friedrich August von Hayek. Die Tradition der Freiheit*, Düsseldorf: Wirtschaft und Finanzen.

Höbelt, Lothar (2003), *Defiant Populist: Jörg Haider and the Politics of Austria*, West Lafayette IN: Purdue University Press.

Jaszi, Oscar (1971 – 5th edition), *The Dissolution of the Habsburg Monarchy*, Chicago: University of Chicago Press.

Jelavich, Barbara (2003), *Modern Austria*, Cambridge – New York: Cambridge University Press.

Karlhofer, Ferdinand (1996), "The Present and Future State of Social Partnership", in: Günter Bischof and Anton Pelinka (eds.), *Austro-Corporatism. Past-Present-Future* (Contemporary Austrian Studies 4), New Brunswick, NJ: Transaction, p. 119-146.

Karlhofer, Ferdinand and Emmerich Tálos (2000), "Sozialpartnerschaft unter Druck. Trends und Szenarien", in: Anton Pelinka, Fritz Plasser and Wolfgang Meixner (eds.), *Die Zukunft der österreichischen Demokratie. Trends, Prognosen und Szenarien*, Vienna: Signum, p. 381-402.

Kattinger, Matthäus (2003), "Österreichs Sozialpartnerschaft hat Patina angesetzt", *Neue Zürcher Zeitung*, 2/3 August, p. 19.

Kersbergen, Kees van (1995), *Social Capitalism – A study of Christian Democracy and the Welfare State*, London: Routledge.

Kindley, Randall W. (1996), "The Evolution of Austria's Neo-Corporatist Institutions", in: Günter Bischof and Anton Pelinka (eds.), *Austro-Corporatism. Past-Present-Future (Contemporary Austrian Studies Vol. 4)*, New Brunswick, NJ: Transaction, p. 53-93.

Knoll, Reinhold and Anton Mayer (eds.) (1976), *Österreichische Konsensdemokratie in Theorie und Praxis*, Vienna-Cologne-Graz: Böhlau.

Korpi, Walter (1983), *The Democratic Class Struggle*, London: Routledge.

Kreisky, Bruno (1986), *Zwischen den Zeiten. Erinnerungen aus fünf Jahrzehnten*, Berlin: Siedler.

Lehmbruch, Gerhard (1985), "Sozialpartnerschaft in der vergleichenden Politikforschung", in: Peter Gerlich, Edgar Grande and Wolfgang C. Müller (eds.), *Sozialpartnerschaft in der Krise. Leistungen und Grenzen des Neo-Korporatismus in Österreich*, Vienna-Graz-Cologne: Böhlau, p. 85-107.

Lijphart, Arend (1977), *Democracy in Plural Societies: A Comparative Exploration*, New Haven-London: Yale University Press.

Maier, Charles S. (1975), *Recasting Bourgeois Europe. Stabilization in France, Germany, and Italy in the Decade after World War I*, Princeton NJ: Princeton University Press.

Marko, Joseph (1992), "Verbände und Sozialpartnerschaft", in: Wolfgang Mantl (ed.), *Politik in Österreich*, Vienna-Cologne-Graz: Böhlau, p. 429-478.

Markovits, Andrei S. (1996), "Austrian Corporatism in Comparative Perspective", in: Günter Bischof and Anton Pelinka (eds.), *Austro-Corporatism. Past-Present-Future. (Contemporary Austrian Studies Vol. 4)*, New Brunswick, NJ: Transaction, p. 5-20.

Nick, Rainer and Anton Pelinka (1993), *Österreichs politische Landschaft*, Innsbruck: Haymon-Verlag.

Paulinyi, Àkos (1973), "Die sogenannte gemeinsame Wirtschaftspolitik Österreich-Ungarns", in: Alois Brusatti (ed.), *Die Habsburgermonarchie 1848-1918*, Vol. 1, Vienna: Verlag der österreichischen Akademie der Wissenschaften, p. 567-604.

Pelinka, Anton (1998), "Austrian political culture: from subject to participant orientation", in: Kurt Richard Luther and Peter Pulzer (eds.), *Austria 1945-1995. Fifty Years of the Second Republic*, Aldershot: Ashgate, p. 109-119.

Pelinka, Anton, Fritz Plasser and Wolfgang Meixner (eds.) (2000), *Die Zukunft der österreichischen Demokratie. Trends, Prognosen und Szenarien*, Vienna: Signum.

Prisching, Manfred (1996), *Die Sozialpartnerschaft. Modell der Vergangenheit oder Modell für Europa*, Vienna: Manz.

Riedlsperger, Max E. (1989), "FPÖ. Liberal or Nazi?", in: Fred Parkinson (ed.), *Conquering the Past. Austrian Nazism Yesterday and Today*, Detroit: Wayne State University Press, p. 257-278.

Rudolph, Richard L. (1975), "The Pattern of Austrian Industrial Growth from the Eighteenth to the Early 20th Century", *Austrian History Yearbook*, Vol. 11, p. 3-25.

Sandgruber, Roman (1995), *Ökonomie und Politik. Österreichische Wirtschaftsgeschichte vom Mittelalter bis zur Gegenwart* (Österreichische Geschichte 10), Vienna: Carl Ueberreuter.

Seidel, Hans (1996), "Social Partnership and Austro-Keynesianism", in: Günter Bischof and Anton Pelinka (eds.), *Austro-Corporatism. Past-Present-Future*

(Contemporary Austrian Studies 4), New Brunswick, NJ: Transaction, p. 94-118.

Seidel, Hans (1998), "Die österreichische Stabilisierungspolitik 1951/1953", in: Franz Baltzarek, Felix Butschek and Gunther Tichy (eds.), *Von der Theorie zur Wirtschaftspolitik – ein österreichischer Weg. Festschrift zum 65. Geburtstag von Erich W. Streissler*, Stuttgart: Lucius & Lucius, p. 267-300.

Seidel, Hans (2000), "Austria's Economic Policy and the Marshall Plan", in: Günter Bischof, Anton Pelinka, and Dieter Stiefel (eds.), *The Marshall Plan in Austria* (Contemporary Austrian Studies 8), New Brunswick NJ: Transaction, pp 247-289.

Seidl, Conrad (2003), "Alles friedlich, alles strittig", *Der Standard*, 24/25/26 December, p. 32.

Senft, Gerhard (2002), *Im Vorfeld der Katastrophe. Die Wirtschaftspolitik des Ständestaates Österreich 1934-1938*, Vienna: Braumüller.

Sperl, Gerfried (2000), *Der Machtwechsel. Österreichs politische Krise zu Beginn des 3. Jahrtausends*, Vienna: Molden.

Tálos, Emmerich (1985), "Sozialpartnerschaft: Zur Entwicklung und Entwicklungsdynamik kooperativ-konzertierter Politik in Österreich", in: Peter Gerlich, Edgar Grande and Wolfgang C. Müller (eds.), *Sozialpartnerschaft in der Krise. Leistungen und Grenzen des Neo-Korporatismus in Österreich*, Vienna-Graz-Cologne: Böhlau, p. 41-83.

Tálos, Emmerich (1992), "Sozialpartnerschaft", in: Herbert Dachs, Peter Gerlich, *et al.* (eds.), *Handbuch des politischen Systems Österreichs*, Vienna: Manz, p. 390-409.

Tálos, Emmerich (1992), "Sozialpartnerschaft. Kooperation – Konzertierung – politische Regulierung", in: Herbert Dachs, Peter Gerlich, *et al.* (eds.), *Handbuch des politischen Systems Österreichs*, Vienna: Manz, p. 390-409.

Tálos, Emmerich (1995), "Interessenvermittlung und partikularistische Interessenpolitik in der Ersten Republik", in: Emmerich Tálos, Herbert Dachs *et al.* (eds.), *Handbuch des politischen Systems Österreichs. Erste Republik 1918-1933*, Vienna: Manz, p. 371-394.

Tálos, Emmerich, and Bernhard Kittel (1996), "Roots of Austro-Corporatism: Institutional Preconditions and Cooperation Before and After 1945", in: Günter Bischof and Anton Pelinka (eds.), *Austro-Corporatism. Past-Present-Future* (Contemporary Austrian Studies 4), New Brunswick, NJ: Transaction, p. 21-52.

Unger, Brigitte (1999), "Social Partnership: Anything Left? The End of a Dinosaur or just a Midlife Crisis?", in: Günter Bischof, Anton Pelinka and Ferdinand Karlhofer, *The Vranitzky Era in Austria* (Contemporary Austrian Studies 7), New Brunswick NJ: Transaction, p. 106-135.

Vaughn, Karen I. (1994), *Austrian Economics in America. The Migration of a Tradition*, Cambridge-New York: Cambridge University Press.

Weber-Felber, Ulrike (1995), "Gewerkschaften in der Ersten Republik", in: Emmerich Tálos, Herbert Dachs *et al.* (eds.), *Handbuch des politischen Systems Österreichs. Erste Republik 1918-1933*, Vienna: Manz, p. 319-338.

Winckler, Georg (1985), "Sozialpartnerschaft und ökonomische Effizienz", in: Peter Gerlich, Edgar Grande and Wolfgang C. Müller (eds.), *Sozialpartnerschaft in der Krise. Leistungen und Grenzen des Neo-Korporatismus in Österreich*, Vienna-Graz-Cologne: Böhlau, p. 295-312.

CHAPTER 5

Dancing with Economics

Dutch Politicians, Policies and Institutions Reacting to Economic Turnarounds (1973-2004)

Jan Peter VAN DEN TOREN

Introduction

Most European countries had similar economic cycles in the second half of the last century. World War II was followed by a period of reconstruction and strong economic growth. The disadvantages of this growth became visible in the 1960s: salaries and inflation rose and West-European countries were forced to use imported labour to keep their industries afloat. In the 1970s and 1980s, all European countries had to deal with world-wide economic crisis and dramatically rising unemployment. After struggling to find an adequate response – often based on national social pacts – to the changes in economic structure in the 1980s and the first half of the 1990s, economy again flourished in the second half of the 1990s, followed in 2001 by another downturn.

Of course, deviations to this general pattern occurred. Even countries with similar economic policies differed in the manner in which decisions regarding those policies were made. Social-economic decision-makers in the individual European countries danced to their own tune in the area of economics. In this chapter I analyse Dutch post-war socio-economic policymaking.

For the Netherlands, comparative studies reveal several points with regard to the structure of the Dutch economy and labour force. The Netherlands already started feeling the impact of the European recession in the 1970s. That forced the Netherlands to restructure wage policy earlier than other European states, allowing the Netherlands to reap higher profits in the period that followed, due to wage levels that were lower than those in competing countries. Thereby industrial restructuring in the 1970s and 1980s was based in part on retirement routes such as disability and early retirement plans rather than just unemployment insurance. Also, the service sector was relatively strong in the Netherlands, making the economy less sensitive to the decline of European industry. There were also specific circumstances in the Dutch labour force. Until the 1970s women constituted a rather small part of the work force. When women – particularly married women – entered the work force in the 1980s and 1990s, they generally held part-time jobs and had modest wages. This permitted a relatively rapid growth in the number of jobs. A summary of socio-economic development from 1973-2003 is given in figure 1.

Figure 1: Unemployment, Disability and Wage Growth 1970-2003

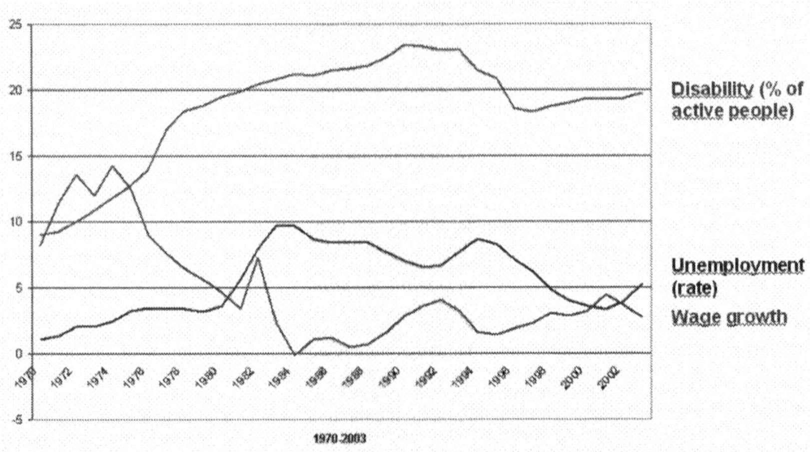

These economic aspects comprise part of the explanation. In the Netherlands the institutional constellation played an important role in economic reconstruction. Institutional circumstances made certain policy modifications possible and obstructed others. Frequently reached tripartite agreements form an example of clearly favourable institutional circumstances.

In the 1990s social pacts became an important component of social consultation in many European countries. In the Netherlands, where economic crises had already peaked in the late 1970s, the "first" social pact was reached earlier: the "Wassenaar Agreement" in 1982. In studies executed in 1990s, the origins of this agreement were traced back to the post-war period (1945), when the Labour Foundation re-established corporatism in the Netherlands, and even to 17th century nation-building in the Low Countries (including Belgium at that time) (Hemerijck, 1993; Metze, 1999). Dutch industrial relations form a well-known specimen of social partnership (van den Toren, 1997). Labour relations in several continental nations can be characterised as "organised decentralisation" (Traxler, 1995). Social-economic policy-making has been decentralised to sector and concern level, without losing its "responsiveness" (Selznick, 1992) for macro-economic objectives.

Although the idea that the Dutch are consensus-seeking by their nature may explain much of Dutch corporatism, the issue really deserves more specific analysis. What were the circumstances that supported the completion and implementation of agreements? What external shocks and institutional conditions can be identified as "triggers", not only for the 1982 agreement, but also for the "near-agreement" of 1979? Why exactly did the tripartite agreement ultimately fail in 1979? And why did later tripartite arrangements in 1993 (wage moderation and decentralisation), 1996 (labour market flexibility and security), 1998, 2003 and (after huge strikes) 2004 succeed?

In this chapter, I analyse the dynamics of post-war Dutch consultation arrangements in the context of economic, institutional and political circumstances, with a focus on the 1980s and 1990s. I present an answer to the question what conditions support the realisation of tripartite arrangements. I will conclude that the Netherlands have developed a combination of exogenous institutions, institutional playing rules and institutional behaviour. This can answer question as: why do right-wing cabinets seem to be able to establish better relations with social partners than left-wing cabinets? And why is it easier to reach agreement on wages than it is to reach agreement on social security policy?

Analytical Framework

The Dutch consultation model has been the object of considerable attention in recent years. Most of this attention focused on policy choices – wage moderation, increasing flexibility and reconstruction of the welfare state. These policy choices arise from decisions made by politicians, union leaders and employer representatives. However, recent – often comparative – analysis, has pointed to different mechanisms to shed light on the logic of these decisions. It is on four institutional rules that I wish to focus in this chapter: (1) minorities and mediation; (2) the shadow of the hierarchy, (3) contract freedom and pluralism; and (4) binding and autonomy.

The core of the Dutch system can be worked out in these terms as follows. In the Netherlands minorities must form coalitions that – in contrast to those in most surrounding countries – are not dominated by one party. Parties in these coalitions mediate with employers and employer representatives. During most of the post-war period the position of the labour unions was extremely important: the labour unions had to agree to wage moderation and to changes in social security. The composition of the cabinet appears to influence the "game" that the cabinet can play with the various social partners. One of the mechanisms that the government can exploit is the "shadow of the hierarchy" (Scharpf, 1997). Consultation at the macro-level is only part of the consultation economy. Another important factor is the level to which social partners at meso-level are prepared (or can be forced) to implement the agreements made at central level. To what extent are they bound by agreements, i.e. to what extent are they prepared to surrender autonomy to peak organisations? At the macro-level and, due to Dutch pluralism, at the meso-level as well, three or more parties are often involved. In this situation, the question of whether unanimity is needed also plays a role, which is parallel to the question of whether the parties have contract freedom.

These institutional factors are known from literature, but have not yet been systematically detailed and tested. This chapter addresses these matters and takes a detailed look at these factors for two policy areas: wage policy and social security. Policy options available for collective bargaining may not be feasible when it comes to social security. This distinction between policy areas particularly applies when the role of the government hierarchy and the relationship between trade union federations and the unions are involved.

This chapter maps outs the relevant features of the Dutch model and tests them on the post-war development for the two policy areas mentioned. First I discuss the social-political relationships, based on a division of the post-war period into eight phases (section 3). The manner in which institutional aspects have also exerted an influence is documented in sections 4 and 5 for the policy areas wage development and social security. section 6 examines the extent to which the four institutions mentioned have played a role. The paper closes with an evaluation of the current constellation with a glance at the future.

Social-Political History in Phases

In a country made up of minorities, coalitions are important. The three trade union federations NVV, NKV and CNV (later FNV, CNV and MHP)[1] have always been represented all at the social-economic negotiation tables. The biggest confederation FNV has never been able

[1] NVV: Nederlands Verbond van Vakverenigingen, socialist; NKV: Nederlands Katholiek Vakverbond, Catholic, successor to the KAB (Katholieke Arbeiders Beweging); CNV Christelijk Nationaal Vakverbond, Protestant. The FNV, Federatie Ne-derlandse Vakbeweging, resulted from the federation (1976) and merger (1982) of the NVV and the NKV. The MHP, established in 1974, is the trade union federation for professional and managerial staff.

to take advantage of its majority position to exclude other federations.[2] In contrast, politicians always look for a majority. The political colour of the cabinet is important for the role of the social partners, particularly for the individual trade union federations. In the overview below, the post-war trade union federations and cabinets are grouped into eight periods.

Table 1: Labour Unions and Cabinet Composition

Period	Labour Unions	Cabinet
1945-1958	NVV-KAB-CNV	Centre-left
1958-1973	NVV-NKV-CNV	Centre-right
1973-1977	FNV-CNV-MHP	Centre-left
1977-1981	FNV-CNV-MHP	Centre-right
1981-1982	FNV-CNV-MHP	Centre-left
1982-1989	FNV-CNV-MHP	Centre-right
1989-1994	FNV-CNV-MHP	Centre-left
1994-2002	FNV-CNV-MHP	"Purple"
2002-2007	FNV-CNV-MHP	Centre-right

1945-1958. During this period the labour unions consisted of three centrally organised trade union federations, i.e. NVV, KAB and CNV. Each trade union federation belonged to a political block and thus had its own political representation. During this period cabinets enjoyed broad-based support. Social-democrats (PvdA) and Christian democrats (the Catholic People's Party KVP – and as of 1952 – the Protestant 'Anti-Revolutionary' Party ARP) were always represented in the government. In the decade immediately following the war, the trade union federations adopted a policy of wage control. Within those margins, they could increasingly play an advisory role via the Labour Foundation and – from 1950 onwards – via the Social-Economic Council.

1958-1973. In the final days of the former period the religious parties opted for a social market economy. That widened the gap to the socialist PvdA.[3] After years of centrally controlled wage policy and therefore centrally controlled trade union federations, in the 1960s all of the trade union federations had to deal with the increasing emancipation

2 Until 1973 none of the recognised labour union federations organised more than 50 per cent of the union members. As of 1976 (the federation) and 1982 (the formal merger), this also applied to the FNV. See Ebbinghaus and Visser, 2000 for numbers of labour union members.

3 Roebroek and Hertogh (1998: 359 and 363) state that until 1973 the welfare state expanded primarily in periods in which the cabinet mainly consisted of the religious parties.

of the unions at the meso-level and with growing polarisation.[4] The cabinets nearly all had a centre-right hue in this period. This gave the Catholic KVP and the Protestant ARP a great deal of influence at that time, in part because these parties formed a channel to get the support the Catholic KAB and the Protestant CNV, respectively, for the policy of the consecutive cabinets.

NKV and CNV had political kindred spirits in the consecutive cabinets. Conversely, along with PvdA, NVV was part of the rapidly disintegrating social-democratic block that increasingly displayed a more opposition-like attitude. KAB and CNV "mediated" between the centre-right cabinet and the labour unions, exacting a high price from the cabinet in the bargain, which stimulated the growth of the welfare state (Roebroek and Hertogh, 1998: 358).

1973-1977. The formation of a federation comprised of the former trade union federations would ultimately backfire in 1974 when the CNV refused to participate in the federation and merger between NVV and NKV and their unions, which ultimately resulted in the FNV trade union federation. In combination with the emergence of the MHP, this gave rise to the plural labour union movement that still functions today, with the FNV as the largest party, the CNV traditionally in second place and the MHP a steadily growing third trade union federation.

The mergers on the side of the labour unions were not accompanied by a strengthening of internal coordination. Uncertainty regarding the nature of the growing economic problems and the unequal effects of these problems on the different sectors and unions, led to a weakening of the labour unions, both in terms of membership as well as in terms of internal coordination. Because the employers' position was also becoming stronger, the labour unions were no longer able to exert as much influence over economic strategy as before. At this point, we can speak of blocked labour relations (Hemerijck, 1993).

1977-1981. The centre-right cabinet Van Agt-Wiegel (1977-1981) was the first cabinet that displayed awareness of the problems facing the economy and government finance, but did not come up with a fundamentally different policy, despite its ideological ambitions. Moreover, both the Den Uyl cabinet and the Van Agt-Wiegel cabinet were internally divided. The consecutive ministers of Social Affairs Boersma (1973-1977) and Albeda (1977-1981) argued for a much more active, Keynesian approach than that being followed by the restrictive Minis-

---

4 This was further strengthened because different unions, motivated in part by loss of members, concluded in the 1960s that they had become too far removed from their members and that the wage control policy had eviscerated the militancy of the labour unions. This is an important point in Harmsen, Perry and van Gelder, 1980.

ters of Finance. This division led to a wait-and-see attitude regarding rising unemployment (Roebroek and Hertogh, 1998: 443). The cabinet opted for constant wage controls that seriously strained relations between the cabinet and the social partners.

1982-1989. The serious economic crisis weakened the position of the labour unions at the beginning of the 1980s. Not only did they lose a large number of members; they were regarded by the political and economic elite as an important impediment to the resolution of the crisis. The second Van Agt cabinet (1981-1982) did not display sufficient decisiveness to induce the labour unions to accept agreements. It was former metal industry employer representative Ruud Lubbers with his centre-right government of Christian democrats (CDA)[5] and liberals (VVD) who was able to force the central employee and employer organisations to agree on a recommendation that was adopted by the affiliated organisations. This "Wassenaar Agreement" would have significant consequences in the domain of wage development. The labour unions regained a respected and influence seat at the various central and local negotiation tables.

In the domain of social security, however, the labour unions continued to oppose the cabinet's austerity policy. None of the trade union federations dared to approve serious cutbacks in social security, and certainly none of them wanted to take the risk of being the first or the only one to do so. The CNV was considered the Achilles heel of the CDA, the party in power at the time. Unlike the FNV, the CNV had a "related" party in the cabinet, which gave the CNV some attention, but little real influence.

1989-1994. When the PvdA became a part of the third Lubbers cabinet (1989-1994), the dominant policy path shifted to centre-left, even though the social democrats were prepared to make far-reaching concessions in their traditional standpoints. At first glance it appeared that both the two largest trade union federations (FNV and CNV) had kindred spirits in the cabinet. However, in political practice the cabinet felt strong enough in the social arena to follow its own course. In the domain of social security and labour market policy, there was continual trench warfare between the cabinet and the social partners. The labour unions had no position in this area; their approval was not needed to make policy changes. And until 1994, the trade union federations did not yet have the strong internal direction regarding wage development that they would have during the second half of the 1990s. In 1993 the cabinet even threatened the unions with wage controls.

---

5 The CDA was formed in 1980 after the merger of the Catholic KVP and two Protestant parties.

1994-2002. The "purple" cabinet of social democrats (PvdA) and liberals (VVD), which ended the pivotal position of the CDA and its predecessors in 1994, could make an even stronger argument that it had broad-based social support: after all, left and right were united in one cabinet. Although it started with a strong anti-institutional approach, the cabinet quickly sought a pragmatic relationship with its social partners.

In the period around 1994 the social partners' palette was also modified by mergers on the employers' side. The newly formed employer confederation VNO-NCW in particular gained strength from these mergers, which dramatically reduced the number of players on the employers' side. The stronger internal control on the side of the employers and employees, a number of valuable recommendations by the SER and the Labour Foundation and foreign recognition of the so-called "polder model" increased the authority of the social partners. The strong and cooperative role of the social partners contributed to rapid growth in employment and labour market participation. In 2001, however, the Netherlands was faced with an economic reversal.

2002-2007. Overindulgence and uncertainty led to a dramatic shift in the political palette in 2002. After a short-lived cabinet comprised of CDA, VVD and the political heirs of Pim Fortuyn, in 2003 again a centre-right government came to power under the leadership of Jan Peter Balkenende. The cabinet introduced the most stringent austerity programme ever, but in the fall of 2003 was able to obtain the approval of the social partners in the form of a ratified central agreement. In 2004, a second "grand design" agreement was reached, but not without huge manifestations and strikes.

Table 2 shows a summary of these periods. The process of "policy learning" is shown per policy domain (Visser and Hemerijck, 1997): a few decades of instrumental re-adjustment and modification were followed by an institutional crisis focussing on questions as: how do we organise socio-economic policy and who will make the decisions? In the area of wage development this took place during the 1970s. In the domain of social security this occurred during the 1980s and the first half of the 1990s. Both policy areas had undergone a comparable phase of institutional reorganisation in the 1940s and 1950s.[6] These phases of institutional reorganisation are shown in italics in the table. They are worked out in the next sections.

6 This institutional debate regarding wage increases had already occurred during the World War II and was completed in 1945 with the establishment of the Labour Foundation (van Bottenburg, 1995).

Table 2: Institutional Changes in Terms of Wage Development and Social Security

Period	Wage development	Social security
1945-1958	Controlled wage policy	– Building of the system – Debate regarding where the responsibility for execution is placed
1958-1973	Pressure on the sectors for more space	Expansion
1973-1982	Blocked relationships	First, disputed, cuts
1982-1989	Renewed co-ordination	Blocked relationships
1989-1998	Continuing wage moderation	Normalising the tripartite relationships
1998-2002	Controlling the pressure on wages	Separating the role of the government and social partners
As of 2002	Sudden wage moderation	Reducing the amount of benefits in Disability Insurance (WAO)

Wage Development

Post-war wage development can be divided into a long period of wage moderation (until 1967), a period of high wage growth and rising unemployment until 1982 and again a period of wage moderations from 1982 onwards. After World War II, the priority in the Netherlands was recovery of industry. Industrialisation, restoring worker productivity and wage moderation were considered extremely important. During the war, agreement had already been reached to set up the Labour Foundation after the war (van Bottenburg, 1995). This Foundation would play an important role in post-war wage developments. There was little difference of opinion between the various factions within the labour unions, employer organisations and politics regarding the post-war choice for controlled wage policy. But during the first half of the 1950s it became increasingly difficult for employers and trade union federations to hold their constituents to the wage increases agreed upon. Black salaries frustrated the implementation of the controlled wage policy. Social partners had to differentiate and increase salaries in the 1950s. Moreover, at the end of the 1950s the government also frequently intervened in the Collective Labour Agreements even when employers and employees had already agreed. The repeated intervention created more resentment than the central wage policy had ever evoked (Woltjer, 1992: 382).

In 1967 the socialist NVV become the first trade union federation that openly balked at cooperating with controlled wage policy. At that time NKV and CNV shared the NVV's grievances, but still wanted to persevere with the wage policy. The trade union federations' opinions regarding the system of wage development also differed during the 1970s. They all believed that the government's role was too large. However, the trade union federations differed in terms of the extent to which they were able to get their members' approval of the draft agreements in the Labour Foundation. In 1972 the Labour Foundation reached a shaky central agreement,[7] but the opinions within the NVV differed so dramatically that NVV chairman Ter Heide ultimately resigned. The unions – and in particular the socialist union in the industrial sector (Industriebond NVV) under the leadership of Arie Groenevelt – strengthened their position, thus crippling the trade union federations. The oil crisis of 1973 could have prompted the recovery of good tripartite labour relationship, but the political constellation and the dominant Keynesian policy paradigm stood in the way. The Den Uyl cabinet relied on its own ability (i.e. expenditures) and got with the 1973 Proxy Act (*Machtigingswet*) even the authority to intervene in wage development. Simultaneously the many trend mechanisms that arose from the solidaristic income policy, made the cabinet depend strongly on the co-operation of the labour unions (van Kersbergen, 1998). The cabinet was held captive by the labour unions, which by that time had lost all confidence in the cabinet.

In the second half of the 1970s a process of "push and shove" started. Although parties realised that wage moderation and cuts were necessary, the analyses regarding the scope and the manner in which this had to be realised differed sharply. In 1979 the compromise – wages for job opportunity – that would determine the path for the 1980s was already incorporated in the Collective Labour Agreement for steel corporation Hoogovens, but could not be centrally approved because the FNV could not get its members to approve it without the pressure of wage controls.[8]

---

7 In contrast to the situation in 1982, in 1972 the labour unions only wanted to talk about the central agreement if the government would eliminate the threat stipulated in Article 8 of the Wage Act, which gave the cabinet the right to intervene in exceptional collective labour agreements. An agreement could not be reached until the government promised not to exercise the right stipulated in that article. Later, Article 8 was eliminated. See also Lansink, Noordegraaf en van Vilsteren, 1991.

8 In 1979 Minister Albeda of Social Affairs did not explicitly say that he would impose wage controls if the negotiations did not result in an agreement (van Bottenburg, 1995: 191), which means that he did not use this as a lever at that time. When he did finally threaten this, the relationship with the labour unions deteriorated further because FNV chairman Kok felt betrayed.

Social partners not only had to conclude on wages but also on the level of collective bargaining. The labour unions felt the responsibility for the dramatically increasing unemployment, but were only willing to place the automatic price compensation on the negotiation table in exchange for a centrally agreed and at sector level applicable reduction in working hours. They wanted firm, verifiable agreements. Employers however were only willing to discuss a reduction in working hours at sector and company level. At central level, parties were not able to agree on a collective reaction on economic reality until 1982. At that time economic crisis was being felt stronger and stronger. Moreover, at company level mutual trust had grown because of agreed social plans on redundancies. This favoured the willingness to agree at central level.

In 1982 the newly installed centre-right cabinet under the leadership of former metal industry negotiator Lubbers was able to impose the "shadow of its hierarchy" over the consultations within the Labour Foundation.[9] After a decade of constant wage controls in the 1970s, the approval by the Labour Foundation in November 1982 was a turning point. This agreement was reached on Thursday afternoon November 18, 1982 between four negotiators at the home of VNO chairman Van Veen in the village Wassenaar, near The Hague.

The approved "Central recommendations regarding aspects of an employment policy" – the Wassenaar Agreement – had two primary objectives for socio-economic policy: improving companies' profit position and providing better distribution of existing employment. In addition, the agreement recognised negotiating freedom at sector and company level, which was important getting employers agree to it.[10] Formally, this local negotiating freedom meant strengthening the role of sectoral parties to the Collective Labour Agreement (CLA), but in practice it also led to strengthening the role of the peak organisations and the government as well. Stronger internal direction and the restoration of the mutual trust between social partners and trust in the government allowed the government to challenge social partners to arrive bipartite or tripartite agreements. A tradition of central consultation

9 It is interesting that the Wassenaar Agreement, now regarded by many as the rebirth of the Dutch consensus model, was regarded by someone like former Minster Albeda as a breach in his attempts to reach agreement through consensus between the labour unions and the employers (Albeda, 1989).

10 Moreover the social partners did not completely trust this acknowledgement by Lubbers, in part because the premier was not regarded as an ideological proponent of self-regulation. This limited trust can be seen in the many two-year Collective Labour Agreements concluded before 1983. Another reason for concluding two-year Collective Labour Agreements was that this space for wage increases could be accrued to "buy" a 5 per cent reduction in work hours.

arose in the 1980s and 1990s, which in a number of cases also led to bipartite or tripartite agreements. The Labour Foundation dealt with a large number of issues leading to recommendations for CLA-parties: unemployment among the young (1984), pensions (1985), employee training and placement of those who had been out of work a long time (1986), sickness and disability (1989) and minorities (1990). In 1989 also a Common Policy Framework (*Gemeenschappelijk Beleidskader*) was agreed, in which the respective parties agreed that efforts designed to achieve balanced, sustainable economic growth, employment growth and a decrease in unemployment, must be not only continued, but intensified.

After a decade of wage moderation, salaries began to rise in 1992 and 1993. At the same time the German unification led to a rise of interest rates and a rapidly deteriorating economic situation in the Netherlands. To stop wage rise the minister of Social Affairs and Employment threatened with a wage control. This threat was averted by the approved *A New Direction* in the Labour Foundation, which called for wage moderation and far-reaching decentralisation of the labour negotiations. Approval led to a strong decrease in wage increases (from 2.6 per cent in 1993 to 0.6 per cent in 1994) but also to strengthening of co-ordination. From then on the percentage of co-ordination among the trade union federation would apply as the maximum for the affiliated unions (van Rij and Royer, 1998).

During the second half of the 1990s there was only one (brief) economic slump in the second half of 1998 (as a result of the financial crisis in Southeast Asia). It was relatively easy for the social partners to translate this into a restrained wage increase for 1999 (van den Toren, 2000). In 1999 the (new) economy again recovered quickly, after which there was a period of substantial growth and an increasingly tight labour market. During the second half of the 1990s, the employers and the employee trade union federations regularly made agreements in the Labour Foundation on continuing the policy of wage moderation. Near the end of the century the reins were loosened somewhat; the labour market was growing tighter and tighter, which put an autonomous pressure on salary increases.

In 2001 economic circumstances deteriorated suddenly. The international recession, was strengthened by the attack on September 11. In 2002 the contractual salary increase declined (from 4.5 per cent in 2001 to 3.75 per cent in 2002) and the incidental wage increase declined even more (from 1.9 per cent to 0.5 per cent). In the fall of 2002 the centre-right Balkenende I cabinet approved a one-year agreement that focused on wage moderation. This cabinet was succeeded within a year by the centre-right Balkenende II cabinet, that proposed the most stringent post-war austerity programme to date, with 7.25 billion euros of cutbacks in the social-economic arena. In spite of the level of austerity, the cabinet was able to win legitimacy for this plan and co-operation from social partners for its measures in the form of a two-year agreement with social partners which was signed on October 14, 2003, including the agreement that the contractual increases would (virtually) not increase for two years. The cabinet's intentions (from 2003) to eliminate the fiscally favourable treatment of early retirement was more problematic, since both employers and the labour unions are opposed to this. This was one of the reasons that a subsequent central agreement failed in May 2004 and could only be reached in November 2004 after huge manifestations and strikes.

Social Insurance

Post-war social insurance history can be divided into a construction period (until 1974) and a cost-cutting period (after 1974). From 1945 to 1974 (the year of the completion of the General Social Welfare Act), the social insurance system grew continuously, based on the widely accepted idea that citizens had the right to insurance from the cradle to the grave. The social insurance plans and the amounts they disbursed were not open to discussion during this period. The manner in which they were executed, however, was open to debate and the debate continued long after 1974.

Social insurance was an important issue of government policy. Opinions regarding social insurance differed and were strongly based on ideology. The unions could present their own divergent viewpoints regarding social insurance without any risk because ultimately, the political establishment made the decisions. The only area in which the social partners were able to reach agreement was the organisation of social insurance. Mostly, they shared criticism on the cabinet's proposals on this topic.

With the implementation of the Disability Act in 1967 (WAO), the assumption was that the social insurance system was almost complete. The time was ready to harmonise the different implementation systems for the various insurance forms. A request for an advice submitted to the SER in 1967 did not lead to a unanimous advisory report until 1984 (so 17 years later). The social partners apparently took all of the time they needed to exchange opinions regarding ideological differences of opinion. Also, benefit levels and conditions were being debated.

In the late 1970s, the government decided for the first time to cut social insurance costs. In 1979, benefits were cut for the first time and cuts continued in the years that followed. In 1981, the second cabinet Van

Agt, ironically in particular the social democrats Den Uyl and Dales of Social Affairs and Employment, proposed to intervene in the Health Insurance Act and to forbid re-insurance by company group plans. Both employer and employee organisations criticised the proposal and induced the cabinet to withdraw it. From 1983 onwards, however, the government was able to realise its cost-cutting proposals more easily, partially because of a difference of opinion between employers and employees. Particularly after the arrival of the centre-right Lubbers I cabinet in 1982, the government did not allow itself to be stopped from implementing cost-cutting measures by pressure from society. The SER was unable to play a role of any importance in this area, primarily because of an inability on the part of the unions to make the concessions that were required to arrive at politically relevant, unanimous SER advisory reports. Strikingly, despite the fact that wage levels were already used in 1982 as a concession to expand employment, the unions resisted to changes in social insurance benefits for years.

In 1983 – at the lowest point in the recession – the Lubbers I government issued its plans for social insurance restructuring. The government wanted to make far-reaching changes in the unemployment and disability plans, including 3 to 5 billion euro in cost cuts for the period 1984-1986. The plans called for a decrease in the benefit percentage for both unemployment and disability from 80 to 70. Under the threat of these cuts, the SER was asked for an advisory report, which it issued in 1984, but the advisory report was not unanimous (SER, 1984). There was consensus regarding the need for restructuring, but only the employers felt that restructuring was needed to decrease collective costs. Opinions differed radically with regard to the core of the advisory report request, i.e. the disability and unemployment insurance amounts and duration. The advisory report placed employers directly opposite employees. The trade union federations were willing to accept a wage-linked benefit of 75 per cent, but felt further limitations in amount and duration unacceptable. The SER advisory report of 1984 did not arouse debate between the cabinet, parliament and social groups regarding principles, but caused social opposition to the cost cuts, often organised by the unions. Despite union opposition, the cabinet cut down benefits for unemployment, disability and health insurance to 70 per cent in 1985. The cabinet also ignored the social partners regarding system restructuring. The restructuring resulted in benefits at welfare level for the long-term unemployed and long-term disabled. Decreased benefits and increased revenues caused by strong economic growth resulted in a drop in collective social insurance costs starting in 1984.

Unlike wage development, the social partners differed strongly in their opinions regarding the necessity of change. Consequently the cabinet Lubbers I was able to (and had to) follow its own course. In addition, certain policy changes actually were reversals of the generous eligibility conditions that social partners were able to apply based on their role in the execution of the social insurance system.

In 1989 the newly elected centre-left cabinet Lubbers III was quickly confronted with rapid rises in the number of people in the disability insurance system. Prime Minister Lubbers characterised the situation with the much-quoted phrase "The Netherlands is sick". During the negotiations of October 2, 1990 between the cabinet and the social partners, agreement was reached regarding a large number of instruments to decrease the number of people receiving benefits from the disability insurance system. In 1991, continuous and rapid increases resulted in a decision by the cabinet in 1991 to implement more far-reaching measures, despite the agreements reached during the tripartite negotiations. The measures included limitations for the disability insurance benefit amounts and duration. This resulted in strong social protest and a wide separation between social partners. The cabinet asked the SER for an advisory report on disability insurance, based on cost cuts of 2 billion euro in 1994. The request submitted to the SER by the government did not include a concrete proposal because of great differences of opinion between the Christian democrats (CDA) and socialists (PvdA). At the same time, social partners were unable to agree on the need for changes to the benefit amounts and duration (the employers were in favour, but the trade unions were against the changes). They were also unable to reach agreement because of different expectations with regard to the policy the cabinet would implement if the social partners did not issue an advisory report. Consequently, a unanimous advisory report was impossible. The FNV was not even willing to issue a majority advisory report because it thought that the government would not actually implement its plans. The CNV, which was willing to issue a majority advisory report, was afraid to do so without FNV or MHP.

After reaching a non-unanimous SER advisory report, the unions organised large protests. Still, the changes made by the Parliament and the cabinet in government plans were minimal. The cabinet agreed not to intervene in collective labour agreements if the social partners issued central advisory reports for employment conditions that supported efforts to fight absenteeism due to illness. The pressure exerted by the government, plus the fact that the employers decided to allow retention of existing rights for illness in response to mass protests organised by the unions in The Hague, helped the Labour Foundation to reach an agreement (van den Toren, 1991).

The role of the social partners was strongly influenced by the results of a parliamentary inquiry into social insurance implementation. The critical report issued by the Buurmeijer Commission in 1993 resulted in a definitive break with the past. The first "purple" cabinet came to power in 1994, accentuating the break. The role of the social partners in the management, supervision and advisory bodies was decreased. In an attempt to consolidate their losses, employer and employee organisations found solace with each other. In 1994, the first unanimous SER advisory report since 1984 was issued. The advisory report handled cabinet plans to regionalise the execution of social insurance. In 1995, the SER reached agreement regarding premium differentiation and private insurance. Based on good relationships in the SER and the Labour Federation, the social partners were able to develop rather harmoniously a long-term vision for social insurance. In 1997, the SER issued a comprehensive advice regarding the future of social security (SER, 1997). Under pressure from cabinet plans, the SER issued another unanimous advisory report, regarding social security organisation, in the spring of 1998. When the second purple cabinet issued a completely different proposal in 1999, social partners were unanimous in their objections in the Labour Federation. However, the government had enough political support for its plans and was not obliged to make fundamental concessions to obtain the approval of the social partners. Change in social security law in 2000 resulted in further limitations to the role of the unions and employer associations. The government was able to exploit the shadow of its hierarchy to the disadvantage of the social partners. The purple cabinet did not ascribe much importance to unanimous advisory reports and did not allow the social partners to make major adjustments to its plans. The purple cabinet made no secret of the fact that part of its mission was to decrease the role played by social partners.

In 2001, the social partners were able, for the first time, to reach agreement in the SER regarding major changes to amounts and duration of disability benefits. In an area in which the purple cabinet was unable to reach agreement, the social partners knew that they would be able to exert influence over the new legislation when they would reach a unanimous advisory report. However, a unanimous advisory report was not possible because of certain government appointed members in the SER. Because of successive cabinet changes, the advisory report did not have an immediate effect on policy. Just in October 2003 a tripartite agreement was closed between the newly formed right-wing Balkenende government and (central) social partners. For the first time ever, the tripartite agreement incorporated a combination of wage moderation, social security policy and pension schemes. Before 2003 these topics were negotiated at separate bargaining tables. In January 2004, the SER again issued a unanimous advisory report, this time regarding disability and unemployment insurance. In 2004 a second "grand design" agreement was reached, but not without huge manifestations and strikes.

Analysis: Four Institutions

In the last two sections I analysed post-war wage policy and social security in terms of convergence and divergence between the various actors at central and sector level. The highlights in the period 1970 – 2003 are shown in figure 2. The interactions between these actors are influenced by institutional circumstances. In this section I will analyse four institutions that play an important role at macro and meso-level and in the relationship between these levels. They are pictured in figure 3.

1. Mediation: the search for majorities. The Netherlands are a nation of minorities. This results in what the Dutch political scientist Van Kersbergen refers to as "the politics of mediation". His reference focuses on the Christian democratic political movement, which held onto its position of power in part due to its ability to bridge the gaps between labour and capital in its own rank and file, which made it possible for it to rule the nation with alternative social democrats (PvdA) and liberals (VVD) (van Kersbergen, 1995; 1996).

The need for coalition forming applies not only to politics, but also to social economics. The politics of mediation play a role in collective labour negotiations too. In this context, the unions who are part of the two smaller federations (CNV and MHP) negotiate collective labour agreements less fettered by the ideological baggage of controversies between labour and capital. Also, the "politics of mediation" can be found in bodies such as the Social-Economic Council (SER) and the Labour Foundation. The members of the SER are representatives of employer and employee organisations and cabinet appointed experts. The Labour Foundation consists solely of representatives of employer federations and employee unions.

Van Kersbergen's "politics of mediation" applied to national politics until 1994, the last year in which the religious parties were needed to form a majority government. In general terms, the politics of mediation resulted in a post-war welfare state with many elements of self-regulation by social partners.

Figure 2: Some Social Pacts and SER Agreements

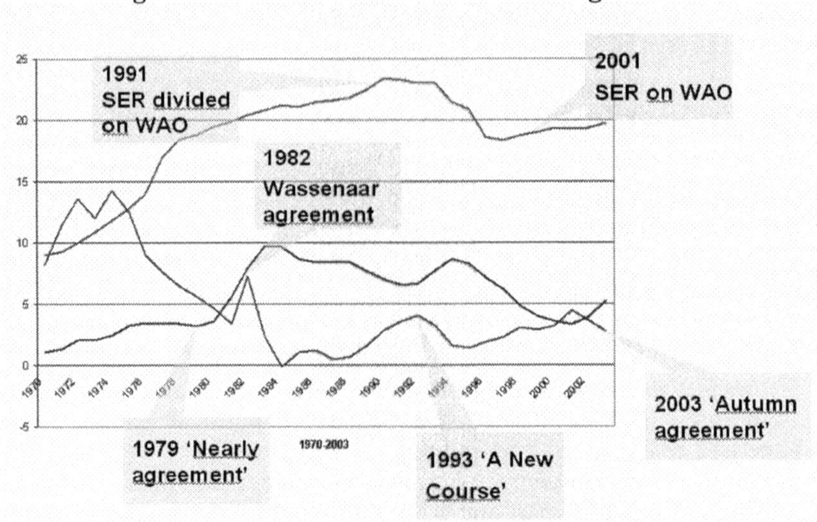

Figure 3: Institutions of a Consultation Economy

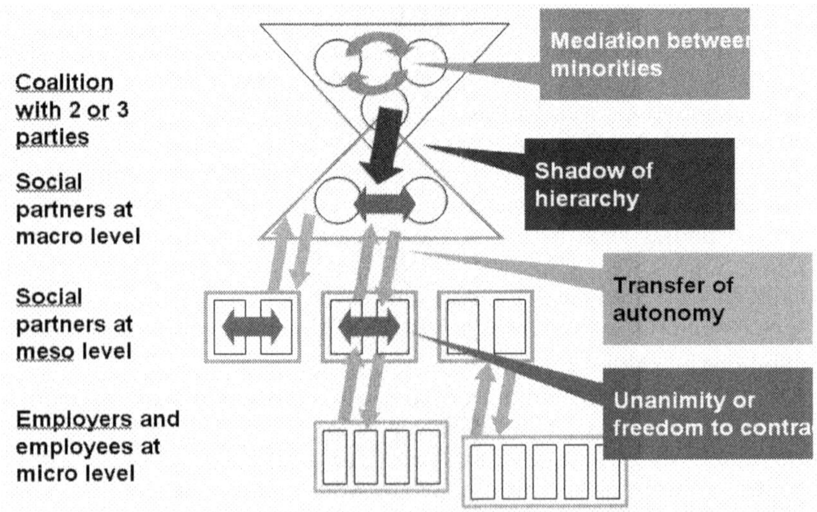

In cases in which the unions were able to exert a relatively strong influence over government policy, the influence was particularly strong in cases involving a centre-right government, primarily because centre-right governments ascribed considerable significance to agreements with the unions. When the PvdA is a member of the ruling coalition, the FNV has an alternative for compromising with employers by focussing on this party, trusting on the fact that the union and the party are closely related in terms of ideology. In hindsight, we can conclude that the FNV was not able to achieve relatively much with centre-left cabinets. The CNV was able to exert influence as a "mediation" union on centre-right cabinets.

A summary of cabinet colour and important pacts is shown in table 3.

Table 3: Shadow of Hierarchy: Cabinet Composition and Social Pacts

Period	Cabinet	Pacts
1977-1981	centre-right	1979 "Nearly agreement"
1982-1989	centre-right	1982 Wassenaar Agreement
1989-1994	centre-left	1991 SER divided on disability 1993 "A New Course"
1994-2002	left-right	2001 SER on WAO
As of 2002	centre-right	2003 Autumn Agreement 2004 SER agreed on WAO 2004 Autumn Agreement

2. Lobbying or negotiating: the shadow of hierarchy. A government that wants to formulate and execute policy is faced with a dilemma. Should it present its own decisions to society, risking rejection of those decisions and frustration of their execution? Or should it allow the organisations that make up society to negotiate decisions, risking failure of the negotiation process or risking results that fall short of government expectations? It is precisely this dilemma that frustrated efforts to influence wage policy and restructure the social welfare system in the 1980s. An institutional setting that rises above this dilemma is referred to by Fritz Scharpf as the "shadow of the hierarchy" of the government (Scharpf, 1993; 1997). The government can stimulate social partners to reach agreements by threatening to intervene if an agreement is not reached. For this approach to be successful, the government must display a predictable and unambiguous position and must have the courage to threaten to intervene – but actually intervene very seldom. A government that is divided and indecisive cannot not play this game. Even, such a government will face threats from both employers and employee unions.[11] Social partners are able to lobby the cabinet directly, but the amount of influence they can exert depends strongly on the composition

11 Christa van Wijnbergen states that the primary focus is the perception of the government held by the social partners (van Wijnbergen, 1999).

of the cabinet and the degree of agreement between and within employer and employee organisations. An unambiguous government drives the social partners into each other's arms. From the perspective of the social partners, the institutional setting and the composition of the cabinet are important. The social partners have to choose to negotiate with each other or to place their fate in the hands of political kindred spirits in the cabinet.

Although the Dutch welfare state shows many of the characteristics of self-regulation by social partners, the role of government has always been quite important. In fact, the government's release of its grip on wage policy in 1963 was followed by a period of blocked and inefficient labour relations. In the 1970s, subsequent cabinets used wage ceilings as a last resort when the social partners were unable to reach agreement on their own. Only when confronted with the threat of wage ceilings the unions were able to reach agreements that could be approved by the underlying organisations. This "shadow of the hierarchy" was also applied in later years, e. g. the threat of a wage measure in 1993 and the threat of a government refusal to declare collective labour agreements generally binding in 1994 if the agreements did not include low salary scales. This lead to *A New Course*. The "shadow" was effectively applied again in 2003 when the government threatened to intervene in early pension benefit plans if the social partners did not reach agreement regarding wage restraint.[12]

The "shadow" was primarily applied by government in cases involving wage policy and was not used as often to exert influence over agreements regarding social insurance. The "shadow" approach is more difficult to apply in cases involving negotiations between the social partners in the area of social insurance. In the collective labour agreement negotiations, Labour Foundation recommendations (which are almost always unanimous) are not implemented by the government, but by the social partners themselves. If the cabinet feels that a Labour Foundation recommendation or its implementation is inadequate, it can intervene by enacting regulatory legislation or by not declaring the results of the negotiations generally binding. Social insurance legislation is a government task. Once the cabinet has successfully finished difficult negotiations to reach a compromise itself, it is not apt to grant unquestioning approval of a proposal submitted by the social partners

[12] In 2004 the cabinet reached an agreement in itself and with parliament to intervene in social security and pensions. For one side this was a sharp shadow on social partners to move toward an agreement that could convince cabinet to change their plans. At the other side government had a strong interest to enact this severe change with the support of social partners.

(even if it is unanimously supported by the social partners). In the late 1990s, after years of preparations, the purple cabinet was able to reach a compromise regarding the implementation of social insurance policy. The government was unwilling to abandon this compromise, which had taken a great deal of time and effort, in favour of a compromise reached earlier by social partners in the SER.

Obviously, the cabinet takes into account the degree to which the social partners can ignore the policy desired by the cabinet when it defines its standpoints. In the area of social insurance there is less space available for deviations from cabinet policy than in the area of employment conditions and that space is shrinking steadily. In 2001, the social partners issued an almost unanimous SER advice regarding Disability Law (WAO) restructuring. In the years thereafter, the advisory report was regularly used to exert pressure on the cabinet and to confront the cabinet with very difficult dilemmas. In 2004, a similar SER-advice was issued in an attempt to stop the cabinet from more far-reaching intervention.

The examples above reveal that the government must be extremely careful when using the shadow of its hierarchy. Legislation that overrules the agreements reached by the social partners does not stimulate the social partners to stick their necks out during subsequent negotiation rounds. Legislation can stimulate further self-regulation (also into other domains) if it respects the agreements reached by the social partners and if the social partners are involved in the content of legislation. This was the case during development of the government's "flexibility and security" policy in the 1990s. While the government was unable to reach an agreement in the years prior to 1996, the social partners were able to reach agreement in the Labour Foundation in a relatively short period of time. Threats on the part of the Parliament to enact its own legislation also played a role. The social partners were able to create support for a different balance between flexibility and security, based on internal debate. They used this support to effect changes in collective labour agreements and as a basis for recommendations for the cabinet regarding changes legislation. In this context, they realised that unanimity would be a strong argument for approval of their recommendations by the cabinet. The cabinet was then able to exploit the support created by the social partners to enact its legislation, without overruling or ignoring the bipartite agreements reached by the social partners.

3. Unanimity and contract freedom. Multiple decision rules in the Dutch negotiating model differ in their effects. The Labour Foundation, which consists of employer and employee federations, formally cannot negotiate with the government until it has reached mutual agreement. In the Labour Foundation, the Social Economic Council and other, similar advisory bodies in the area of social insurance, unanimous advisory reports carry far more weight than advisory reports in which one of the parties takes a minority standpoint with regard to essential points. In collective labour agreement negotiations, however, an agreement that does not have the approval of one union bears the same legal weight (for generally binding declaration) as one that is unanimously approved.[13] An important counterpart of the plurality of the Dutch unions is the decision rule of contract freedom at decentral CLA negotiations, when exocentric standpoints can result in exclusion. Important changes in CLA negotiations are reached in collective labour agreements that were not signed by all of the unions and after strikes that did not involve all of the unions.[14] Examples are the strikes on price compensation in 1972 and 1973 in the metal industry; the education, railroad, and civil servant strikes in 1982 and 1983 and the strikes on price compensation in the food industry in 1992 (For the period up to 1989: van der Veen and Klandermans, 1990).

Differences in opinion have resulted in separate collective labour agreements, giving employer organisations the opportunity to close agreements with individual unions and groups of unions. In most cases, the agreements reached with the majority were eventually accepted in later years by the unions that originally refused to accept them. The risk of exclusion is one of the explanations for lower wage increases in cases involving more unions (Royer, 1996; Teulings and Hartog, 1998). Contract freedom and the related risk of exclusion stimulate policy change because unanimous approval on the part of the unions (and employer unions) is not required. The Labour Foundation, on the other hand, cannot close agreements until all of the parties involved approve the agreement. This system "rewards" the party that requires the greatest amount of persuasion to approve the agreement. This is why the FNV, that blocked a pact developed by the Labour Foundation in 1979, could play a key role in the Wassenaar Agreement in 1982.

---

13 In an Anglo Saxon institutional constellation, multiple (competing) unions results in higher wages (see Booth, 1995; Teulings and Hartog, 1998). The Rijnland model also runs the same risk under certain circumstances. In Belgium, collective labour agreements must be approved by all of the CLA parties (representatives) admitted to the negotiations, which is why the smaller socialist unions are often able to put a radical stamp on the negotiations; little was accomplished in the area of wage moderation in Belgium until 1998. See also Scharpf, 1993; 1997.

14 The right to negotiate with part of the unions does not involve an obligation to negotiate. In 1985, two of the three construction unions agreed to the employer's collective labour offer for the construction industry. But because the employers did not consider the two (smaller) unions representative, they refused to negotiate the agreement, and their stance was later backed up by the courts.

While union plurality supports innovation in collective labour agreements, it has an opposite effect on social insurance policy. Although "competition" does result in new ideas, the individual organisations are usually less willing to make concessions because they are unsure that other organisations will make them as well. Until 2001, this resulted in a "joint decision trap" in the world of social insurance, with none of the parties willing to take the first step.

4. Binding and transfer of autonomy. In addition to the horizontal dimension (in which the parties involved reach agreement), negotiating systems as the Dutch system also have a vertical dimension: can the organisations involved in the negotiations count on the support of the rank and file within the organisation? Trade union federations, for instance, need the approval of their unions for SER advisory reports and Labour Foundation pacts. In cases involving ratification of a collective labour agreement or a call to strike, the approval of a majority of the union members is also required. Social organisations need members, which means that they cannot ignore the desires of the rank and file. These organisations must have influence to appeal to members – but they only acquire influence by making compromises (Schmitter and Streeck, 1981). The organisations are attractive negotiating partners if they are able to bind the rank and file to the agreements they make. Franz Traxler uses the term "governability" in this context (Traxler, 1993). Fritz Scharpf describes the governability concept in detail for a range of social political organisations by in *Games real actors play* (1997) (see figure 4). He refers to organisations that are able to make hierarchical decisions regarding the opinions of their members as "corporate actors". He makes a distinction between these organisations and "collective actors", which he divides into "movements" and "clubs". Movements can only operate as long as all members want them to and therefore require consensus or unanimity, while clubs consist of members that transfer part of their autonomy to the collective, which requires majority approval of subsequent decisions to operate. Unlike employees in certain other European countries, employees in the Netherlands are not members of the trade union federations, but are members of individual unions that are members of the trade union federations (FNV, CNV and MHP).[15] This means that the trade union federations are unable to automatically speak on behalf of the employees, but need the approval of the unions. In the pillarized post-war period, during which the various unions generally operated as individual blocks, the authority of the Dutch trade union federations over the unions was strong and decision-making was hierarchical (top down). In the first few decades after 1945,

---

15 In 2000, the name of the last trade union federation was changed to Unie MHP.

the union movement could be characterised as a corporate actor. In the period thereafter, however, the Dutch trade union federations increasingly took on the characteristics of a collective actor.

Figure 4: Transfer of Autonomy ('action resources') – Actor Orientations according to Scharpf

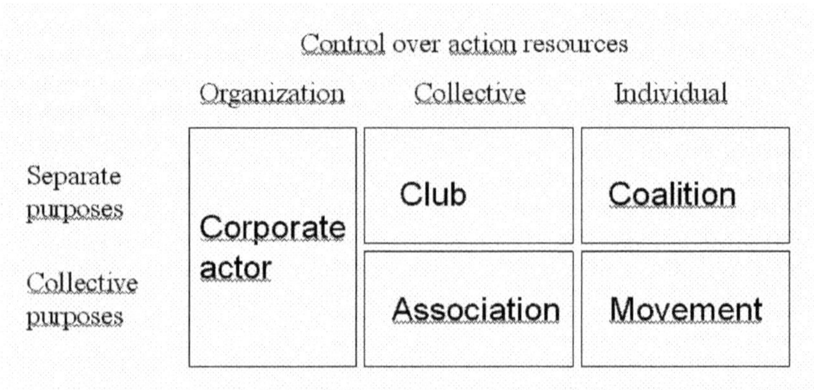

Philippe Schmitter and Wolfgang Streeck (1981) describe a number of factors that facilitate binding, despite the rank and file, e.g. a strong shared ideology and unique member benefits. In Dutch post-war society, there were enough shared ideologies, usually based on one of three political blocks, but the role of ideology diminished rapidly in the 1970s for both NVV and NKV. Aso the product of their merge, the FNV, had to keep its supporters united with a far weaker ideology.[16] The CNV, the smallest trade union federation, which from 1974 had to fight the far larger FNV for legitimacy, has always been able to call on its Christian-social ideology to bind its members, facilitating internal *governability*.

Interestingly, the role of unions differs depends on the policy domain involved (see figures 5 and 6). In the area of social insurance policy, for instance, trade union federations operate as *associations*: after approval of the majority of their members (the unions), the trade union confederation can take a standpoint in an advisory body or even close an agreement with the government. In the area of employment conditions, the trade union federations primarily function – to use Scharpf's terminology – as *movements*: members (the unions) that do not agree with the opinion held by the majority of the trade union federation members

16 This is also why the FNV places a stronger emphasis than the CNV on member benefits such as legal assistance, insurance plans, holidays and discount cards. The central budget for promotional activities of the FNV trade union federation also helps the union retain control over the member unions.

regarding a give area, e.g. wage restraint, can frustrate the decision of the majority by applying their own divergent policy in their specific sector.

Figure 5: Transfer of Autonomy ('action resources'): Collective Bargaining on Wages

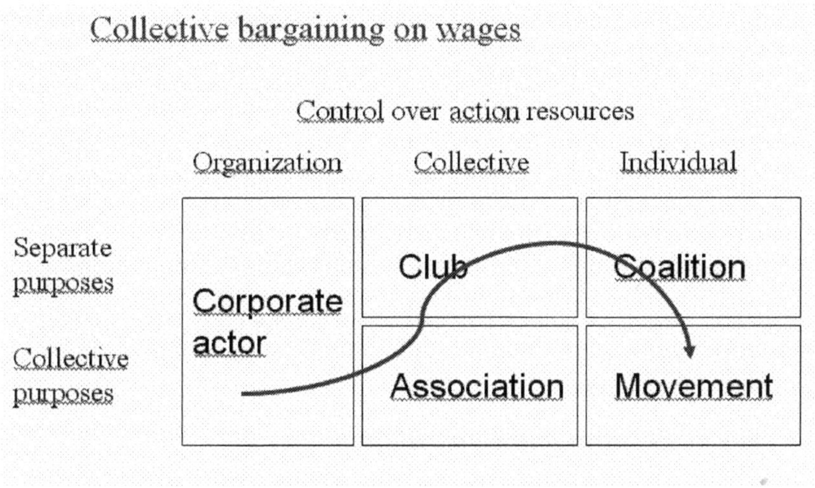

Figure 6: Transfer of Autonomy ('action resources'): Social Security

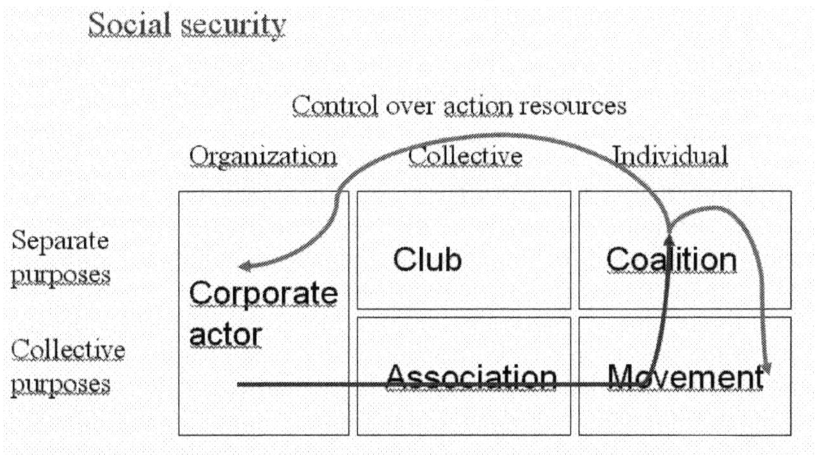

The paradox of the Dutch model is that the Dutch union movement did not acquire and consolidate its influence by striving to maximise the direct wage benefits of its supporters. That objective can be achieved more easily by a corporate actor than a collective actor. That the Wassenaar Agreement was not concluded until 1982[17] was not because the federation negotiators were unable to reach an agreement until that year, but because 1982 was the year in which the negotiators finally were able to obtain enough approval of all of the member organisations. In the 1960s and 1970s the trade union federations had lost control over their member organisations, control that had previously been viewed as almost self-apparent. In the 1960s and 1970s the various blocks began to disintegrate and were transformed from corporate actors to collective actors and federations *de facto* needed the unanimous approval of their member organisations to operate, particularly in the area of wage policy. These collective actors were unable to independently reach agreements in the 1970s. Since 1982, however, even the most left-side confederation (FNV) has been able to accept wage moderation. The concept of restrained wage growth has become a basic attitude for professional trade union negotiators.

A Coherent Institutional Constellation

This research into the institutional mechanisms of Dutch social economics reveals that the Dutch system does not consist solely of romantic notions, heroism or altruism. A number of playing rules, often based on historic precedents, force the various parties involved to contribute to general interests as they strive to protect their own specific interests. Although the mechanisms differ in character, they are closely related. The mechanisms and their relationships are shown in table 4.

The combination of exogenous (historically or social-culturally driven) institutions and the figuring playing rules (the institutional constellation that is defined by law) results in effects that can be considered the institutional baggage of the Netherlands. The institutions are related. The plurality of the Dutch labour unions, combined with contract freedom, makes self-regulation effective.

"Responsiveness" (Selznick, 1992), which is stimulated by the plurality of the labour unions, is strongest in the area of wage policy. The institutional constellation for wage policy is structured in such a way that the government needs the social partners to realise its objectives. In the same constellation, union plurality favours socially responsible behaviour. In the post-war period, 1967 to 1982 were the only years in

[17] From an international perspective, the Wassenaar Agreement was one of the first 'central pacts' closed after the recession in the 1970s (Grote and Schmitter, 1999).

which the (institutional) relationships were problematic, but, here again, the plurality of the unions contributed to a solution. Plurality benefits the powers needed to bring wage policy into balance, but it also limits those powers by making the individual labour unions less visible. In the absence of external disruptions, employers, labour unions and the government tend to leave the existing constellation unchanged. In the area of social insurance policy, the social partners helped to build a system that consisted of a mixture of self-regulation and government legislation until the mid-1980s. In addition, the social partners exploited social insurance policy in various bodies to obtain collective and, in some cases individual interests. This resulted in a collapse of the hybrid system. In 1994, the government started to push the social partners out of their role as organisers of social insurance policy. This forced the social partners to co-operate with each other more closely, but their new spirit of co-operation was primarily driven by a desire to limit their losses. They did not regain their influence over cabinet policy until 2001, then based on (nearly) unanimously approved SER-advises. It took another three years and even huge manifestations till government followed this advises.

Table 4: Institutions in the Dutch model

Exogenous institutions +	Endogenous institutions → (playing rules)	Institutional behaviour
Minorities require coalition forming	Shadow of hierarchy	Responsiveness
Plural organisations (particularly on trade union side)	Contract freedom	Agreements Policy competition → Policy innovation
Organisations as "collective actors"	Self-regulation Generally binding declaration	Binding rank and file

Closing Remarks: Dancing with Economics?

Institutional constellations have hindered modernisation in the area of social insurance policy for decades. The social insurance field, closely fettered by self-regulation, has been divided by the social partners on one hand, based on collective agreements with supplemental wage provisions, and by the government on the other, based on government legislation and basic social welfare provisions. The social partners are limited in their influence by what they are able to achieve via SER advisory reports and what they are able to achieve in terms of building support in the rank and file, for or against government proposals.

In the area of employment policy, historic plurality and contract freedom contribute to the achievement of agreements at macro and meso-levels. Changes in the behaviour of the organisations, in response to changes in the economic situation, have had a particularly strong effect in the area of wage restraint and wage flexibility. However, this does raise the question of whether the system also contributes to economic innovation and productivity. Is the system able to support the ambitions of the Netherlands to fit the needs of the Lisbon Strategy towards productivity and labour participation? Can consultation arrangements deal with the opportunities and threats of a "knowledge economy"? Can corporatism deal with the changes that we currently face in a world of internationalisation, shareholder-ism, and individualisation? And can corporatism support the shift from early retirement to longer participation in the labour market by elderly workers?

In the context of these new themes, the control of CLA negotiators on employee and firm level is far lower. The social partners are now faced with the challenge of offering constellations that stimulate employees and firms to increase their productivity and that "seduce" employees to work longer. The relationships between meso and micro-level must intensify further and will become more "give-and-take" instead of based on regulation and norms. In "1982", the central social partners realised that they could no longer rely on a hierarchical relationship with their labour unions and branch organisations. Serious consideration of meso organisations made macro agreements effective. We may need the same type of change today in the relationship between meso and micro-level.

References

Albeda, Wil (1989), "Lubbers als econoom", in: Arendo Joustra and Erik van Venetië, *Ruud Lubbers. Manager in de politiek.* Baarn: Anthos.

Booth, Alison L. (1995), *The Economics of the Trade Union*, Cambridge: Cambridge University Press.

Bottenburg, Maarten van (1995), *"Aan den Arbeid!" In de wandelgangen van de Stichting van de Arbeid 1945-1995*, Amsterdam: Bert Bakker.

Ebbinghaus, Bernhard and Jelle Visser (2000), *Trade Unions in Western Europe since 1945*, Oxford-New York-Basingstoke: Macmillan.

Grote, Jürgen R. and Philippe C. Schmitter (1999), "The Renaissance of National Corporatism: Unintended Side-effects of European Economic and Monetary Union or Calculated Response to the Absence of European Social

Policy?", *Transfer. European Review of Labour and Research*, Vol. 5, 1-2, p. 34-63.

Harmsen, Ger, Jos Perry and Floor van Gelder (1980), *Mensenwerk. Industriële vakbonden op weg naar eenheid*, Baarn: Ambo.

Hemerijck, Anton C. (1993), *The Historical Contingencies of Dutch Corporatism*, Oxford: Balliol College.

Kersbergen, Kees van (1995), *Social Capitalism. A Study of Christian Democracy and the Welfare State*, London-New York: Routledge.

Kersbergen, Kees van (1996), "Hopen op macht. De neergang van de Nederlandse christen-democratie in vergelijkend perspectief", in: *NDPP, Jaarboek 1995*, Rijksuniversiteit Groningen: NDPP, p. 92-112.

Kersbergen, Kees van (1998), "De cultuur van gelijkheid. De herverdeling van inkomen", in: Jan Ramakers, Gerrit Voerman and Rutger Zwart (eds.), *Illusies van Den Uyl? De spreiding van kennis, macht en inkomen*, Amsterdam: Het Spinhuis, p. 67-88.

Lansink, Henny, Herman Noordegraaf and Eef van Vilsteren (1991), *Herman Bode. Vakbondsman*, Baarn: Ambor.

Metze, Marcel (1999), *Let's talk Dutch now. Harmonie in de polder: uitvinding of erfenis?* Amsterdam: De Arbeiderspers.

Peet, Jan, Bert Altena and Hein Wieldijk (eds.) (1998), *Honderd jaar sociaal. Teksten uit honderd jaar socile beweging en sociaal denken in Nederland*, The Hague: Sdu Uitgevers.

Rij, Coen van and Maurice Royer (1998), "'Follow the leader?' Een analyse van volging en coördinatie van afspraken over loonstijgingen", in: *CAO's*, The Hague: Ministry of Social Affairs and Employment.

Roebroek Jos M. and Mirjam Hertogh (1998), *"De beschavende invloed des tijds" Twee eeuwen sociale politiek, verzorgingsstaat en sociale zekerheid in Nederland*, The Hague: COSZ/VUGA.

Royer, Maurice (1996), *CLA-onderhandelingen. Een voorspelbaar, logisch and rationeel proces?* Amsterdam: Thesis Publishers.

Scharpf, Fritz W. (1993), "Coordination in Hierarchies and Networks", in: F. W. Scharpf (ed.), *Games in Hierarchies and Networks. Analytical and Empirical Approaches to the Study of Governance Institutions*, Frankfurt/M-Boulder Colorado: Westview Press, p. 125-166.

Scharpf, Fritz W. (1997), *Games Real Actors Play. Actor-centered Institutionalism in Policy Research*, Boulder: WestviewPress.

Schmitter, Philippe C. and Wolfgang Streeck (1981), "The Organization of Business Interests. A Research Sesign to Study the Associative Action of Business Interests in the Advanced Industrial Societies of Western Europe", in: *IIM Discussion Papers*, IIM/LMP 81-31, Wissenschaftszentrum Berlin.

Selznick, Peter (1992), *The Moral Commonwealth. Social Theory and the Promise of Community*, Los Angeles-Oxford: Berkley.

SER (1984), *Advies hoofdlijnen gewijzigd stelsel van sociale verzekering bij werkloosheid en arbeidsongeschiktheid*, The Hague, June 29.

SER (1997), *Werken aan verzekering*, 2 Volumes, The Hague, June 20.

Teulings, Coen and Joop Hartog (1998), *Corporatism or Competion? Labour Contracts, Institutions and Wage Structures in International Comparison*, Cambridge: Cambridge University Press.

Van den Toren, Jan Peter (2000), "Netherlands", in: Giuseppe Fajertag (ed.), *Collective Bargaining in Europe 1998-1999*, Brussels: European Trade Union Institute.

Van den Toren, Jan Peter (1991), *ZW / WAO-acties. Kwalitieve beschrijving en analyse*, Utrecht: CNV Research Department.

Van den Toren, Jan Peter (1997), "A 'Tripartite Consensus Economy': The Dutch Variant of a Social Pact", in: Giuseppe Fajertag and Philippe Pochet (eds.), *Social Pacts in Europe*, Brussels: ETUI/OSE, p. 181-194.

Traxler, Franz (1993), "Business Associations and Labor Unions in Comparison. Theoretical Perspectives and Empirical Findings on Social Class, Collective Action, Associational Organizability", *British Journal of Sociology*, Vol. 44, p. 673-693.

Traxler, Franz (1995), "Farewell to Labour Market Associations? Organized versus Disorganized Decentralization as a Map for Industrial Relations", in: Colin Crouch and Franz Traxler (eds.), *Organised Industrial Relations in Europe: What Future?*, Aldershot: Avebury, p. 23-44.

Van der Veen, Gerrita and Bert Klandermans (1990), *Tussen overleg & strijd. CNV en collectieve acties*, Kampen: Kok.

Visser, Jelle and Anton Hemerijck (1997), *"A Dutch Miracle" Job Growth, Welfare Reform and Corporatism in the Netherlands*, Amsterdam: Amsterdam University Press.

Wijnbergen, Christa van (1999), *The Politics of Reform: Battling Unemployment in Germany and the Netherlands*, Atlanta: Paper American Political Science Association, September 2-5.

Woltjer, J. J. (1992), *Recent verleden. Nederland in de twintigste eeuw*, Amsterdam: Balans.

CHAPTER 6

The Wassenaar Agreement (1982), the Timing of a Social Pact

Doreen ARNOLDUS

Introduction

The periodisation of the study of political economy and socio-economic developments in the Netherlands for the second half of the 20th century could be based on social pacts. In fact, the institutional framework of the Dutch consultation economy is built upon organisations whose existence and entire raison d'être is closely connected with social pacts. The Labour Foundation ("Stichting van de Arbeid"), for example, was founded in 1945 based upon a Manifesto that was a social pact between employers and employees. From then up to the present day, the peak organisations of employers and employees that constitute the Labour Foundation have concluded many agreements with each other and the government, generally on wage formation issues. Wage formation is an important subject, because for a small, open economy relying on exports such as the Netherlands, competitive wage levels and productivity levels determine the chances for sustained economic growth.

For the first two decades of its existence, from 1945 until 1963, the Labour Foundation played an import role in the centrally guided wage-policy which had wage constraint as its primary object. In 1970, wage formation was formally decentralised. This set the stage for a period that was characterised by lack of consensus between employers and employees. For twelve consecutive years until 1982, the "social partners" – as employers and employees are called in the Netherlands – were unable to reach a national agreement.

This chapter focuses on the question of how the deadlock in the relationship between employers and employees was overcome in 1982, when the social partners finally came to an agreement. Why was it possible in November 1982 to dispel the atmosphere of polarisation that had been so typical for almost fifteen years? To answer this question I will make an adaptation of the explanative framework for policy concertation that was formulated by Compston in 2003, as expounded in the next section (Compston, 2003). Next, I will give a survey of the social pacts in the Netherlands, followed by a description and analysis of the route to the Wassenaar Agreement.

For the purpose of this chapter, social pacts are defined as formal agreements on socio-economic issues; such as employment, wage formation and social policy. These can be bipartite agreements negotiated between the social partners, or tripartite agreements which also include the government. In Dutch practice, formal tripartite agreements are rare. More often bipartite employer-union agreements are given the appearance of a tripartite agreement by state approval or by state assistance in the implementation phase.[1] Below, I will give a survey of the Dutch tradition of agreements. In Dutch these agreements have names such as *centraal akkoord* or *sociaal akkoord* or *najaarsakkoord* (national general, social or autumn agreement) rather than *sociaal pact*.

A Framework for Social Pacts

In 2003, Hugh Compston formulated a configurational theory of policy concertation, inspired by the theory of agenda-setting by John Kingdon (Compston, 2003). Compston's definition of policy concertation focuses on the government's policy-making by means of agreements with representatives of employer organisations and trade unions. Social pacts are only one manifestation of this. Compston distinguishes four types of co-determination of public policy (as opposed to mere consultation): (a) by agreement within government committees; (b) by informal agreements; (c) by formal tripartite or government-union agreements such as social pacts; or (d) by implementation by the state of bipartite employer-union agreements.

Compston's model can be summarised as follows. The occurrence of co-determination of public policy is determined by the coincidence in time of specific configurations of events and conditions. Policy concertation (in this case a social pact) is likely to occur when the government is confronted with an economic problem which in its perception can only be solved by this instrument (note that the primacy of politics is a logical implication of Compston's perspective). This must coincide with a certain degree of shared economic understanding between the socio-

1 Bipartite government-union agreements are also called social pacts by Compston but these do not exist in the Netherlands.

economic actors and the expectation that the future participants are capable or willing to implement the agreement.[2]

Compston argues that the four possible states of policy concertation are a function of the specific configuration of the three explanatory variables. For creation and persistence of policy concertation arrangements the three independent variables are all necessary, but individually they are not sufficient. For termination and non-existence of policy concertation, the absence of each individual independent variable is sufficient. Constructing policy concertation is therefore more time-consuming than breaking down the institutions of policy concertation. In my view, a highly intriguing implication of this is that the very persistence of a policy concertation framework means that the participants still perceive it as functional.

Policy concertation can be analysed from several perspectives. Compston's model aims to explain (changes in) the making of public policy. Policy choices are made by politicians alone, or – in the case of policy concertation – in combination with representatives of employers' organisations and trade unions. The conditions must be right for the latter two "natural opponents" to collaborate. As Van den Toren shows in his contribution to this volume, the logic of political decisions can be analysed by identifying the underlying institutional rules. The configurational theory of policy concertation adopts a more actor-centred perspective. Not by reducing policy concertation to merely particular decisions, but by underlining the importance of the perception that socio-economic actors have of the economic and political situation. The attractiveness of Compston's model is that it attempts to identify the factors that may change these perceptions, for example about the likelihood of the implementation of a potential social pact.

Social Pacts: Milestones in Consultation and Wage Formation, 1945-1982

In the Netherlands, social pacts are concluded within the Labour Foundation ("Stichting van de Arbeid"). This Foundation was established immediately after the liberation of the Netherlands after World War II, on May 6, 1945. Being a joint organisation of the central employers' and employees' organisations, it developed into a suitable body for effective negotiations between the social partners. This was an important difference with the other institution of the Dutch consultation

2 The three explanatory variables that Compston distinguishes ("perceived problems"; "shared economic understanding" and "expectations about implementation") are in my view not entirely independent from each other (see also below).

economy, the Social and Economic Council ("Sociaal Economische Raad", SER). The SER, established in 1950, is a tripartite institute. The third party consists of independent experts, called crown members, appointed by the Crown, though not accountable to the government. These crown members are supposed to look after the general interest, while the representatives of employers and employees are promoting the interests of their own members. As an institute under public law, the SER offers a good floor for public debate, but its advice to the government is not binding. Especially in the first decades, unanimously voiced recommendations of the SER were usually implemented by the government. The private character of the Labour Foundation, on the other hand, made it possible to organise negotiations between the social partners while keeping the government at arms length. By their very nature, these negotiations were less noncommittal.

Although the Foundation produced advice for the government, it was primarily meant as an institution to formulate recommendations on social issues – wages, conditions of employment, social security and education – to the negotiating parties in industries and companies. Of course, the government attempted to influence the negotiations. In his eloquent institutional history of the Labour Foundation, Van Bottenburg depicts the changing liaisons between employers, employees and the state from the period of the centrally guided wage-policy in the 1950s to the long-drawn-out process of decentralisation of wage formation since the 1982 Wassenaar Agreement. Within the Labour Foundation the relations between the two parties also changed in the course of time (van Bottenburg, 1995). With this in mind, it is possible to distinguish a number of important social pacts.

Manifesto of the Labour Foundation (1945)

The first social pact is the founding Manifesto of the Labour Foundation in 1945. Remarkably, in his *exposé* on the Netherlands, Compston does not mention this social pact, although it implied that the social partners recognised each other (with the exception of the communist union EVC) – one of the basic criteria of the variable "shared economic understanding" of his model. In this sense, the manifesto of 1945 was as significant for the country's industrial relations as the Swedish bipartite Saltsjöbaden Agreement of 1938 between employers and unions. The Swedish case was exceptional because the basic economic agreement was already established before World War II (Compston, 2003: 798). The Dutch Manifesto was not unique in its time; social pacts between employers and employees were also concluded in France and Belgium immediately after the liberation: the French *Programme commun de la Résistance* of March 1944 and the Belgian Social Pact of April 1944

(Luyten, 2003; Pasture, 1993). The Dutch Manifesto resembled the Belgian and French social pacts in that it institutionalised the relationship between employers and employees and that it benefited the establishment of a national consensus in the socio-economic realm. In contrast with Belgium and France, however, labour relations in the Netherlands had not been severely damaged in the late 1930s and during the war. Dutch employers were therefore under less pressure to make concessions to the unions. The 1945 Manifesto was indeed not very radical; the primary goal was to boost social peace and to avoid mass unemployment. According to Luyten, the importance of the establishment of the Labour Foundation must be sought not so much in a compromise between capital and labour, but in the attempt by the social partners to establish a formal relationship between the government and the social partners (Luyten, 2003).

Unlike the original high ambitions of the Labour Foundation, the government initially did not want to allow the social partners much co-responsibility. In one important policy area, however, the Labour Foundation was granted substantial influence. In October 1945, the BBA ("Buitengewoon Besluit Arbeidsverhoudingen", Extraordinary Decree on Labour Relations) was passed. The name of this law shows the reason why the government allowed the Labour Foundation such an important role: It reveals the perceived urgency of the economic situation. The government and social partners shared the idea that wage restraint was an essential aspect of post-war reconstruction (Compston, 2003: 799). The BBA was meant as a temporary decree, but after several adaptations it survived until 1970. The BBA put the Labour Foundation in a central position in the process of wage formation. It was obligatory for the executive committee of the post-war wage control, the Board of Government Mediators ("College van Rijksbemiddelaars") to ask the Labour Foundation for advice before approving a collective labour agreement (CLA). Wage formation was consequently completely centralised; the government, the Board of Government Mediators and the leaders of the umbrella organisations in the Labour Foundation left very little room for negotiation at company level (Windmuller, 1969: 113; van Bottenburg, 2003: 71, 90).

Agreement of Oud-Wassenaar (1961)

To understand the second social pact, the Agreement of Oud-Wassenaar (November 17, 1961), it is necessary to summarise the history of the centrally directed wage policy (Hulst, 1984: 202-206). During a first phase (1945 to 1953), the centrally directed wage policy brought about the desired wage moderation. A second phase (1954 to 1959) resulted in "welfare pay rounds" during which wages increased significantly, but wage formation was still centralised. This phase was followed by the years of what was called the "differentiated wage policy" (1959 to 1963), in which wage increases were linked to productivity increases in the individual branches of industry. According to Van Zanden, this *de facto* constituted the end of the centrally directed wage policy because it meant a decentralisation of wage formation (van Zanden, 2002: 288). However, wage formation had not yet been entirely liberalised. It was still coordinated by the Board of Government Mediators and the Labour Foundation – with an unprecedented amount of bureaucratic rules (van Bottenburg, 1995: 134-136). Moreover, the decentralisation of wage formation was hindered by the centralised organisational structure of the trade unions (van Zanden, 1998: 83). The unions strategically concluded CLAs in the strongest industries first, and used the acquired wage rises in the negotiations in the weaker industries.

The upshot was that "wage leadership" became the standard of wage increase, which led to larger wage increases than productivity growth could account for. The attempts of the government to adjust this undesired wage formation process created a great deal of annoyance with the social partners. In an effort to improve the relationship between the government and the Labour Foundation, the three parties negotiated a way to coordinate the differentiated wage policy. In November 1961, a tripartite social pact was concluded in the castle of Oud-Wassenaar (near The Hague). This pact of wage moderation was an agreement on how to calculate the maximum wage rise in an industry. The formula $(3x+y)/4$ determined that the estimated annual national productivity rise counted for a quarter and the industrial productivity trend for three quarters of the maximum wage rise.

However, no social pact could avert the abolition of the declining years of the centrally directed wage system. The differentiated wage policy remained unworkable. From 1963 to 1969, the wage policy system appeared to fade away several times, to revive only briefly a while later. Internal coordination by the Labour Foundation (1963-1965) did not succeed either and led to unwelcome wage explosions. It was subsequently replaced again by the supervision of the Board of Government Mediators (1966-1967). In expectation of the Wage Formation Act of 1970, wage formation was liberalised in 1968 – although the government, in this case the Minister of Social Affairs, was still entitled to issue wage measures when he deemed necessary.

Notwithstanding the many shortcomings of the centrally directed wage policy, it must be said that the social partners in the Labour Foundation had almost always been able to reach a collective recommendation on wage developments. This general consensus came to an end in the 1970s. The polarisation in Dutch society also contaminated the ranks of the Labour Foundation. Theoretically, in 1970, an era of free wage formation began, but reality was different. Since the social partners were not able to reach agreements, the government issued measures on wages each year (with the exception of 1972). Thus, in practice wage formation was still centralised, based on direct intervention of the government instead of on consensus between the social partners.

Wassenaar Agreement (1982)

The next social pact was the 1982 Wassenaar Agreement. The build-up to the conclusion of this watershed agreement will be dealt with in the next section. Here, I want to pay some attention to the significance of the Wassenaar Agreement as a turning point in the Dutch consultation history. After more than a decade with a lack of consensus, one would expect that the announcement of an agreement within the Labour Foundation in 1982 had a great impact. However, the recognition that this was a historical agreement dawned only slowly. This is not surprising if one reads this very concise agreement containing just over 500 words (including all signatures and affiliations!). The text needed true exegesis; the document that later was said to have heralded a new phase of wage moderation did not even contain the very word "wages". The message of agreement about "work before income" was hidden in the statements about the fact that "improved returns" (of enterprises) were essential for a structural improvement of employment and that "a better distribution of existing employment should not result in higher costs".

For a long time this social pact was referred to as the "Foundation agreement" (*Stichtingsakkoord*) and it was only from the late 1980s onwards that it began to be referred to at all in newspaper articles, scholarly articles and books.[3] The name Wassenaar Agreement (after the village where it was concluded) probably came en vogue in the wake of the popularity of the term *Poldermodel* around 1995, when the Labour Foundation celebrated its 50th anniversary. International recognition came in 1997 when the Labour Foundation was awarded the prestigious German Carl Bertelsmann Prize for its work on the subject "Individual

[3] Even Dutch scholars who were interested in the wage policy, consultation economy, and general economic developments initially ignored the agreement. For example, van Hulst, 1984; Visser, 1989; van Zanden and Griffiths, 1989. The regularly revised textbook on labour relations in the Netherlands *Arbeidsverhoudingen in Nederland, een inleiding* (Albeda, Dercksen and Frank Tros, 1986) gives an impression of the changed designation of the Wassenaar Agreement. In the fifth edition (1994), the "Central Agreement of 1982" is mentioned, in the added paragraphs of the sixth edition (1998) it is suddenly named "Wassenaar Agreement".

Responsibility and Solidarity – New Approaches in Social and Collective Bargaining Policy".

Wassenaar Agreement became the current term while the agreement gained acclaim. In the words of an SER crown member: "The further 1982 lies behind us, the more significant the Wassenaar Agreement seems to become" (Prof. dr. V. Halberstadt, as quoted in van Bottenburg, 1995: 198). It is indeed often described as a "turning point" and "historical breakthrough". Among employers, it is not unusual to refer to the Wassenaar Agreement as "the mother of all agreements",[4] a qualification that in my opinion would better suit the founding Manifesto of the Labour Foundation. Notwithstanding the appreciation and the consequent mythical proportions of Wassenaar in popular language, balanced judgement dominates in scholarly texts. Although it is brief and could at the time not be judged as more than a symptom of improving labour relations, it turned out to be of great significance for the ensuing decades. With the benefit of hindsight, the Wassenaar Agreement was considered a defining moment, both in the form and content of wage formation in the Netherlands. It is in this sense that scholars often qualify the Wassenaar Agreement as a historical turning point (van Bottenburg, 1995: 160, 192-203; van Zanden, 1989: 170-174; Visser and Hemerijck, 1997).

The most significant change was in form. Wassenaar signified that polarisation was worn out as a behavioural strategy, which could also be observed in society at large. In terms of wage formation, Wassenaar marked the end of a rather long transitional period from centralised wage policy (the last decade by emergency laws, the measures on wages) to an accepted system of decentralised wage formation. During the first decades of its existence, the Labour Foundation had made binding agreements with the government. Later they concluded "central agreements", subsequently toned down to "central recommendations" or even "enquiries" (*verkenningen*), which were recommendations to the bargaining social partners in the industries with no mandatory character at all (van Bottenburg, 1995: 203). It is quite ironical that the very first central recommendation came to fame as an agreement, the Wassenaar Agreement![5] Within the Labour Foundation, the peak organisations of employers and employees had come to the fundamental conclusion that

4 Alexander Rinnooy Kan, president of the employers' central organisation VNO (later VNO-NCW) 1991-1996, as quoted in Visser and Hemerijck, 1998: 156; Hans van den Akker, former president of the employers organisation in metal and electrotechnical industries FME in 2001, as quoted in van Gaal, 2001: 98.

5 The official name of the Agreement was *Centrale aanbevelingen omtrent aspecten van een werkgelegenheidsbeleid* (General recommendations on aspects of an employment policy).

they could no longer *impose* agreements on their rank and file. This acknowledgement of the leaders of the central organisations proved essential for the actual decentralisation of wage formation. Van Bottenburg already noted the paradox that the withdrawal in fact increased the Foundation's authority (van Bottenburg, 1995: 197).

Visser and Hemerijck identify the Wassenaar Agreement as a central moment of institutional learning, a turning point from "immobile corporatism" to "responsive corporatism". Immobile corporatism refers to the situation of "consultation without consensus" prevailing in the Netherlands from the late 1960s onwards. Parties continued to participate in the existing corporative institutional framework and negotiated with each other without the necessary underlying consensus. They were subsequently unable to reach new agreements. According to Visser and Hemerijck, the signing of the Wassenaar Agreement put an end to the immobile corporatism in the field of wage policy (by contrast, the reform of the social security system continued to suffer from immobile corporatism). Responsive corporatism refers to a situation in which the consultative institutions enjoy more societal support, the cause as well as the consequence of their effectiveness.

With their identification of the Wassenaar Agreement as a transition from immobile corporatism to responsive corporatism, Visser and Hemerijck interpret 1982 not only as a turning point in form but also in content. Other authors likewise placed emphasis on the content; the Wassenaar Agreement is often said to have inaugurated a new period of wage restraint (van Zanden, 1998: 172). This is not to say that the Wassenaar Agreement was the actual cause of this development. It was more the marker of a defining moment in opinions and in the mental climate, a turning point that set in motion a new development of wage moderation, working hours reduction and employment growth (van Bottenburg: 1999).

The Long and Winding Road to Wassenaar

In his configurational model, Compston explains the conclusion of a social pact by the changed configuration of three variables; firstly, the perceived nature of contemporary problems; secondly, a shared understanding of the aims and mechanisms of economic policy among government and social partners; and thirdly, the perceived likelihood of implementation. In this section I apply this model on the genesis of the Wassenaar Agreement. The analysis will not only describe the changed values of the mentioned variables, but also attempts to explain how the transformation of the three variables occurred. It is important to note here, that Compston himself does not seem to consider the Wassenaar

Agreement as a social pact in the strict sense of co-determination of public policy, precisely because the government agreed to abstain from intervening in wage formation (Compston, 2003: 796). However, one can interpret this as a radical policy concession of the government in exchange for the intensely desired wage moderation. It was hence a very particular solution to what the government perceived as a serious problem (cf. Compston, 2003: 791). Moreover, the government was not entirely absent during the substantiation of the agreement.

In general terms, the timing of the Wassenaar Agreement can be explained by a rising sense of urgency in the Dutch society in the early 1980s. As I will argue below, this trepidation can be categorised under the variables of "perceived problems" and "shared economic understanding".

Perception of Economic Problems

The first explanatory variable in the model is the perception of economic problems by the parties involved. Contrary to Compston, I do not only consider the perception by the government, but also by the (representatives of) employers and employees, which is important in the case of a bipartite social pact. The perceived economic problems can be translated into the following question. When (and why) was the sense of urgency so great that parties decided to drastically change their policy? In other words, how deep must an economic crisis be before a social pact stands any chance?

The question is relevant because the economic problems were certainly not new in 1982. The open, relatively energy-intensive economy of the Netherlands was vulnerable to external shocks such as the first oil crisis of 1973/1974 (van Zanden, 1998: 167). But government expenditure (facilitated by the natural resource boom of North Sea oil and gas) in combination with increased consumer spending mitigated the impact of the first oil crisis. The upshot was that until well into the 1970s, the expansive Keynesian economic policy obscured the economic recession and subsequently slowed down awareness, especially that of the trade unions. In 1977, the trade unions still dared to organise strikes in which the persistence of the automatic cost-of-living adjustment was at stake.[6] The employers lost this battle. The indexation of wages in the collective labour agreements (CAOs) was one of the main causes of a continuous rise in real wage costs, which undermined the profitability of Dutch firms (van Zanden, 1998: 164-165). The employers learned two things

---

6 10 February 1977, this led to the "Protocol of The Hague", the automatic cost-of-living adjustment was to be continued in 1977. This agreement was concluded within the Labour Foundation (van Bottenburg, 1995: 187-188).

from the 1977 events. Firstly, the largest employers' organisation, the VNO, acknowledged the importance of a timely, coordinated approach of the CLA-negotiations and in the preceding central consultation rounds in order to prevent undesired wage rises in individual sectors. An internal Committee was created for the Preparation of Policies concerning Conditions of Employment ("Commissie Voorbereiding Arbeidsvoorwaardenbeleid", CVAB). Like trade unions, the CVAB was supposed to produce an annual memorandum on the subject (van den Braak, 2002: 43). A second lesson learned from 1977 underlines that employers reached a peak in their crisis awareness, because they were prepared to make concessions in order to reach a social pact. In the autumn of 1979 (on 29 November 1979) the social partners within the Labour Foundation reached an agreement concerning wages. This agreement, however, was rejected by the peak organisation of employees after consulting the rank and file of FNV, the largest trade union. For that reason, it came to be known as the "almost-agreement". According to Willem van den Braak, the present director Social Affairs of the employers association VNO-NCW, at the time a young employee of VNO, the almost-agreement could be considered as a "voluntary measure on wages" by the social partners – a first cautious reduction in working hours in exchange for a moderate wage rise (van den Braak, 2002: 42). For employers, it was not a cheap agreement, but within the ranks of the central organisation, it was feared that the outcome could be even worse in decentralised negotiations. If explains why the direct predecessor of the 1982 social pact was a very centralistic agreement, diametrically opposed to the Wassenaar Agreement.

Immediately after the collapse of the almost-agreement in December 1979, the second oil shock and a sudden rise of interest rates severely hit the Dutch economy. For each of the three parties, government, employers and employees, the economic crisis manifested itself in a different shape. The government faced an enormous budget deficit. In business life, insolvency problems reigned, and among employees, many workers faced a real threat of unemployment. The employers felt the crisis more directly than the first oil crisis since many companies had financed their expansion with loans. As a result, the bankruptcy rate suddenly increased. While the number of annual bankruptcies increased from 1,700 in 1970 to 2,600 in 1979, it more than doubled in the early 1980s to a peak of 6,900 bankruptcies in 1982 (Sluyterman, 2003: 251). As Sluyterman sums up in her recent synthesis of Dutch business history in the 20th century, in the early 1980s, several spectacular business failures shocked Dutch society, such as the bankruptcy of Van Gelder Papier (paper industry) in 1981 and the problems of OGEM (a conglomerate of building and trade subsidiaries), which in the same year could only ward off bankruptcy with complex financial constructions (Sluyterman, 2003: 251-252). After such massive redundancies, the trade unions could no longer deny the seriousness of the crisis. Their members and the rest of the Dutch population were confronted with frightening levels of unemployment (see Table 1).

Table 1

	1974	1975	1976	1977	1978	1979	1980	1981	1982	1983	1984	1985
Economic growth [a)]												
Real national income, annual growth rate	1.2	-1.0	5.0	2.4	1.9	0.7	-0.1	-1.4	-0.1	1.8	2.7	3.7
Annual growth rate GDP	4.1	0.2	4.8	2.3	2.4	2.2	1.2	-0.5	-1.2	1.7	3.3	3.0
Wages [a)]												
Annual growth rate, CAOs in private sector	13.3	13.1	8.7	7.3	5.9	4.6	4.0	3.1	5.8	2.4	0.7	1.1
Annual growth rate wage costs per employee in private sector	15.6	12.8	10.9	8.7	7.2	6.1	6.4	4.3	7.0	4.0	1.2	1.9
Unemployment [b)]												
Registered unemployed (in thousands)	135	195	211	204	201	194	217	317	468	612	591	511
% unemployed of economically active population	2.8	4.0	4.3	4.1	4.1	3.9	4.3	6.1	9.0	11.7	11.2	9.7
Inflation [a)]												
Consumer price index, annual growth rate	9.2	9.6	8.6	6.1	3.7	4.0	6.8	6.8	5.9	2.9	3.4	2.3
Purchasing power for modal employees, annual growth rate	1.4	3.7	-0.5	1.8	1.9	0.7	-1.9	-4.2	-2.2	-3.6	-1.1	1.5
National Budget deficit (% GDP) [a)]				-3.1	-3.4	-5.0	-5.0	-6.8	-8.4	-8.9	-8.0	-6.2

Sources: [a)] CEP, 2003; [b)] CBS, 1994.

The new coalition government Lubbers I (1982-1986) that came into office on 4 November 1982 was confronted with the highest budget deficit in the 20th century (see Table 1). This cabinet was not the first that attempted to implement cuts in government consumption, but in contrast to its predecessors, it achieved a substantial decrease in the growth of expenditure. The Lubbers administration also aimed to cut back the real wage costs in the private sector and put severe pressure on the social partners to accomplish wage restraint. By threatening to apply a government measure on wages – euphemistically called a "breathing space" – the social partners were driven (back) to the negotiating table of the Labour Foundation. By this time, as will be explained below, the social partners had changed their minds about wage measures.

The depth of the depression created the beginning of a solution. The high levels of unemployment changed the general opinion about the private sector. During the polarised 1970s, employers, who at first were characterised as the exploiters of labour, were increasingly recognised as job creators. The new appreciation of entrepreneurship became evident when the government asked several entrepreneurs to chair important government committees (Sluyterman, 2003: 256). One of these advisory committees was chaired by the president of the supervisory board of the Royal Dutch, G. A. Wagner. The (interim) reports of this Wagner-Committee contributed substantially to the change in economic thinking.

Shared Economic Understanding

The second variable of Compston's model which is necessary to explain the conclusion of a social pact, is a shared economic understanding between the government, employers and employees, about the general aims and mechanisms of economic policy. In the Netherlands, the two minimum criteria of economic understanding were met long before Wassenaar came in sight. All actors had accepted the principle of capitalism and the legitimacy of both trade unions and collective bargaining; otherwise distrust would prevent agreements, and on a more practical level, any agreement on wage restraint would be difficult to coordinate. In Compston's framework, beyond these minimum criteria of economic agreement, a social pact becomes more likely when there is all parties, including trade unions, understand the desirability of economic reasons for wage moderation and low inflation according to the philosophy of international competitiveness as advocated in monetary theory and supply-side economics.

Between the second oil shock in 1979 and the conclusion of the Wassenaar Agreement, the disagreement on economic priorities between the socio-economic parties subsided to a remarkable extent; a new consensus dawned. This was not a particularly Dutch phenomenon. It was part of the internationally growing influence of the new economic views which influenced economic policy everywhere in the capitalist world. Economists increasingly bade farewell to Keynesianism and admitted that the supply effects of wage rises and tax increases were particularly detrimental to business profits and incentives to invest. Increasingly, these negative effects were deemed larger than the potential positive effects of anti-cyclical demand policy. The Dutch economic situation also played a minor role in the international paradigm shift. The Dutch gas profits of the 1970s had been used to finance the expanding welfare state, thus financing permanent public expenses. The gas exports had also created a surplus on the Dutch balance of payments. The subsequent hard currency was at first harmful to the Dutch export sector and in the longer run to the Dutch economy at large. In the second half of the 1970s, the term "Dutch Disease" was coined in the international discourse to describe these negative effects of a natural resource boom to a national economy.

In the Dutch consultation framework, the new economic ideas trickled down slowly, amongst others through the channels of the Dutch Central Bank and the Netherlands Bureau for Policy Analysis ("Centraal Planbureau", CPB). Since consensus still seemed a long way off, the consultative institutions sought refuge in research committees. In 1980, the social partners within the Labour Foundation agreed to research the complex issues of employment and labour market. According to Willem van den Braak, these investigations were deliberately not directed towards an agreement, because this was considered as a "mission impossible" (van den Braak, 2002: 36). Although the study group "Employment and Working Hours" of the Labour Foundation could only produce a report with divided opinions in 1981, the same report became one of the building blocks of the Wassenaar Agreement one year later. To a lesser extent, the same holds true for the preparation within the SER of its 1982 advice on socio-economic policy in the mid-to-long term (van Bottenburg, 1995: 195-196; SER, 1982).

Outsiders were needed to break the deadlock situation and to achieve acceptance of the new economic insights in the decision-making levels of the consultation economy. These outsiders appeared on the stage in the form of the 1980 Netherlands Scientific Council for Government Policy ("Wetenschappelijke Raad voor Regeringsbeleid", WRR) which published an influential report on industrial policy. In this report it criticised the lack of pro-active behaviour among Dutch politicians, who were allegedly only waiting until the corporatist institutions would come up with something (Visser and Hemerijck, 1998: 140). This induced the government to install a state committee on industrial policy in January 1981. The two successive state committees (1981-1984) were both named after their chairman, G. A. Wagner, the above-mentioned Shell-director.

In hindsight, the added value of the Wagner Committee was that this advisory committee was independent of the consultative institutions and the representative organisations of employers and employees. The composition of the committee therefore did not need to be on an equal footing. The membership of the two committees – with 14 and 9, partly overlapping, members respectively – suggests that they were designed to be powerful and not impeded by deadlock-situations.[7] The majority of the two committees (8 out of 14, 5 out of 9 respectively) were businessmen still active in Dutch companies, either as executive directors or as members of the supervisory board. They were experts on industry policy from practical experience. The background of the remainder of the committee possibly had to prevent that the committee could be criticised for simply echoing "the employers' voice". One prominent, experienced socialist politician was present in both committees, namely H. Vredeling, former minister of Defence and former EC commissioner for Social Affairs and Employment. Both committees also contained one equally experienced and leading Christian-democratic politician: P.J.A.M. Steenkamp, former Minister for Social Affairs and W. Albeda respectively. Both were renowned for their concern for social matters. The point of view of the employees was also included. In the first committee, two members came from the largest trade unions, although their membership was not on behalf of these unions (L.R.A. Ester, president of CNV and P.J. Vos, policy officer of FNV). In the second committee, employees were represented by two former employee members of the SER (A. H. Kloos, representing NVV, and the aforementioned W. Albeda who had represented CNV). Finally, A. van der Zwan, the director of the Netherlands Scientific Council for Government Policy (WRR) had a seat in both committees. Overall, the Wagner-committee was an independent state committee that was not based on formal representation, but which was potentially very influential because of its representative character.[8]

By publishing several interim reports, the Wagner-committee stirred up a lively debate about socio-economic changes. The most prominent proposal on wage formation was free wage formation without interference of the government. Free wage formation could only be effective, so the Committee argued, if it was based on decentralised wage formation in the industries, and when the cost-of-living adjustment would no

7 The first committee: W.J. Beek, A.C.R. Dreesmann, L.R.A. Ester, J. Klevering, A.E. Pannenborg, P.J.A.M. Steenkamp, F. Swarttouw, H. Verwey-Jonker, P.J. Vos plus five members of the second committee: G.A. Wagner, W.A.J. Bogers, H. Langman, H. Vredeling and A. van der Zwan. The second committee consisted apart from the latter five of W. Albeda, M. Bijl, A.H. Kloos and J.H.S. van Ruiten. See van Dellen, 1984: 66, 74.

8 It must be noted, however, that in at least one important sense it was not representative at all. Only the first Committee contained a female member, the much acclaimed dr. Hilda Verwey-Jonker. Verwey-Jonker is the personification of the very unequal gender representation in the Dutch consultation institutions. From 1958 to 1972, she was crown member of the SER; throughout those years, she was the sole female permanent member of the SER.

longer be automatic but the result of annual negotiations. In his textbook on labour relations, W. Albeda, a member of the second committee, later assessed the importance of the Wagner-committee was proposing an exchange; the social partners would jointly give up the automatic cost-of-living adjustment and in return the government would sacrifice its legal right to issue measures on wages (Albeda, Dercksen and Tros, 1998: 84-86). In the Wassenaar Agreement, this exchange was combined with the exchange of the "almost-agreement" of 1977 (in which a reduction in working hours was exchanged for wage moderation) in order to make the loss of the automatic cost-of-living more acceptable for the trade unions.

The general agreement that the governmental wage measures, the wage measures, should be abolished was an important step to reach the necessary "shared economic understanding" to make Wassenaar possible. The fact that Albeda, a former minister who had issued quite a number of wage measures himself, also urged to shelve the instrument away, must have had a significant impact.

It is important to note that the view on governmental wage measures had changed. The peak organisations of employers and employees had not always been opposed to them. In the early 1970s, trade unions had welcomed the equalising effects on incomes, since wage measures often prescribed absolute wage rises instead of relative figures. Employers had welcomed the side-effect that they could take up a strong position in the negotiations without fearing strikes, since the government could intervene (Bruggeman and Camijn, 1999: 265). In the course of time, however, both social partners woke up to the fact that annual government wage measures had many disadvantages. Trade unions realised that the – in their view beneficial – equalising effect in practice boiled down to wage restraint. Additionally, the emphasis of the traditional trade unions on equalising incomes was not appreciated by the higher echelons of employees. As a consequence, the polarisation strategy was questioned within the trade union movement by a growing group of white collar unions. In 1980, after almost a decade of strife for recognition, the Trade Union Federation for Intermediate and Higher Employees (MHP) finally acquired membership of the Labour Foundation (van Bottenburg, 1995: 175-176).

In turn, employers realised that if they wanted to have more autonomy in economic affairs, they had to be consistent (van Bottenburg, 1995: 193). Early 1982, the Minister of Social Affairs and Employment of the Cabinet-Van Agt II, the social-democrat and former prime-minister J. den Uyl, issued a very special *loonmaatregel* (wage measure), maximising holiday allowances and price adjustment. This greatly irritated the employers, who considered this a measure of forced income equalisation, since it would hardly reduce labour costs and was completely at the expense of the higher incomes. For the first (and only) time in history, the largest employers' organisation VNO filed a complaint against the Dutch government with the International Labour Organisation ILO in Geneva on the grounds of violation of the freedom of collective bargaining (van den Braak, 47).

Both social partners consequently had come to realise that government measures on wages were no longer useful. In this time of crisis, after more than a decade of polarisation, the credibility of the representative organisations was seriously at stake. When the new Cabinet Lubbers I threatened with yet another wage measure in 1982, this increased the sense of urgency for employers and employees alike. Government intervention was now perceived as an outdated instrument, endangering their own legitimacy to their members. In these circumstances, the shadow of hierarchy cast over the negotiations by Lubbers could be very effective (Scharpf, 1997).

As described above, the Wagner committee played an important part in creating a more shared understanding of new (political) economic ideas. The independent position of the state committee enabled it to break through barriers and to talk to the relevant actors of the socio-economic parties. Shortly after the new Cabinet Lubbers I was sworn in on 4 November 1982, Gerrit Wagner and three members of his committee had a long, informal, secret meeting with the two chairmen of the Labour Foundation, Chris van Veen (representative of the employers and chairman of VNO) and Wim Kok (representative of the employees and chairman of FNV). At that time, they already knew that a new "loonmaatregel" by the Lubbers-administration was pending. The delegation of the Wagner Committee discussed their views on wage development, the labour market and a reduction of working hours in great detail. When they left, they had no idea whether their ideas would bear fruit.[9]

They did. After the tripartite consultation of the Labour Foundation with the government about the "breathing space", on November 17, 1982, Van Veen and Kok started negotiating – without any official mandate from their organisations. Two days later, in Van Veen's villa in Wassenaar (hence the name) they accepted a concept-agreement.

9 In an interview in 1984, Wagner was quite surprised that the journalist knew of the secret meeting of a delegation of the Wagner Committee with the leaders of the Labour Foundation. When confronted with it, Wagner's first reaction was "How do you know?", but he immediately admitted that it had happened and subsequently described the meeting (van Grieken, 1984: 327).

Expectations about Implementation

In the course of only a few years, a shared economic understanding had developed between government, employers and employees. It fulfilled the second condition for a social pact. The last variable required for the actual conclusion of a social pact is "expectations about implementation". How do the parties perceive the likelihood of the social pact's implementation or the implementation capacity of the other participants? Compston distinguishes two important factors: structural and contingent factors. For the structural factors "[...] corporatist theory is relevant, as implementation of promises would be expected where employer associations and trade union confederations are large, centralised and disciplined, and where collective bargaining is coordinated, preferably on a national basis" (Compston, 2003: 793). As we have seen above, the performance of the Dutch corporatist institutions in the 1970s and early 1980s could hardly inspire confidence in this sense. The inclination to turn to study groups when no consensus could be reached seems highly inefficient. Polarisation crippled true consultation, and the consequence was a lack of results. Visser and Hemerijck rightly refer to this period as immobile corporatism because policymakers and social partners seemed paralysed. On the other hand, the persistence of the consultative framework was very useful when the actors were finally able to revert from polarisation to consensus. How likely would it have been that the social partners would (re)invent an institutional framework at the depth of the depression and start from scratch? The sense of urgency which is described above triggered the recovery of the trust enhancing effects of the institutional framework (den Butter and Mosch, 2003).

According to Compston, contingent factors such as experience with previous agreements and the degree of trust between leaders are more important in determining the timing of a social pact than the structural factors. As regards the previous agreements (i.e. before polarisation), the institutional framework guaranteed and accounted for a proper implementation of those agreements. More important for the Wassenaar Agreement was the amount of trust between the leaders of the peak organisations. Notwithstanding the severe polarisation, key persons such as Chris van Veen (chairman VNO) and Wim Kok (chairman FNV) had always kept in contact with each other, managing to maintain good relations (van Bottenburg, 1995: 185-187, 194). Between these two men, concluding a social pact such as the Wassenaar Agreement was not very difficult – the real challenge was getting it accepted by their member organisations. For both chairmen this was not an easy task. Especially in the rank and file of the employers, substantial resistance surfaced. Paradoxically, the weak position of the trade unions endangered the acceptance of the social pact. Some employers within the VNO thought that the hard economic times would make it possible to squeeze a more profitable agreement out of the weak position of the unions, for example by eliminating the automatic cost-of-living adjustment without any compensation. In the end, Van Veen, who was the first professional chairman of the employers and who had ample political experience (he was a former Minister) managed to convince his colleagues that no further bargaining was possible, and that it was vital to sign the agreement (van den Braak, 2002: 51). There are two interesting remarks to be made about this incident. Firstly, in order to increase the chance of policy concertation in general and social pacts in particular, the position of the trade unions in relation to the employers should not be too weak. Secondly, this incident shows the added value an actor perspective can bring to a class perspective. However significant the balance of power between the social partners in labour relations may be, sometimes the personal ability of the individual leaders of the social partners to persuade their rank and file of their assessment of socio-political situation may be decisive.

The largest achievement of Wim Kok and Chris van Veen, however, was that they managed to make the government surrender a precious policy instrument. In the course of the negotiations, they informally obtained the consent of the government. The brand new government promised that if the social partners would conclude such a social pact, the government would arrange an immediate withdrawal from the wage formation process. In addition, CLAs entered into before 1983 would be reviewed in order to enforce wage moderation without further delay (van Bottenburg, 1995: 196). It is clear that the contingent factors, in particular the actors Van Veen and Kok, were greatly beneficial to guarantee implementation. The result was that the three parties had high expectations of the implementation of the Wassenaar Agreement, which was officially signed on 24 November 1982 in The Hague.

Conclusion

On 24 November 1982, the chairmen of the nine national employers' associations and trade union confederations that were represented in the Labour Foundation signed the document "General recommendations on aspects of an employment policy", later known as the Wassenaar Agreement, after the village where the compromise had been negotiated between the leaders of the employers' and employees' associations.[10] Because of the immediate supporting legislation of the new Lubbers administration, this bipartite employer-union agreement later obtained the appearance of a tripartite social pact. The Wassenaar Agreement demonstrated several changes. The government withdrew from wage formation, which was in line with changes in society at large, where the co-ordinating role of government was replaced by new deregulation and liberalisation. The Wassenaar Agreement was only the beginning of a changing climate in labour relations in the Netherlands. The results of this change would materialise in the two decades to come. In 1993, for example, a new bipartite agreement called "A New Course" was needed to boost the decentralisation of wage formation to the industry and company level, a process that had begun with the Wassenaar Agreement.

The Wassenaar Agreement also marked the end of a long period of polarisation between the social partners. In this paper the central question was why the turning point from polarisation to renewed consensus took place in November 1982. Using Compston's configurational theory of policy concertation, I analysed how the conditions for the conclusion of a social pact slowly developed, with acceleration in the turbulent year of 1982, a year with three governments in office, which was unprecedented in the Netherlands: Cabinet Van Agt II (1981-2), Cabinet Van Agt III (1982) and Cabinet Lubbers I (1982-6).

After the second oil shock of 1979, a sense of crisis grew among the three socio-economic parties of employers, employees and government. In 1982, this sense of urgency was greater than ever, and more importantly, more generally felt than ever. In this sense of urgency, the two variables "perception of economic problems" and "shared economic understanding" came together. In a few years time, both a shared cognitive and shared normative understanding had arisen. The economic situation was no longer judged from a Keynesian perspective and the budget deficit and ever-increasing wage costs were therefore perceived as larger problems than before. This underlines an important feature of

[10] The document was signed by: C. van Veen (Federation of Netherlands Industries, VNO); W. Kok (Netherlands Trade Union Confederation, FNV); S.J. van Eijkelenburg (Federation of Christian Employers in the Netherlands, NCW); H. van der Meulen (Confederation of Christian Trade Unions in the Netherlands, CNV); W. Perquin (Royal Netherlands Federation of Industries, KNOV); H. van der Schalie, (Trade Union Federation for Intermediate and Higher Employees, VMHP); S. Veninga (Federation of Christian Industries in the Netherlands, NCOV); J.J. Schouten (Catholic Farmers and Market Gardeners Association in the Netherlands; also on behalf of Royal Netherlands Agriculture Committee Christian Farmers and Market Gardeners Association in the Netherlands).

Compston's model; it is the perception of the economic actors that matters.

The early 1980s show that the actions of key persons based on those perceptions can revive paralysed consultative institutions. A crucial role in the dissemination of the new economic ideas among the leaders of the social partners was played by the Wagner Committee. The very establishment of this state committee was a sign of the emergence of a new episode in the Dutch consultation economy, since the committee was not based on representation. In speech and print the Wagner-Committee proposed solutions for the economic problems, for example the exchange of wage moderation by the social partners and the withdrawal from wage formation by the government. The then recently established Lubbers administration was prepared to make this great policy concession, and thereby fulfilled the last condition to set the stage for a social pact. The promise that wage measures would become history, increased the expectations of the social partners that the other party would implement the agreement. The trust that the leaders of the employers and employees Van Veen and Kok had carefully fostered in the polarisation years, finally bore fruit.

References

Albeda, Willem, Willem Dercksen and Frank H. Tros (1998 – 6th edition [1975)], *Arbeidsverhoudingen in Nederland, een inleiding*, Alphen aan den Rijn: Samson.

Bottenburg, Maarten van (1995), *"Aan den Arbeid!" In de wandelgangen van de Stichting van de Arbeid, 1945-1995,* Amsterdam: Bakker.

Bruggeman, Jan, and Aart Camijn (1999), *Ondernemers verbonden. 100 Jaar centrale ondernemingsorganisatie in Nederland*, Wormer: Inmerc.

Braak, Jan Willem van den (2002), *Keerpunt '82, enkele herinneringen van een VNO-man*, Assen: Koninklijke Van Gorcum.

Butter, Frank A. G. Den, and Robert H. J. Mosch (2003), "The Dutch Miracle: Institutions, Networks, and Trust", *Journal of Institutional and Theoretical Economics*, Vol. 159, No. 2, p. 362-391.

Centraal Bureau voor de Statistiek (1994), *Vijfennegentig jaren statistiek in tijdreeksen, 1899-1994*, The Hague: CBS.

Centraal Planbureau (2003), *Centraal Economisch Plan (CEP) 2003*, The Hague: CPB. Online. Available HTTP: http://www. cpb. nl/nl/data/cep2003 (accessed 1 February 2004).

Compston, Hugh (2003), "Beyond Corporatism: A Configurational Theory of Policy Concertation", *European Journal of Political Research* Vol. 42, p. 787-809.

Dellen, H. van (ed.) (1984), *Een nieuw elan: de marktsector in de jaren tachtig: de rapporten van de Adviescommissie inzake het industriebeleid (juni 1981) en de Adviescommissie inzake de voortgang van het industriebeleid: januari 1982-juni 1982, juli 1982-januari 1983, februari 1983-juni 1983, juli 1983-december 1983*, Deventer: Kluwer.

Gaal, Frans van (2001), *Spanning in de polder, 55 jaar CAO ontwikkeling in de metaal- en elektrotechnische industrie,* Apeldoorn/Leidschendam: Stichting ROM.

Grieken, Nico van (1984), *EW (Elseviers Sociaal-Economisch Weekblad)* 24 March 1984 (reprinted in: van Dellen, 1984).

Hulst, Noe van (1984), *De effectiviteit van de geleide loonpolitiek in theorie en praktijk*, Groningen: Wolters-Noordhoff

Luyten, Dirk (2003), "Op zoek naar nationale sociaal-economische consensus. Sociale pacten bij de bevrijding in België, Frankrijk en Nederland", in: Madelon de Keizer *et al.* (eds.), *Thuisfront: oorlog en economie in de twintigste eeuw, Jaarboek van het Nederlands Instituut voor Oorlogsdocumentatie,* Vol. 14, p. 192-205.

Pasture, Patrick T. (1993), "The April 1944 'Social Pact' in Belgium and its Significance for the Post-war Welfare State", *Journal of Contemporary History*, Vol. 28, No. 3, Oct., p. 695-714.

Scharpf, Fritz W. (1997), *Games Real Actors Play. Actor-centered Institutionalism in Policy Research*, Boulder: WestviewPress.

SER (1982), *Advies sociaal-economisch beleid op middellange termijn 1983-1986*, The Hague: Sociaal-Economische Raad.

Sluyterman, Keetie E. (2003), *Kerende Kansen. Het Nederlandse bedrijfsleven in de twintigste eeuw*, Amsterdam: Boom.

Visser, Jelle and Anton Hemerijck (1997), *"A Dutch Miracle". Job Growth, Welfare Reform and Corporatism in the Netherlands*, Amsterdam: Amsterdam University Press.

Visser, Jelle and Anton Hemerijck (1998), *"Een Nederlands mirakel". Beleidsleren in de verzorgingsstaat*, Amsterdam: Amsterdam University Press.

Visser, Patrice E. (1989), *Overlegeconomie*, Assen/Maastricht: Van Gorcum.

Windmuller, John P. (1969), *Labor Relations in the Netherlands*, Ithaca: Cornell University Press.

Zanden, Jan Luiten van (1998), *The Economic History of the Netherlands, 1914-1995. A Small Open Economy in the "Long" 20th Century*, London: Routledge.

Zanden, Jan Luiten van (2002), "Loonmatiging en het poldermodel in historisch perspectief", *Tijdschrift voor Arbeidsvraagstukken,* Vol. 18, p. 284-291.

Zanden, Jan Luiten van, and Richard T. Griffiths (1989), *Economische geschiedenis van Nederland in de 20e eeuw*, Utrecht: Het Spectrum.

CHAPTER 7

Industrial Policy in Italy after 1945 and the Role of Tripartite Agreements

Ruggero RANIERI

General Features

Planning and state intervention may have gone out of fashion during the last quarter of the 20th century, but industrial policy has remained an important topic of enquiry. Industrial policy refers, here, to a wide range of government actions designed to promote industrial activity. It might directly impinge on firms or industrial sectors or, more broadly, it may seek to achieve social and regional aims, or may cover trade, and competition or even some areas of macro-economic management. While government remains the key actors in industrial policy, social partners also need to be considered as part of the decision-making process.

In the case of Italy we face a kind of paradox. Many would agree that the Italian State has been one of the most interventionist, together with Japan or Germany, or even, looking back at the early stage of industrialisation, Russia. Italy was a late industrialiser, she lacked raw materials and energy sources, and was burdened by a structural trade deficit, calling for import substitution and/ or a strong mercantilist export drive. On the other hand, the exact nature and the results of State intervention in Italy has been open to question. Some commentators believe that everything that went wrong in Italy's economy has been the State's doing. Others, without denying the importance of the public sector, argue that there was no coherent State-led strategy. Others still have picked on the definition of Italy's capitalism as "political capitalism", implying that it was subject to a vast amount of short-term, politically-motivated interference.[1]

In trying to assess the evidence, it useful to set out a few preliminary points. The first concerns the remarkably large size of the public sector in Italy. Andrew Shonfield, writing in the 1960s, remarked that Italy

1 For a summary of the debate see Federico and Cohen, 2001; Federico and Giannetti, 1999: 1127-1162; Bonelli, 1978 and Sapelli, 1990.

was "most extreme example (with Austria) of public sector enterprise and intervention in the whole of Western Europe", and he went on to talk of the proliferation of nationalised and semi-public enterprises" (Shonfield, 1965). More recently Patrizio Bianchi has observed how three kinds of State companies can be discerned (Bianchi, 1995). Firstly, those belonging to the public administration proper, directly controlling a number of services and public utilities. Secondly, a network of agencies and companies entirely owned and controlled by the State, but enjoying some kind of autonomy within the public sector, although their rules of governance are very diverse. This vast area, which in 1984 numbered 54 000 different bodies, covers anything from banking to insurance to the railways, opera houses and ports. In some cases these companies were the result of nationalisation, in others they were expressly created by the government to run certain public monopolies. Local government might also be involved. Not uncommonly some of their functions have been leased out to more flexible, efficient firms, either belonging to the private sector or to the State-Owned Enterprise sector. State-owned enterprises (SOES), which constitute the third and by far most important category, consist of a number of conglomerates and companies, operated in conformity to private commercial law, but with a large, although not exclusive, public stake; they have been managed with a large degree of autonomy by a small elite of high-powered managers. Some scholars have even drawn a parallel with Japanese and South-Korean business groups.

The existence of this vast public apparatus has acted as a protective shield for the Italian economy. At its origins, mainly during the inter-war period, it was part of a series of monopolistic arrangements, meant to prevent market competition. When the economy opened up after World War II, it slowed down and hampered the process of liberalisation. Companies running State concessions were not supposed to act outside national borders, although this did not prevent certain SOES, operating in "strategic" sectors, such as oil and gas and public works, from becoming major international players. Government controls, licensing arrangements and publicly sanctioned cartels were key features of the fascist regime. After 1945, there was some loosening of controls and some movement towards more competitive conditions, but not enough to fundamentally reverse the picture (Vito, 1954).

As for the nature of Italy's governance two levels need to be considered: the political system and the civil service. The former was based upon unstable coalition governments, elected by proportional representation, and upon a weak executive. Political instability, however, was partly compensated by a certain amount of continuity in leading party political figures, considering that all post-war coalitions between 1946 and 1992 were essentially centred on the Christian Democratic Party (DC), and that the main opposition party, the Communist Party (PCI), was not considered eligible for government in a western democracy. The outcome is not easy to assess. Professor Ranci is probably correct when he estimates that this led to "a kind of continuity in the general orientation of economic and industrial policy, which goes together with a tendency to paralysis at the operational stage" (Ranci, 1987: 113 ff.; Ruffolo, 1976: 214-215. See also LaPalombara, 1989). The paralysis was compounded by a lack of efficiency and quality in the civil service, which, according to some scholars, was encouraged by the DC, which used the public sector as a vehicle for patronage, recruiting mostly in the South of the country. However this lack of efficiency, in my view, should not be unduly extended to cover all areas of the civil service. There has been a tradition of public service in the Italian State, and, at least in some areas, notably the foreign service, the economic ministries, the Bank of Italy, it was decently upheld after 1945.

Italy's dualisms are also important, particularly in geography and company size. One of the features of Italy's economy is a large development gap between the South, or *Mezzogiorno*, and the rest of the country. This gap was particularly serious after World War II and needed to be urgently addressed, constituting one of the key arenas for State intervention. However, the differences within the Centre-North should not be overlooked, and have taken on increasing significance over the years, particularly between the North-West, the region of oldest industrialisation and tending to decline after the end of the post-war cycle of rapid growth, and the North-East, together with parts of the Centre, which has developed in recent years from a position of relative backwardness into a dynamic area, making it the core of the so called "Third Italy" (King, 1985).

A number of large firms, both public and private, have traditionally tended to have a strong grip their particular markets. Alongside these large oligopolistic players there is a mass of small and very small privately-owned firms, a distinctive feature of the Italian economy. In the early post-war period small firms were considered, by and large, backward and inefficient. Since the 1970s the opposite view prevailed: small firms, bunched together in "clusters" or "districts" became the success story, while declining large firms provided a showcase of Italy's limited organisational capabilities. While it is impossible to generalise, small firms have undoubtedly been a very dynamic factor. They benefited from operating, at least initially, in local niche markets, but they were capable, in many cases, of developing a strong export trade. Further advantages included flexible labour markets, tax evasion, but also strong family ties, support from local communities, innovative, unconventional, product design and aggressive salesmanship (Forte, 1974: 346 ff.).

Despite the existence of these outsiders, of greater importance are the unwritten set of corporate governance rules which apply to both industry and finance. They ultimately rest on a elitist system, which allows a small number of players occupying positions of leadership in major corporations and banks to prevail by way of a system of interlocking directorships and pyramidal group systems, enhancing family control and limiting the rights of minority shareholders. Key to success are co-optation, personal acquaintances, belonging to what has been called the *salotto buono*. While these features apply especially to the private sector, SOES have also displayed clannishness and exclusiveness (Colajanni, 1991).

Italian industry has long been highly dependent on bank credit, due to the slow development of financial markets and of the stock exchange. The bank system, in some ways, mirrors the company system: its large institutions have been very centralised and largely owned by the State. The largest deposit banks were public bodies, with their top management appointed by the government, and, as a legacy of an important banking law of 1936, not allowed to acquire control of industrial activities. Smaller banks, particularly in the provinces, have proved flexible and diverse and were able in many ways to promote the development of industry, benefiting from a strong sense of local identity and civic pride, enhanced by gradual devolution of powers to the regional level. SOES were allowed partly to opt out of the banking system, by floating their own debentures and enjoying access to a special Government Endowment Fund. Still, they ended up borrowing short-term from the big banks and, in the 1970s and 1980s, suffered accordingly from high interest rates, as did their private counterparts (Barca and Trento, 1997a: 537 ff.; Zamagni, 1993: 357 ff.; Conti, 1999).

On the whole the banking system provided a vehicle for political interference. Whether it was an instrument for conducting strategic investment and industrial policies is debatable. A number of State specialised institutions, for channelling funds into specific sectors did exist. The Bank of Italy was firmly entrenched at the top of the system, with considerable monetary and regulatory powers. It enjoyed independence and authority and shared some of the features of the SOE sector, over the expansion of which it presided by allocating it resources and determining its strategies. It also had a commanding voice over Italy's economic international involvement (on the role of the Bank of Italy see Shonfield, 1965: 181-183; Carli, 1993).

Organised labour was not a significant factor and it was possible, for at least 20 years after the war, to discuss policies for industrial change without paying too much attention to the constraints of collective bargaining. A free trade union movement re-emerged after the fascist interlude to play a part in the Reconstruction, but it remained organisationally weak, and, in 1950, split, along party lines, into three competing unions, of which the main one, the CGIL, was closely attached to the opposition PCI, while the CISL was an emanation of the DC. Strong politicisation within the trade union movement, centralised bargaining and weak unionisation as a result of high unemployment and a vast reserve of underemployed in agriculture, were all factors which marginalised labour in the post-war years. With few exceptions, employers were inclined to bypass the unions, or to exploit their weaknesses and divisions. Unions, however, were dramatically enhanced by the surge of industrial conflict in the 1960s and 1970s. As a result, an uneasy tripartite partnership developed (cf. Cella and Treu, 1998; Locke and Baccaro, 1999; Berta 1999: 997-1034).

The main characteristics of Italy's post-war system can be seen as a peculiar "model" of State-intervention which established itself in the period between 1945 and 1960, drawing upon the legacy of the fascist period. This founding period is described in section 2 of my paper. In sections 3 and 4, I will go on to show how changes occurring in the 1960s, and subsequently in the 1970s and 1980s, were part of an attempt to update or improve the original model, turning it into a more concerted and broadly-based one. During the 1990s, as I show in my final section, change has been far more radical, as the fundamental inconsistencies of the model were recognised against a background of looming economic failure.

Shaping the Economic Miracle: Italy's Post-war Model of State Intervention

Italy's economy after World War II was organised around a strong State sector, in which SOES played a leading role. It was a system, designed to expand industrial capacity and build efficient externalities.

The most important legacy that the fascist period bequeathed to post-1945 Italy's economy was the IRI (Istituto per la Ricostruzione Industriale), which had been created in 1933, and made permanent in 1937, as a State-owned agency, possessing an important share of country's assets, with a focus on heavy industry. On the eve of World War II, IRI controlled, amongst others, 80 per cent of the nation's shipbuilding, 45 per cent of its steel, 39 of the electromechanical industry, 23 per cent of the engineering industry, and 16 per cent of electrical power generation. It possessed about a quarter of all the equity capital of limited companies existing in Italy (Amatori, 1997: 117 ff.).

IRI was the outcome of the rescue by the Bank of Italy of the large mixed banks, which had played a key role in the industrialisation of the country. It can be seen as an attempt to harness private savings to industrial investment, using State ownership as a vehicle. At the same time it was an attempt to find a compromise between State and market: it was publicly owned, but its holdings (Finsider, Finmeccanica, Fincantieri etc.) were able to attract some private capital, while its operative companies were legally incorporated as private joint-stock companies and required, with certain exceptions, to return a profit. It was, importantly, a focus for industrial modernisation and rationalisation, and for the emergence of a body of able managers, imbued with a mission to improve Italy's industrial performance (Bianchi, 1987: 269 ff.; Poster and Woolf, 1967).

During the period of autarchy, alongside IRI an elaborate panoply of monetary and trade restrictions had been set up, the operation of which was entrusted to the Bank of Italy. An important role was also given to the fascist Corporations, a new tripartite machinery, which, despite its authoritarian nature, did succeed in forging an industrial policy based on permanent consultation between business and the ministerial bureaucracy as well as on organised collusion between industrialists. Corporations produced guidelines for a number of economic sectors, setting out goals, investment priorities, which were not without practical consequences (Petri, 2002: 117 ff.).

After 1945 much of this machinery was scrapped and replaced by policies designed to achieve market liberalisation. However the transition to an open international economy was very gradual, requiring long negotiations and careful supervision. Thus, the experience and the personnel of the 1930s came useful once again – economic management remaining for a long time in the hands of technocrats clustered within the Bank of Italy and IRI. After brief tinkering with ideas of wholesale nationalisation (on the Left) and with privatisation (on the Right) the SOE system remained intact. At the end of 1945 IRI still employed 135,000, controlling 216 companies. In February 1948 a decree restored it to operational status and effectively strengthened its independence from the government. Alongside IRI, new holdings sprang up, most importantly ENI, established in 1953 to develop the energy sector (Barca and Trento, 1997a: 549 ff.; Bianchi, 1995).

Alongside the older managers, many of whom (but not all) survived the anti-fascist purges, new men emerged to run the SOE sector: mostly able industrialists coming from the private sector, in some cases members of the Resistance movement who enjoyed good connections with the new political elite. They were encouraged to proceed with long-term plans for economic development in crucial sectors such as steel, energy, the creation of a modern transport and telecommunications infrastructure, in which the degree of risk, the amount of finance required and the possible clash with foreign interests deterred private capital. Some of these initiatives were launched and carried out by State enterprises, others required joint efforts between SOES and large private firms. There is already a considerable body of literature on these efforts and it would seem by now established that they were crucial in the success of the Italian post-war economy (On SOE investment in steel see Ranieri, Kipping and Dankers, 2001; more generally Allen and Stevenson (1974: 231 ff.; Holland, 1972).

On what economic assumptions did this kind of informal planning network develop? Keynesian ideas did not have a wide following in Italy, at least until the 1960s. Rather there was a prevalence in academic circles of orthodox, neo-classical views. Such views, however, were only superficially embraced by the new technocratic elite, who instead developed what can be described as a, rather crude, supply-side approach. It was based on selective investment in strategic sectors together with an orthodox fiscal and monetary policy. Savings were encouraged and channelled, preferentially, into projects entrusted to SOES. Demand was squeezed and wages constrained. Manufacturing industry was strongly encouraged, through a variety of subsidies, to increase its exports in order to avoid balance of payments constraints. Schemes for State intervention in the South were further reinforced by the theoretical work on latecomers to industrialisation, which advocated removing bottlenecks through industrial capacity expansion. Because large-scale job creation was expected only in the long term, Italy's unemployed were encouraged to emigrate (De Cecco, 1989: 220 ff.).

It is important to understand the relationship between the technocrats and Italy's political class, as well between the private and public sector. The DC was a pragmatic party, composed of different groupings, with an overall commitment to a mixed economy, combining a strong measure of state intervention to help the *Mezzogiorno* and to develop social policies with the basic principles of a market economy, paying particular attention to the small business sector. It was, thus, prepared to work alongside SOE managers. Some have characterised this relation as one of "benign neglect" on the part of the DC, at least during the first post-war years. State enterprises were organised in powerful conglomerates and were effective tools for conducting policies requiring a vast amount of technical expertise that was, otherwise, out of reach of a relatively new and inexperienced political elite. The DC's priority, in any case, lay in meeting the challenge of the mass parties of the Left. In 1956, thanks to the efforts of the Left wing of the DC, SOES were brought under the umbrella of a newly created Ministry, the Ministero delle Partecipazioni Statali. The change was significant, for it showed the politicians' intention of exercising more direct control, but the powers of the Ministry were limited, and large SOE conglomerates retained most of their freedom (Maraffi, 1990: 197 ff.; see Shonfield, 1965: 197-198).

The relation between the public and private sector ranged from co-operation to confrontation. Undoubtedly SOES proved beneficial to the rest of industry, for they provided the country with a decent infrastructure, for example the network of autostrade, air transport and telecommunications, as well as a supply of energy and basic investment goods at low cost. This has led some to observe that the SOES were simply meant to prop up private capitalism, a view, however, that few would agree with today. There was, in fact, a potential for conflict and in many cased conflict did indeed develop (Amatori, 1997: 109-133; Amatori, 1999: 721 ff.). One might quote the opposition of private steel companies to the large-scale investment in coastal plants initiated by IRI-Finsider's Sinigaglia Plan, or the bitter opposition of Italian and foreign companies to the public monopoly on natural gas extraction granted to ENI. Deep cleavages opened up among private companies, some choosing to co-operate, others to resist the strategies of SOES. SOE managers were not ideologically motivated – many of them were themselves former private sector industrialists. Their driving force was a sense of mission, an urgency to turn Italy into a strong industrial power – an ideology which underpinned Italy's very essence as a modern nation. Understandably, then, there was very little consideration for arguments about fair competition, or the virtues of *laissez-faire*. Alliances were struck on a case by case basis – as for example when Fiat, the automobile giant, collaborated with IRI-Finsider to install a wide strip mill for producing coils for autobodies. The position of the national employers' association, Confindustria, on the other hand, was very guarded and conservative. It remained hostile to State involvement in the economy and tried to pressure the government to restrain the scope of the SOES, not least by offering funding to the DC and its allies. The rift became organisational as well as political when employers in the SOE sector created their own associations, removing their companies from Confindustria (Martinelli, 1979: 71 ff.).

Industrial policy included a vast state programme of State initiative in the South. Initially the *Cassa del Mezzogiorno* was supposed to provide infrastructure and there was no particular emphasis on industrial development, except for some credit and fiscal incentives for small business. After 1956, on the other hand, industrialisation became its chief aim. In 1957 a special law provided capital grants and soft loans towards the investment cost of new industrial activities, establishing a number of development zones where it was hoped that grouping of industries might call into existence external economies. The public sector was required to direct an important part of its investments to the *Mezzogiorno* and a similar obligation was imposed on SOES. Private firms were equally enticed to invest in the South, both by the incentives and by a degree of moral suasion. Fiat and Olivetti, for example, established plants in the *Mezzogiorno*, with good results. Chemical companies invested in new plants in Central Sardinia. Eventually the *Mezzogiorno*'s share of total investments in manufacturing rose from 17 per cent in 1951-1963 to over 30 per cent in 1963-73 (Petri, 1997: 393 ff.).

Plans for the *Cassa del Mezzogiorno* were developed among a circle of economists and industrial managers, who were very close to the leading technocratic elite. In fact one can find their predecessors in the so called "nittiani", the group of technicians collaborating with Saverio Francesco Nitti, a leading liberal politician who had been Prime Minister in 1919-1920. Many of them were southerners and they had also been the leading elements in the creation of the IRI in the 1930s. Not surprisingly, then, SOES were entrusted a key role in industrialising the South.

Two further elements of industrial policy were incentives for small firms and a first stab at indicative planning at the national level. Small firms benefited both from special financial assistance and State subsidy. Special institutions were devised to provide them with credit such as the Mediocredito Centrale, financed by the Treasury and designed to refinance local institutions providing soft loans to small firms, as well as a number of Mediocrediti Regionali, set up by local savings banks for medium and long term lending. Furthermore state finance to small firms was provided under a special law passed in 1959.

In 1955 the Vanoni Plan, was presented by the Finance Minister, Ezio Vanoni, belonging to the left wing the DC and reputed to be very close to leaders of the SOE sector, especially to Enrico Mattei, the chief of ENI. Vanoni's plan introduced a long term macro-economic perspective. The bulk of public expenditure was to go to infrastructure in the *Mezzogiorno*, in order to initiate a push for overall growth and thereby reduce unemployment, creating four million jobs, most of which in the South, over the next ten years. In this respect the plan proved to be overoptimistic, despite the fact that actual growth rates exceeded its forecasts: the overall number of jobs created was far less and most of them were created outside the South, generating large internal migration flows (Petri, 1997: 359 ff.).

The model we have outlined has been referred to aptly as "capitalism working in a state of emergency" (Barca, 1997: 12 ff.; on the limits of the model also Amato, 1972). Its key feature was to give the SOES a special investiture to develop projects that would be crucial for economic development. In some cases reorganisation of industrial sectors by leading SOES was made more compelling by the need to bring costs down to compete with European partners, subject to the new rules of the ECSC and the EEC. In other cases the rationale came from the need to fend off foreign competition, at home and abroad. Other features, such as investment in the South or support to small firms were conceived as complementary measures. High rates of investment, growth in industrial production and in exports based on technological innovation and high productivity, together with a sound macro-economic performance vindicated these policies.

There were, however, serious weaknesses, the importance of which was overshadowed by the excitement surrounding the economic miracle. In the first place, the SOE sector had been given a mission but no clear rules for governance. This was bound to generate serious problems once the leaders of the first post-war generation of SOE managers could no longer be relied upon. Secondly, the system lacked transparency and accountability. A small number of powerful players, both public and private, sometimes acting in concert, dominated many important branches: company law was primitive, the capital market underdeveloped and no anti-trust legislation in place. Government subsidy was erratic and indiscriminate. Finally, industrial performance was enhanced by high labour productivity set against comparatively low wages, but there was no common ground in industrial relations, which remained polarised and unbalanced. It was not a solid or promising basis for the rapid transition towards an industrial, consumer-based democracy (Regini, 1979: 48-61; Rogari, 2003, Vol. II.).

Failure of Planning and Extension of Political Influence in the 1960s

The 1960s was an ambitious period for planning and industrial policy. A new Centre-Left governing coalition, including both the DC and the socialists, took over. Of its vast reformist programme, however, only few pieces fell into place. Essentially SOES remained the pivot of industrial policy, but were increasingly subjected to an informal web of influences and controls, which affected their performance.

The Centre-Left coalition, born in 1962, was committed to a formal planning exercise, presented as *programmazione economica*. In the last few years Italy had been experiencing a remarkable period of economic growth and social change and many, especially the Left wing of the DC and the Socialist Party, believed it was time to spread the benefits of wealth more broadly and tackle a number of long-due economic reforms. Two policies belong to this period: the nationalisation of the electrical industry, and the launching of a national economic plan.

The nationalisation of the electrical industry resulted in the creation of ENEL, a large State company, with the aim of developing the national grid, keeping prices down for all users. The old electrical companies, however, were allowed to survive and were paid fairly generous compensation for their plants; in fact compensation was given to the companies, rather than to individual shareholders. A great deal of reorganisation took place as a result. SIP, an SOE and one of the former electrical companies, took over the telephone network. This was an ingenious way of financing a State-owned utility with public money and bringing about the rationalisation and unification of the network. It also highlighted the uncertain status of SOES within the public sector, as well as the multifaceted nature of industrial policy options that were available. Another former IRI electrical company, SME, took over a number of manufacturing firms mostly in the food sector, trying, without much success to form an integrated group capable of standing up to international competition. The largest private electrical company Edison used its compensation funds to take over the chemical firm Montecatini, thus creating a new large chemical conglemarate, Montedison. However, the results were not very positive: Montedison failed to rationalise its plant while costly investments in basic chemicals, particularly in the *Mezzogiorno*, led to surplus capacity (McCarthy, 1995: 83-86; Amatori, 1999: 742 ff.).

The first economic plan, after a long period of incubation, was presented in 1966 and approved in July of the same year. It was a very far reaching, ambitious document, containing both macro-economic prescriptions in the Keynesian mould and a menu of urgent reforms. It set a target of 5 per cent annual GDP growth for the next five years, compatible with preserving balance of payments equilibrium and low inflation. Rather naively it assumed that it would be possible for the government to direct all SOE investment, as well as influence private firm decisions. Appended to the plan was a long list of reforms, such as public housing and planned urban development, improved schooling, the development of an integrated transport system, the reform of the tax system and a devolution of powers to the Regions.

Most of the reforms were carried out with difficulty and delay. Devolution, the health service and the tax reform had to wait for the early 1970s. The core economic prescriptions of the plan, on the other hand, were too ambitious. There was a fierce, defensive action from private industrialists. Capital flight, culminating in the mid-1960s, seriously wrecked the balance of payments and had to be countered by a deflationary shock, administered by the Bank of Italy, whose Governor, Guido Carli, was highly critical of the national plan, perceiving it as unrealistic and biased against private business. Also the bureaucratic machinery established by the plan was cumbersome and ineffective. A new high-level ministerial committee, the CIPE (Comitato Nazionale per la programmazione economica), was supposed to set strategic guidelines and co-ordinate the work of the single economic ministries. However, it never succeeded in replacing the existing committee structure. SOE conglomerates retained a large degree of autonomous negotiating power, despite the numerous requirements and guidelines they were supposed to follow (Federico and Giannetti, 1999: 1148 ff.; Podbielski, 1974).

According to Giuliano Amato, who worked as an official in the planning office, the forces that were committed to the plan, were not fully aware of the complexities of the exercise, and they even lacked the necessary information on the economy. Giorgio Ruffolo, a socialist who was Secretary General for Planning between 1964 and 1975 also acknowledged that the planners' approach was simplistic and overoptimistic, at least in the early stage. According to his testimony, opposition came both from the Right and from the Left: the PCI, as well as the left wing of the socialists, were political enemies of the Centre-Left formula, which they saw as a surrender to capitalism, and they refused any involvement with the plan, influencing the trade union movement in the same direction. Business hostility was reinforced by the fact that growth rates continued to be positive: why interfere in an economy that was working so handsomely (Amato, 1972: 55; Amato, 1979; Ruffolo, 1976: 216-217)?

The attempt to bring trade unions into the planning mechanism by way of a nationally agreed "incomes policy" strategy failed to overcome a history of adversarial industrial relations. At first tripartite meetings held and a new consultative tripartite body (Commissione Nazionale per la Programmazione) was established (Regini, 1979: 57-58). But support ebbed away rapidly, under the hostile fire of the PCI and its allies on one side, and Confindustria on the other. Furthermore the trade union movement was rapidly gaining strength. The previous ideological divisions among the three confederations diminished, particularly thanks to increasing left-wing militancy in the supposedly moderate CISL and UIL. The first successful big waves of strikes swept the country in the early 1960s, against a background of rapidly falling unemployment and swelling factories in Northern Italy. Unionisation picked up and collective bargaining became more decentralised, as wages increased substantially for the first time since the war (Regini, 1979: 51; Magnani, 1994: 166 ff.). It was the beginning of a trend lasting for two decades that reached its high point during the Hot Autumn of 1969, when militant shop floor representatives forced industrial relations to a breaking point. Factory councils – elected by and composed of union and non-union workers alike – gained substantial power in a number of large industrial enterprises, while the unions exploited the new militancy to successfully demand greater wages, elimination of overtime, restriction to lay-offs and to internal mobility. Thus, the pace of work slowed down, jacking up labour costs and harming industrial output and firm profitability. Between 1970 and 1974 labour costs increased by 64 per cent, as opposed to annual increases of 8.5 per cent between 1963 and 1969 (Locke and Baccaro, 1999: 221).

Failing the planning mechanism, SOES established themselves even more as key protagonists of an informal industrial policy. In the years leading up to 1973 their expansion was remarkable. Between 1955 and 1970 their workforce doubled and the volume of their investment increased ten fold to reach a share of 30 per cent of gross investment in industry. They also covered significant shares in transport and communications and other services. Considering SOES together with the rest of State firms, including the recently nationalised electrical company, in 1971 their overall share of fixed capital investment in the economy was 40 per cent (Forte, 1974: 340-5). IRI was the largest group in Italy, a huge sprawling conglomerate, employing 447,000 in 1973. Its core lay in heavy industry, with steel ship building and heavy engineering covering over half of its sales. ENI in the meantime, had moved upstream into refineries, pipelines, petrochemicals and fertilisers. By 1973 it employed over 80,000 and controlled 180 companies (Toninelli, 2003: 639; Barca and Trento: 1997; also Amatori, 1997). New holdings were created or expanded, such as EFIM, operating in railway rolling stock engines, aluminium, food processing especially in the South, EGAM concentrating in mining and metallurgy, or GEPI, created to take over and restructure ailing companies. They were very poorly managed and had to be closed down a few years later (Shonfield, 1974: 270 ff.; Forte, 1974: 356-358; Bianchi, 1987).

SOES were engaged over a number of areas. As in the earlier post-war period they developed strategic industrial sectors and infrastructure, and they were also called upon to initiate capital intensive projects for the industrialisation of the South. In some cases, for example cement and fertilisers, they acted to break private monopolies. They were also used to create national champions in high-tech areas, although this kind of action did not feature as highly as in Britain or France. In 1967, IRI and Fiat, for example, merged their aerospace interests to create Aeritalia, a company receiving special grants from the government. Finally, especially during the crises of the 1970s, they were called upon to step up their investment for countercyclical purposes.

Through which mechanism did the political class bring the SOES to heel, and how were industrial priorities selected? Various forms of control and influence were gradually established: some of them were from above, using the channels of the ministerial control, others from within, by influencing the appointment of top directors within the SOES and ensuring they were close to the leading political parties. The system was gradually perfected with the distribution of jobs within SOES to reflect the political balance of the governing coalition. Parties and politicians were prepared to be generous in their support but they expected favours in return. Writing in 1974, Andrew Shonfield was convinced that "exchange of favours [between members of the SOES top management and politicians belonging to all parties] is normal and regular and that these favours are an important contribution to the funding of political parties" (Shonfield, 1974: 272).

Setting SOES tasks from above did not automatically mean exercising full control, while penetrating them from within was bound to be a slow and ambiguous process. Some managers offered resistance, but they were gradually replaced by a new brand of 'political technocrats", men like Eugenio Cefis, the successor of Mattei at ENI, who openly flouted a combination of management skills and political influence. Gradually the performance of SOES worsened, just at the time when, thanks largely to their achievements, Italian industry had reached considerable levels of technological excellence. Some choices were bungled; investment strategies became opportunistic and day to day performance in key plants deteriorated.

The weaknesses of Italy's industrial policy system emerged more clearly during this period. There was no accountability, either to the State or the market. Because extensive planning proved a chimera, a kind of informal, pervasive negotiating process developed between the State, SOES and large private firms, with the help of a generous system of state subsidies. There was much talk of implementing anti-trust legislation, but nothing was achieved. SOES themselves were often monopolistic, and their very nature seemed incompatible with any set of established rules and accepted practices. On the other hand, booming foreign trade, particularly within the rapidly expanding Common Market, was leading to a rapid opening up of the Italian economy and acting as a deterrent against monopoly, at least in tradable sectors. But this did not affect the vast sectors producing non-tradable goods or offering non-tradable services, which remained steeped in lack of transparency and over-regulation.

New Approaches in Facing the Crisis of the 1970s and 1980s

During the 1970s Italy was beset by double digit inflation, disruptive strikes, political instability against the background of a serious terrorist threat. Inflation became deeply ingrained in the system so that, after 1979, many years of tight monetary policy within the ERM were required to tackle it. Fiscal policy, however, was inconsistently lax. In the short term repeated currency devaluations during the 1970s and early 1980s succeeded in boosting export performance, and profits remained strong, thanks also to some deft government handling of the fiscal drag and to private corporate restructuring in the 1980s. Despite the crisis of the more capital intensive industries so crucial during the boom, the manufacturing sector continued to perform quite strongly, especially engineering and other miscellaneous branches, with small firm "industrial districts" on the ascendant. On the other hand, productivity performance in the service sector was poor and unemployment rose rapidly, hitting the South particularly badly. Emigration had ceased to be an outlet, indeed there was immigration from poorer countries as well as repatriation of former emigrants (Ranieri, 1998: 84-93; Sassoon, 1997: 58 ff.).

The Italian economy struggled for many years with the imperatives of economic crisis and industrial restructuring. The SOE sector resisted rationalisation as far as possible and drew heavily on the resources of the State, widening the budget deficit. Eventually SOES and the rest of the State sector came to be seen as the problem, rather than the solution. Industrial policy became even more fragmented and piecemeal. There is very little evidence of a coherent national strategy apart from monetary policies, conducted with some consistency by the Bank of Italy. The strength acquired by organised labour meant that it had to be brought into the policy-making arena. This shift to a concerted approach to economic management carried out in conditions of emergency was far from well thought-out; rather it was bumpy, reluctant and incomplete. Nevertheless a certain amount of common ground, especially at the micro-level, was reached.

The wave of shop floor militancy unleashed by the Hot Autumn of 1969 forced an important rethink, on the part of both unions, employers' association and the government, of the industrial relations' system. The direction was, inevitably, a neo-corporatist one, following North European examples, but there was much ground to be made up. Labour confederations sought to regain their influence over spontaneous agitations, by carrying out initiatives at the central level. From 1969 to 1971 they pressed the government, for major reforms and backed up their demands by a series of general strikes articulated on a regional basis (Regini, 1979: 54-6). Results were patchy but they included a change in the pension system, new laws on housing and the health service. Agreements were reached with the employer's association through peak negotiations. As the crisis bit more severely in 1974-1975, unions took a more co-operative attitude. They were encouraged by the shift to the Left of the political landscape, which eventually brought the PCI close to the centre of power as member of a large parliamentary coalition, supporting an executive of "national unity" between 1976 and 1979. At the so called "*svolta dell'EUR*" in 1978, a document was voted by the delegates of the three main Confederations, calling for wage restraint in return for union involvement in industrial policy management.

Changes in the strategy of Confindustria were equally important, especially after 1973, under the presidency of Fiat's Giovanni Agnelli. The employers' embarked on what could be called containment, calling upon all their resources to accommodate some of the unions pay demands, in return for the restoration of badly dented managerial authority on the shopfloor. This tactics appealed more to large firms, including SOES, than to smaller ones, which could less afford high wage settlements and automatic, indexed pay rises (Chiesi and Martinelli, 1989: 204-5).

Three moments marked the transition to a new industrial relations picture: the *Statuto dei Lavoratori* of 1970, a piece of legislation, which granted the unions a number of basic rights, considerably tightened the rules on hiring and firing, and attributed organisational privileges to the three confederations CGIL, CISL and UIL. Only very small companies, with less than 15 employees, were allowed to escape these prescriptions. Secondly, in 1975, an agreement was reached stretching automatic wage indexation to cover nearly 80 per cent of pay rises, so that gradually more and more of workers' pay was covered by this mechanism, rather than by normal contractual pay rises. This extra degree of protection had a serious economic impact, weakening the effectiveness of lira devaluation, and fuelling inflation. It, also, dramatically flattened wage differentials eroding professional hierarchies and generating resentment. Finally the tripartite agreement on CIG (*Cassa Integrazione Guadagni*) or short-term lay-off fund, meant that in the event of temporary layoffs, workers' earnings were paid by the State for up to one year to the extent of 80 or 90 per cent of their salary, pending re-employment. It thus reduced the burden on employers shedding labour, and encouraged bilateral negotiations at the factory level over investment and restructuring issues (Regini and Regalia, 1997: 147-148; Cella, 1989: 172 ff.; Marsden, 1987: 191).

The government, furthermore, adopted the practice of systematically consulting the unions often granting them privileged access in the process of formation of bills. Proposals were floated to establish tripartite bodies with an advisory role over industrial policy. Unions, however, shied away from full co-operation, preferring formal involvement only on policy implementation, although they did accept co-optation in a very wide variety of public agencies and boards of directors (Regalia and Regini, 1998: 488 ff.).

Most severely affected by the crisis of the mid-1970s were the "strategic sectors", such as petrochemicals, steel and automobiles, suffering from shrinking markets, huge sunk fixed capital and spiralling energy costs. In the mid 1970s Law n. 675, was introduced to encourage industrial restructuring and to rationalise the current jungle of subsidies and special measures. However, it set up a complex machinery of sectoral plans, committees of experts, consultation with local authorities and with workers' and employers' associations, a Committee of Ministers and a special Parliamentary Commission. Significantly new was the involvement of Parliament in industrial policy, a reflection of the current political climate of "national unity" (Ferrera, 1989: 120-127; Adams, 1990).

The results of Law 675 were disappointing. A large amount of work was devoted to producing plans of doubtful value. The allocation of funds was insufficient and subject to paralysing delays; furthermore they were channelled into rescue operations, rather than in reconverting industries into new fields. At the national level, tripartite co-operation was at best tentative and unions were often adversarial. What was achieved, however, was a better climate of co-operation at the local level between social partners. A system of "secluded micro-concertation" developed, especially in large companies but also in small business districts (Regalia and Regini, 1995).

The political and social climate changed after the 1979 election. A new coalition was launched excluding the PCI and bringing together the DC with a rejuvenated and aggressive Socialist Party, under the leadership of Bettino Craxi. Soon after, a sharp confrontation between unions and Fiat was resolved in favour of the latter by an unexpected march of 40,000 anti-union white collars in Turin. These developments hindered, but did not entirely reverse, the entrenchment of collaborative-participatory features. During the early 1980s tripartite concertation focused on an attempt to reach an anti-inflation social pact, which would reverse the impact of the wage indexation agreement of 1975. In 1983 an agreement was reached to partially de-link wage escalation and allow a more flexible use of the labour force, while the government responded with financial inducements to both social partners. However, the following year negotiations broke down over wage de-indexation. Political divisions played a decisive role, the CGIL unwilling to accept an agreement with the Craxi government. In response the government introduced the contents of the agreements reached with the other two unions and Confindustria by decree law. In July 1985 a referendum promoted by the PCI and the CGIL failed to overturned it. It could be said, therefore, that the government achieved its objective, but as a result tripartite consultation stalled for the rest of the decade, the unions paralysed by their divergent political affiliations. Older adversarial pattern of industrial relations seemed to re-establish themselves, although at company level tripartite negotiations continued on a pragmatic basis. The government continued to consult the social partners separately, before introducing important economic policy measures, even occasionally reaching bilateral agreements with the unions over specific taxation issues. Thus, Italy remained in the middle: concertation was half-baked, but the return to the market was also partial, taking at best the limited form of a "bargained deregulation" (Cella, 1989: 73 ff.; Regini and Regalia, 1997: 210 ff.).

The development strategy that had guided industrial policy up to the early 1970s was replaced by a piecemeal, fragmentary set of measures, mostly of a defensive nature. SOES were still called upon to perform specific tasks, such as take-over of assets from ailing private companies or partnerships to bolster failing industries. For example, the SIR chemical group, which had rapidly grown from a small family enterprise into an aggressive conglomerate by means of extensive recourse to state incentives for new plants in the South, was technically bankrupt and it was only through political pressure that it was rescued by ENI. IRI acted in a similar way across a wide range of industries: for example it bought all Fiat's steel plants at an overvalued price. In addition it sold off its own automobile company, Alfa Romeo, to Fiat, with the government blocking a counter bid from Ford (Ranci, 1987: 124).

Not surprisingly the capacity for self-finance of SOES all but disappeared. Depending on the government for funds, they became even more colonised by the politicians. Trade unions played a role as well: they opposed any privatisation; they forced onerous collective agreements on SOE managers by putting pressure on the government to influence the association of public sector employers; they influenced appointments (Grassini, 1980: 362-4). Nor did the opposition act as a watchdog over public enterprises; indeed there was often collusion between majority and opposition in this regard. For instance, most of the measures on behalf of public enterprises, including subsidies, were approved unanimously in Parliament and the PCI, at this late stage, became a strong supporter of the role of IRI (Barca and Trento, 1997a:

555). As a result there was indiscriminate subsidy, mounting losses and a further swelling of SOES, culminating in the early 1980s. IRI and ENI together employed over 600,000 in 1982, a 30 per cent increase over the previous decade. In every single year between 1974 and 1987 IRI posted a loss, losses peaking during the years 1981-4. ENI too fell in the red for a few years, although its losses were less pronounced and it was able to turn around after 1984 (Barca and Trento, 1997b: 198-199).

At the government level, the main thrust of industrial policy were low-interest credit subsidies to firms, including rising export credits, and also discounts (or tax breaks) on the purchase of capital goods, as well as the social cushion of CIG. New ministerial committee structures were set up, but their actual capacity to rationalise a byzantine structure, with a large variety of different institutional and social players, each claiming a share of the cake, seems to have been very limited (Schioppa, 1990: 147-148; Bianchi, 1995b).

Industrial policies for the South were part of this pattern. Special development investment from the *Cassa del Mezzogiorno* had been sizeable and sustained while SOES had played a major part in metallurgy (Finsider Taranto steelworks), engineering (Alfa Sud near Naples) and petrochemicals (Eni at Gela and elsewhere). Large private companies, such as Fiat and Montedison also contributed. By the early 1970s fixed industrial investment in the South had doubled its previous share to over 30 per cent of the national total. In the following years however investment fell. Some of the large plants, beset by surplus capacity, also suffered from poor industrial relations and bad management. Subsidies by the *Cassa* were also cut, and in 1986 a more decentralised approach, based on project financing with local authority involvement was adopted, bringing, however, little improvement. In 1993 the *Cassa* was wound down. Capital intensive schemes, such as Taranto, where dismissed as "cathedrals in the desert", since it was claimed that they had failed to generate a local spin-off in terms of services or supplier industries. This was not entirely true and large scale industry did at least provide the basic of an industrial culture to previously underdeveloped areas. However, a more promising solution to the South's backwardness seemed to be offered by the growth of small firm clusters, particularly along the Adriatic coast (Ranieri, 1998: 95-96; De Vita, 1992: 173-199).

The impact of micro-industrial policies on the emergence of a thriving small-firm sector in the 1970s and 1980s remains controversial. One school emphasises the importance of local subsidies and provisions of credit, common externalities and services, not least from regional institutions. Others refer to widespread habits of tax avoidance through legal loopholes and wholesale evasion, which limited the scope of any industrial policy. Given the variety of different local patterns it is possible to find examples of each. The strength of industrial "districts" (involving a high degree of specialisation) was particularly evident in a number of light industries, such as textiles, footwear, tanning, ceramics, and furniture. These districts are characterised by high birth and mortality rates of companies. Positive externalities take the form of common services ranging from marketing, to quality control and training arrangements. Trade associations and trade unions set up useful channels for conflict resolution while local banks were able to offer support by acquiring detailed knowledge of the district's activities. The overall contribution of the small firm sector to the national economy is very difficult to measure, but it undoubtedly played a part in the resilience displayed by Italy, at a time when some of the key features of post-war model were rapidly failing (Goodman and Bamford, 1989; Trigilia, 1995).

The End of the Italian Model and the Reforms of the 1990s

During the 1990s far reaching and radical reforms were introduced which amounted to no less than a complete overhaul of the previous industrial policy model. As we have argued, that model originated to carry out what were perceived as emergency tasks. It had failed, however, to generate mechanisms for a transition to a self-regulating market-economy and had gradually degenerated into a chaotic, badly managed and politicised structure. Already in the course of the 1980s, in response to the pressures for restructuring emanating from the European Commission, efforts were made, with very limited success, to discipline and reorganise the SOE sector, privatising some companies. External pressures continued to mount with the severe fiscal crisis of the State.

The combination of monetary stringency and fiscal profligacy chosen by the Italian governments became unsustainable as high interest rates were forced upon the ERM by German Unification. This was followed by a sharp recession in 1992-1993. The lira was consequently devalued, at a time when the Government had committed itself to the tight convergence criteria agreed upon at Maastricht in preparation for the single currency. Time was becoming short for the Italian authorities, especially since the stock of accumulated debt in 1993 had risen to 114 per cent of GDP, with crippling yearly interest charges. Politically the country entered a long tunnel. Against a background of judicial disclosures of endemic corruption, the parties of the governing coalition, primarily the DC and PSI, saw their support crumble, while populist anti-establishment movements entered the fray. Bank of Italy technocrats were called in to help manage the crisis: first former Governor Ciampi became Prime Minister in 1993; then after a short interlude by an erratic right wing coalition led by Berlusconi in 1994, again former Bank of Italy official Lamberto Dini was called to head a so-called "technical" government (Ferrera and Gualmini, 2004; De Cecco, 2001).

The task of these executives was to manage the transition towards a new set of rules, including a first-past the post electoral system, and to carry out a radical privatisation process. The emergency also called for an attempt to revive the concertation process, partly shelved during the 1980s: the three partners being now all sufficiently weak to need mutual cooperation. In July 1992 a tripartite agreement abolished wage-indexation and froze decentralised bargaining for the following year. A year later a new, more comprehensive deal, established a permanent incomes policies, based on a commitment to contain wage increases within the expected inflation rate. Further agreements followed, focusing on public sector pay structures and pension reforms (Locke and Baccaro, 1999: 257-258; Regini and Regalia, 1997: 214-227).

Starting in 1990 and with increasing speed, the State sector was forced to loosen its grip. Essential pressure was applied from Brussels. Already as part of the Single European Act directives, the Commission had established the principle that publicly owned companies should follow the same criteria as private ones, so that subsidy from the State would, under normal conditions, be unlawful. The concept whereby improper social burdens justified State subsidies to SOES was thus undermined. Furthermore the Treaty of European Union tightened legislation further, giving new powers to the Commission on competition policy and banning any State aid which might distort competition (Bianchi, 1995a; Bianchi, 1998; Marrelli and Stroffolini, 1998). The system, however, which had proved highly resilient in the past, would have probably survived even this new spate of supranational rulings, but for the imminent threat of bankruptcy. In fact the share of SOES and of the wider public sector on total national investment and value added had escalated further by 1992-1993. At the same time, however, IRI posted unprecedented 1993 losses of 10,000 billion lira, and the Treasury was burdened by both interests on the stock of debt, as well as by the need for new payments into the Endowment Fund. The overall situation of public finances did not make these payments feasible. Between 1992 and 1993 two major banks were privatised and a bill was passed preparing the way for the sale of all SOE shares on the market. In the following years a good number of companies were privatised, either entirely or partially, in the latter case leaving the Treasury with a controlling stake. The revenue of these sales, averaged 1.5 per cent of GDP every year between 1992 and 2000, and was thus highly beneficial for public finances (Toninelli, 2003: 647 ff.).

Parallel to privatisation, extensive economic reform was undertaken. An anti-trust law was hurriedly passed in 1990 together with a High Authority for Market Competition. A new thrust of measures were taken to improve the transparency of the Stock Exchange and reform the corporate governance system. The financial system was also reformed, banks being encouraged to reorganise as multifunctional groups, capable of providing a variety of services. The capital market was allowed to develop further with the creation of new financial institutions, such as pension funds. Many previously overregulated sectors, including the labour market, have been liberalised and, in some cases, independent authorities have been created to supervise them, ensuring adequate competitive conditions (Bianco and Trento, 1995: 81 ff.; Toninelli, 2003).

The speed with which many of these measures were cobbled together meant that the reform process lacked depth and consistency. For example privatisation, despite having succeeded in spreading stock ownership widely among the public, was not far reaching enough to eliminate public monopoly in many crucial services. Also the government encouraged the formation of controlling syndicates of small core groups of investors in some major companies, to the detriment of small investors. Nor has politics entirely relinquished its influence on the banking system. A balance sheet of these reforms is premature, but there is no question that they ended a long stage of Italian capitalism and opened a very different one. In this respect it is not entirely arbitrary to find some parallel between the situation in Italy and that of post-communist Eastern Europe.

In retrospect the Italian model proved appropriate to contend with the imperatives of catch-up and expansion. In the following years of faltering growth punctuated by recession and restructuring, it was unable to adapt. The basis of industrial policy management was made more inclusive, with repeated, frantic attempt at concertation, but what could not be achieved, except under extreme external pressure, was reform of SOE structure and performance. The private sector proved flexible enough to find an answer to the crisis in the growth of the small firm sector, but the sprawling public sector could not find a new mission, nor was the government able to impart it. In fact attempts at planning were far off the mark, both in their more ambitious versions of the 1960s and in the narrower ones which followed. On the other hand, public spending increased to the point where it became unsustainable. The social partnership was built on extremely fragile foundations. Unions wanted to establish an inclusive welfare state, but they became parties to inefficiency and waste. Having chosen political control over economic negotiation, during the neo-liberal and deregulatory 1980s, they were caught on the defensive. A resumption of neo-corporatism at a time when elsewhere it is perceived as an inadequate solution to the needs of a flexible, post-Fordist economy is perhaps the latest paradox of the Italian case.

References

Adams, P. (1990), "La politica industriale", in: B. Dente (ed.), *Le politiche pubbliche in Italia*, Bologna: Il Mulino.

Allen, K. and A. Stevenson (1974), *An Introduction to the Italian Economy*, London: M. Robertson.

Amato, G. (1979), "Le istituzioni per il governo dell'economia", in: L. Graziano and S. Tarrow (eds.), *La Crisi italiana, Vol. 2, Sistema politico e istituzioni*, Turin: Einaudi.

Amato, G. (ed.) (1972), *Il governo dell'industria in Italia*, Bologna: Il Mulino.

Amatori, F. (1997), "Growth via Politics: Business Groups Italian-Style" in T. Shiba and M. Shimotami, (eds.), *Beyond the Firm. Business Groups in International and Historical Perspective*, Oxford: Oxford University Press, p. 109-134.

Amatori, F. (1999), "La grande impresa", in: F. Amatori *et al.* (eds.), *Storia d'Italia. Annali 15. L'industria*, Turin: Einaudi, p. 691-753.

Barca, F. (1997), "Compromesso senza riforme nel capitalismo italiano" in F. Barca (ed.), *Storia del capitalismo italiano dal dopoguerra ad oggi*, Rome: Donzelli, p. 3-115.

Barca, F. and S. Trento (1997), "La parabola delle partecipazioni statali: una missione tradita", in: F. Barca (ed.), *Storia del capitalismo italiano dal dopoguerra ad oggi*, Rome: Donzelli, p. 185-236.

Barca, F. and S. Trento (1997), "State-Ownership and the Evolution of Italian Corporate Governance", in: *Industrial and Corporate Change*, Vol. 6, 3, p. 533-559.

Berta, G. (1999), "Imprese e sindacati nella contrattazione collettiva", in: F. Amatori *et al.* (eds.), *Storia d'Italia. Annali 15. L'industria*, Turin: Einaudi, p. 997-1034.

Bianchi, P. (1987), "The IRI in Italy: Strategic Role and Political Constraints", *Western European Politics*, Vol. 10, 2, p. 269-290.

Bianchi, P. (1995a), "Impresa pubblica", in: *Enciclopedia delle Scienze Sociali*, Vol. 4, Rome: Istituto della Enciclopedia Italiana, p. 587-596.

Bianchi, P. (1995b), "Italy: the Crisis of an Introvert State", in: J. Hayward (ed.), *Industrial Enterprise and European Integration. From National to International Champions in Western Europe*, Oxford: Oxford University Press.

Bianchi, P. (1998), *Industrial policies and economic integration: learning from European experiences*, London: Routledge.

Bianco, M. and S. Trento (1995), "Capitalismi a confronto: I modelli di controllo delle imprese", *Stato e Mercato*, Vol. 43, p. 65-93.

Bonelli, F. (1978), "Il capitalismo italiano. Linee generali di interpretazione", in: F. Amatori *et al.* (eds.), *Storia d'Italia. Annali I. Dal feudalesimo al capitalismo*, Turin: Einaudi, p. 1193-1255.

Carli, G. (1993), *Cinquant'anni di vita italiana*, Rome-Bari: Laterza.

Cella, G. P. (1989), "Criteria of Regulation in Italian industrial relations: A Case of Weak Institutions", in: P. Lange and M. Regini (eds.), *State, Market and Social Regulation. New Perspectives on Italy*, Cambridge: Cambridge University Press, p. 167-186.

Cella, G. P. and T. Treu (eds.) (1998), *Le nuove relazioni industriali: l'esperienza italiana nella prospettiva europea*, Bologna: Il Mulino.

Chiesi, A. and A. Martinelli (1989), "The representation of business interests as a mechanism of social regulation", in: P. Lange and M. Regini (eds.), *State, Market and Social Regulation. New Perspectives on Italy*, Cambridge: Cambridge University Press, p. 187-217.

Colajanni, N. (1991), *Il Capitalismo senza capitale. Storia di Mediobanca*, Mayland: Sperling & Kupfer.

Conti, G. (1999), "Le banche e il finanziamento industriale", in: F. Amatori *et al.* (eds.), *Storia d'Italia. Annali 15. L'industria*, Turin: Einaudi, p. 443-547.

De Cecco, M. (1989), "Keynes and Italian Economics", in: P. Hall (ed.), *The Political Power of Economic Ideas – Keynesianism across Nations*, Princeton, N. J.: Princeton University Press, p. 195-229.

De Cecco, M. (2001), "L'economia italiana negli ultimi trent'anni", in: S. Cassese (ed.), *Ritratto dell'Italia*, Bari: Laterza, 2001.

De Vita, P. (1992), "L'industria nel Mezzogiorno: mutamenti strutturali nel decennio 1980-1990", *Rassegna Economica*, Vol. 56, 1, p. 173-99.

Federico, G. and J. Cohen (2001), *The Growth of the Italian Economy 1820-1960*, Cambridge: Cambridge University Press.

Federico, G. and R. Giannetti (1999), "Le politiche industriali", in: F. Amatori *et al.* (eds.), *Storia d'Italia. Annali 15. L'industria*, Turin: Einaudi, p. 1127-62.

Ferrera, M. (1989), "Politics, institutional features, and the government of industry", in: P. Lange and M. Regini (eds.), *State, Market and Social Regulation. New Perspectives on Italy*, Cambridge: Cambridge University Press.

Ferrera, M. and E. Gualmini (2004), *Rescued by Europe? Social and Labour Market Reforms from Maastricht to Berlusconi*, Amsterdam: Amsterdam University Press.

Forte, F. (1974), "L'impresa grande piccola pubblica privata", in: F. L. Cavazza and S. R. Graubard (eds.), *Il caso italiano*, Mayland: Garzanti.

Goodman, E. and J. Bamford (eds.) (1989), *Small firms and industrial districts in Italy*, London: Routledge.

Grassini, F. (1980), "Vincoli politici e direzione delle imprese pubbliche nell'esperienza italiana", *L'industria. Rivista di economia e politica industriale*, Vol. 1, 3.

Holland, S. (ed.) (1972), *The State as Entrepreneur. New Dimensions for Public Entreprises: the IRI State Shareholding Formula*, London: Weidenfeld and Nicolson.

King, R. (1985), *The Industrial Geography of Italy*, London: Croom Helm.

LaPalombara, J. (1989), *Democracy Italian Style*, London: York University Press.

Locke, R. M. and L. Baccaro (1999), "The Resurgence of Italian Unions?", in: A. Martin and G. Ross (eds.), *The Brave New World of European Labour. European Trade Unions at the Millennium*, Oxford: Berghahn.

Magnani, M. (1994), "La vera occasione mancata degli anni Sessanta", in: P. Ciocca, (ed.), *Il progresso economico dell'Italia*, Bologna: Il Mulino.

Maraffi, M. (1990), Politica e economia in Italia: La vicenda dell'impresa pubblica dagli anni Trenta agli anni Cinquanta, Bologna: Il Mulino.

Marrelli, M. and F. Stroffolini (1998), "Privatisation in Italy. A tale of 'capture'", in: D. Parker (ed.), *Privatisation in the European Union. Theory and Policy Perspectives*, London: Routledge, p. 150-169.

Marsden, D. (1987), "Collective bargaining and industrial adjustment in Britain, France, Italy and West Germany", in: F. Duchene and G. Shepherd (eds.), *Managing industrial change in Western Europe*, London: Frances Pinter Press.

Martinelli, A. (1979), "Organised Business and Italian Politics: Confindustria and the Christian Democratic Party in the post-war period", *West European Politics*, Vol. 2, p. 3, p. 67-87.

McCarthy, P. (1995), *The Crisis of the Italian State: From the Origins of the Cold War to the Fall of Berlusconi*, London: Macmillan.

Padoa Schioppa, F. (1990), *L'economia sotto tutela. Problemi strutturali dell'intervento pubblico in Italia*, Bologna: Il Mulino.

Petri, R. (1997), "Dalla Ricostruzione al miracolo economico", in: G. Sabbatucci and V. Vidotto (eds.), *Storia d'Italia 5. La Repubblica 1943-1963*, Bari: Laterza, p. 313-440.

Petri, R. (2002), *Storia economica d'Italia. Dalla Grande guerra al miracolo economico (1918-1963)*, Bologna: Il Mulino.

Podbielski, G. (1974), *Italy: Development and Crisis in the Postwar Economy*, Oxford: Clarendon Press.

Poster, M. V. and S. J. Woolf (1967), *Italian Public Enterprise*, London: Duckwork.

Ranci, P. (1987), "Italy: the weak State", in: F. Duchene and G. Shepherd, (eds.), *Managing industrial change in Western Europe*, London – New York: Frances Pinter, p. 111-144.

Ranieri, R. (1998), "Italy: After the Rewards of Growth, the Penalty of Debt", in: B. Foley (ed.) *European Economies Since the Second World War*, London: Palgrave Macmillan, p. 84-93.

Ranieri, R., M. Kipping and J. Dankers (2001), "The Emergence of New Competitor Nations in the European Steel Industry: Italy and The Netherlands, 1945-65", *Business History*, Vol. 43, 1, p. 69-96;

Regalia, I. and M. Regini (1995), "Between Voluntarism and Institutionalisation: Industrial Relations and Human Resource Practices in Italy", in: R. Locke *et al.* (eds.), *Employment Relations in a Changing World Economy*, Cambridge: MIT Press.

Regalia, I. and M. Regini (1998), "Sindacati, istituzioni, sistema politico", in: G. Cella and T. Treu (eds.), *Le nuove relazioni industriali: l'esperienza italiana nella prospettiva europea*, Bologna: Il Mulino, p. 467-494.

Regini, M. (1979), "Labour Unions, Industrial Action and Politics", *West European Politics*, Vol. 2, 3, p. 49-66.

Regini, M. and I. Regalia (1997), "Employers, Unions and the State: the Resurgence of Concertation in Italy?", in: M. Bull and M. Rhodes (eds.), *Crisis and Transition in Italian Politics*, London: Frank Cass, p. 210-231.

Rogari, S. (2003), "Sindacati e imprenditori. Le relazioni industriali in Italia alla svolta degli anni '60", in: A. M. Falchero *et al.* (eds.), *La Storia e l'Economia. Miscellanea di studi in onore di Giorgio Mori, Vol. II*, Varese: Edizioni Lativa.

Ruffolo, G. (1976), "Strutture delle istituzioni e sviluppo democratico: il nodo della pubblica amministrazione", in: AA. VV, *Il governo democratico dell'economia*, Bari: De Donato.

Sapelli, G. (1990), "Lo Stato come imprenditore politico", *Storia Contemporanea*, Vol. 21, 2, p. 243-296.

Sassoon, D. (1997 – 2nd edition), *Contemporary Italy. Economy, Society and Politics since 1945*, London: Longman.

Shonfield, A. (1965), *Modern Capitalism: the changing balance of public and private power*, London: Oxford University Press.

Shonfield, A. (1974), "L'impresa pubblica: modello internazionale o specialità locale", in: F. L. Cavazza and S. R. Graubard (ed.), *Il caso italiano*, Mayland: Garzanti, p. 269-90.

Toninelli, P. A. (2003), "Ascesa e declino dell'impresa pubblica in Italia (1860-2000): una nota sul ruolo dello stato nella crescita", in: A. M. Falchero *et al.* (eds.), *La Storia e l'Economia. Miscellanea di studi in onore di Giorgio Mori, Vol. II*, Varese: Edizioni Lativa, p. 629-61.

Trigilia, C. (1995), "Dinamismo privato e disordine pubblico. Politica, economia e società locali", in: *Storia dell'Italia Repubblicana, Vol. 2, La trasformazione dell'Italia: sviluppo e squilibrio*, Turin: Einaudi.

Vito, F. (1954), "Monopoly and Competition in Italy", in: E. H. Chamberlin (ed.), *Monopoly and Competition and their Regulation*, London: Palgrave Macmillan, p. 43-60.

Zamagni, V. (1993), *The Economic History of Italy 1860-1990*, Oxford: Clarendon Press.

CHAPTER 8

Between Planning and Muddling Through

Institutional Change and Economic Growth in Belgium (1945-1961)

Ivan WIJNENS†[1]

In 1933, the Belgian Socialist Party (Belgische Socialistische Partij or BSP) adopted the "Labour Plan". Developed by Hendrik De Man, its intention was to lead the way to a recovery from the economic crisis and to fight unemployment (see among others Claeys-Van Haegendoren, 1972: 188-193; Hansen, 1978: 235-257). It proposed a new economic organisation founded on the principles of a directed economy and acceptance of the need for a mixed economic regime: the extension of public ownership, credit policy, large public works schemes etc. De Man came near to implementing his plan in some form. However, his inclusion as Minister of Public Works and later Minister of Finance in the Van Zeeland Governments proved insufficient to break the resistance of the traditional political and economic elite (Vanthemsche, 1982: 339-387; Hogg, 1986: 168-172). The other political parties in Belgium were unwilling to consider any radical change and De Man's attempts to find common ground with the corporatist-inspired industrial organisations, particularly advocated in Christian democratic political and union circles, failed to succeed.[2] A further obstacle was the fact that the established leadership of his party remained circumspect. The traditional story tells us that Belgian governments after World War II were able to shake off structural reforms and continue much as before. However, in reality it was only from the end of the 1950s that a number of changes did occur that marked a new phase in the relation state-economy. The government set up a full-scale exercise in economic planning almost thirty years after the "De Man Plan".

1 Due to his untimely death, the author has not been able to finalise this text himself. It has been slightly adapted by the editors.

2 For an overview of the initiatives on industrial organisation in the interwar period, see among others Luyten, 1988: 587-654.

The emphasis placed upon both plans actually is referential. More importantly, they reflected the determination to take charge rather than be driven by economic events. The time-span between both plans marked the transition in Belgium from economic orthodoxy to Keynesian economic management. It has often been pointed out that World War II was important for the breakthrough of Keynesian types of interventionism. Clearly, in Belgium, the trend towards sustained Keynesian government intervention for a prolonged period was observed from the sidelines. This chapter is constructed around the propelling of Keynesian policy to the forefront of government concern in Belgium. Our aim is to focus on the political and socio-economic factors inhibiting or facilitating economic policy changes. "Planning" will be regarded in a broad sense to mean the strategic use of the instruments of social and economic policy by the government, in tandem with economic and social organisations, to attain explicit objectives in the medium and long term. Consequently, the analysis deals with questions such as how the government took charge of the economy and how the government organised itself in order to be able to do so. Besides the economic agenda of the government and the methods used to accomplish it, we pay attention to social policy and the emergence of socio-economic consultation. They were, after all, inextricably linked to the nature of the Keynesian welfare state.

Divergent Priorities: Towards a Pragmatic two-tier Policy (1944-1948)

The reconstruction of Belgium after World War II is often typified as an era "between restoration and renewal" (e.g. Witte, Burgelman and Stouthuysen, 1990). This characterisation refers to the atmosphere in which the reconstruction took place: one realised that this was a time for fundamental choices about the structures of power that would determine the shape of the future Belgian state. Although it relates to the entire social context, the most striking aspect was the contrast that existed between social and economic policy. The term renewal mostly related to the realisation of social progress of which most aspects, however, originated in the interwar period. Social security was laid down by law, wages were increased and socio-economic consultation was institutionalised. With this, two pillars of the welfare state had been erected. By contrast, there was very little evidence of renewal in the economic sense. Economic liberalism was restored, while genuine structural reforms never materialised. How can this two-tier policy be explained?

By the late 1930s, it was quite clear that the attempts by De Man to implement a planned economy had been successfully thwarted by members of Belgium's leading circles. Subsequently, his collaboration with the Germans during the war would result in further stigmatisation not only of himself, but also of his economic doctrine. After the liberation, the leadership of the BSP was reclaimed by the more pragmatic figures within the party, whose convictions tied in with the tradition of pre-war reformism (Kramer, 1978: 116-124).[3] Achieving tangible social improvements was their trademark. However, they were less proficient in putting forward revolutionary economic insights. Up until 1949, these reformists constituted the core of the government coalition and thus spearheaded the reconstruction of Belgium.

Achiel Van Acker, who led the government in 1945 and 1946, was the initial architect (see Luyten and Hemmerijckx, 2000: 19-46). As a socialist, he sought practical solutions to concrete problems. A radical approach was not to be expected from him, as he made quite clear in one of his first speeches: "Ne me parlez pas de nationalisations. L'État est un mauvais industriel et un mauvais homme d'affaire" (quoted in Hemmerijckx, 2003: 175). His main goal was to get the country back on its feet. Dirigisme was a necessity, in Belgium as elsewhere, in order to cope with the dislocation and to stimulate economic activity. It was the fight against inflation which was of particular concern, especially as the memories of the towering inflation after World War I were still so very vivid. Consequently, the socialist economic policies were predicated on strong support for Camille Gutt's financial program, the goal of which was to maintain the stability of the franc, by cutting down on excess monetary circulation (Kramer, 1978: 125-131). The logical result of this program was the need for a policy of wage and price controls. In addition, measures were worked out to boost industrial output. Increasing stocks of coal, the most important source of energy, was considered a priority. These kinds of measures had a favourable impact on the traditional sectors of industry, which after all had suffered less war damage than its neighbouring countries. Belgium soon returned to the pre-war free-market model. Pricing was liberalised as early as 1947.

In other words, the socialists introduced certain economic controls, though they were ones that did not go against the interests of the groups that dominated the large industries. The foundations of the free market mechanism were left unaffected. Certainly the vigorous action of the state was no longer viewed simply as a reversible intervention, as it had been after World War I. Now it became part of a long-term perspective. However, the form that state intervention assumed after World War II qualitatively marked no fundamental split from the 1930s. In fact, the views that these pragmatic socialists held in relation to the country's

3 On the tradition of pre-war reformism, see: Vanthemsche, 1998: 57-102.

economic problems did not diverge a great deal from those of the traditional economic elite. There was no major reorganisation of economic policy making.

In face of the challenge of reconstruction, the BSP fully cooperated by restoring the economy to its pre-war basis using traditional instruments of economic policy. Orthodox principles, such as the stability of the currency, the stability of prices and the balance of the budget remained the yardstick of the Belgian government. The adherence to these objectives clearly indicates that the main preoccupation was to safeguard the position of the traditional sectors of Belgian industry in the international market. For instance, there were hardly any signs of an innovative policy directed to the renewal of economic activity or the use of active demand stimulus. The political chances for large-scale economic change were otherwise small. Up to 1947 an anticlerical coalition of socialists, liberals and communists was in power.[4] Provocative economic proposals could only undermine this cooperation.

The pragmatic reformism of the BSP became clear in practice from the division of political power. The socialists led the economic recovery, but they did not stamp their mark on it: there was a *modus vivendi*. Although they held the Economic Affairs portfolio in 1945 and 1946, the epicentre of policymaking at the Economic Affairs Ministry lay in the hands of J.C. Snoy d'Oppuers, a Catholic and confidant of industry. Before the War, Snoy had held the position of Secretary General of Economic Affairs but was removed from office by the Germans. During World War II, he was closely involved with the economic study groups which, under the auspices of the Galopin Committee, prepared a socio-economic policy that was to be implemented after the conflict. He also led a clandestine group of deposed civil servants from the Economic Affairs Ministry who sought ways of kick-starting the economy after the conclusion of the war (Luyten, 1997: 251-252). The activities of the administration concerning various directives was, for that matter, quite considerable in the late 1940s (Luyten and Hemmerijckx, 2000: 29).

Within Economic Affairs, civil servants recruited from the Catholic University of Louvain held the executive positions. Like Snoy, they

4 Socialists did not want to cause an affront to its liberal coalition partner with the prospect of economic renewal because of the 'Royal question', an important reason for the existence of the first post-war coalition governments of socialists, liberals and communists. In short, the Belgian monarchy had lost most of its prestige by the controversial behaviour of King Leopold III during World War 2. In May 1945, the King went into exile in Switzerland instead of returning to Belgium. This created a political crisis, dividing the population into partisans (Christian democrats) and enemies of the King (socialists, liberals and communists). At the end of the 1940s, the 'Royal question' would move to the forefront of matters.

were committed to the theory of "general dynamic interdependence", developed by the Louvain economist Léon Dupriez. Dupriez was the major proponent in Belgium of the more empirical cross-current business-cycle theory, which had surged by the late 1920s. In theory, his economic analysis did not correspond to economic orthodoxy, as the state was given the opportunity to counter-cyclical management. His work, nevertheless, did not anticipate in any coherent sense Keynesian economic management. According to Dupriez and his disciples, the proposals outlined in the General Theory were best suited to a closed industrial economy. The theory did not seem appropriate to Belgium's small and open economy. Moreover, in line with the Christian Democratic distrust of state interference, they took Keynesianism to be a relatively interventionist doctrine. As a stable and closed structure with an adherence to a particular line of economic policy, Economic Affairs was placed in a hegemonic position from which it could exercise great influence over the post-war economic policy. However, before putting their ideas to work, it was necessary to return to the norm.

In the economic field, traditionalists were clearly in control. Social Affairs, on the other hand, was firmly in the grasp of the socialists. They held the portfolio and controlled the Ministry up until 1949. From this position, they were able to steer the reconstruction in accordance with their own views. Social policy had also been thoroughly prepared during the war years. As the leader of the clandestine BSP, Van Acker was closely involved during the occupation in the blueprinting of the so-called Social Pact. This document, to which a number of prominent representatives of both employers and employees had signed up to in April 1944, foresaw the introduction of mandatory social security and expressed the desirability of creating equal-representation forums for socio-economic consultation at all levels of the economy.[5] This was a two-tier process. Both social security and the joint committees had been legally regulated in 1945. Under trade union pressure, wages would increase, particularly from 1947 onwards. Furthermore, at the national level, the General Joint Council (which was subsequently replaced with a National Labour Council in 1952) and the National Labour Conferences began work almost immediately after the end of the war. In the economic field, however, an entirely different scenario unfolded.

The main raison for the fact that this process proceeded with so much difficulty was the strong emphasis that was put on trade union participation in companies, an ideologically loaded issue. The two main trade unions and the employers' organisations were fundamentally

5 For an analysis of the 'Social Pact' and its significance on the post-war consultative economy, see Luyten and Vanthemsche, 1995 and Pasture, 1993.

divided over the required shape and competency of worker participation on the shop floor. Obviously, the employers were extremely reluctant to grant workers representation within the workplace and held on to their management prerogatives. The socialist union ABVV/FGTB, created out of a merger of the pre-war reformist union with the communist and extreme left "unitary" unions that emerged during the Occupation (Hemmerijckx, 2003), was deeply divided on the subject and emphasised the right of the workers to contest management decisions. The reformist leadership under Paul Finet argued for union representatives within the workplace and works councils (see esp. Hemmerijckx, 1995: 227-245; Luyten, 1995: 130-135; and Peiren, 1995: 247-287). The Christian union, however, strived towards co-determination through bipartite works councils and management boards. Both employers and social Democrats opposed co-determination and in particular the workers' participation in the management board (Keulemans, 1990: 189-223; Luyten, 1996, 123-159; Dambre, 1985 and Devolder, 2004).

Besides the dissension amongst both trade unions and employers' organisations, socialist pragmatism and strategy also had a part in the slow coming about of economic industrial organisation. Socialist ministers were in no hurry to introduce industrial organisation because they did not want to offend their Liberal coalition partner, who was not exactly thrilled by the prospect of works councils and the endorsement of more trade union influence within companies. Moreover, they felt that this would be to the benefit of the radical leftwing and the communist factions of the socialist trade union (Luyten, 2001, 46). These factions had emerged during the war and were calling into question the legitimacy of the pre-war reformist tradition, including the Christian trade union. The radical leftwing was striving for a fundamental reform of capitalist society at the same time as reformist socialists were reconstructing the economy on its pre-war base. Therefore, socialist ministers gave priority to restoring their pre-war power base, i.e. joint committees. It was surely no coincidence that industrial organisation was only regulated by law after the reformist wing within the socialist trade union had gained the upper hand over the radical leftwing and communist factions.

The first post-war coalition governments of socialists, Liberals and communists had always put off making a decision on industrial organisation. In March 1947, however, a coalition of socialists and Christian Democrats came to power. An agreement between the chairman of the Christian trade union and the figurehead of the Catholic employers cleared the way for the Industrial Organisation Law of September 1948, which laid down a pyramidal system with three levels of economic consultation (Dambre, 1985: 75).

As it turned out, industrial organisation as laid down in 1948 was easily acceptable for the capitalist system. As the economic councils were perceived as a tool to maintain the social peace, they contributed to the stabilisation of capitalism. The underlying concept tied in with the Christian ideology on class co-operation and the Christian Democratic distrust of state interference. More radical demands for worker control as well as joint management were curbed towards further integration of the trade unions into the capitalist order.

Belgium's consultative economy noticeably had a twofold structure, whereby the social aspect was detached from the economic perspective. The similarity with policy is striking. Of course, there are several explanations for this twofold structure (Vercauteren and Wijnens, 2004: 238). Nonetheless, the main obstacle to establishing a single structure was the fear, particularly strong in trade union circles, that the "economic" would condition the "social". The plea by Louis Major, figurehead of the reformist wing of the socialist trade union, in favour of a twofold structure is quite illustrative in this respect: "As long as we are not living in a socialist society, it is important that we should have at our disposal special bodies where reasoning is not merely based on figures and production methods, but primarily on the social aspects of the reforms".[6] Economic reality should, in other words, not be allowed to preclude social progress. The long-term implications of the new social system for the Belgian economy had not yet sunk in.

An Inhibiting Lead: Policy, Diagnosis and Recommendation (1948-1954)

By around 1948, the most significant economic issues in the aftermath of World War II had been resolved. The Belgian economy had made a flying start. Thanks to an optimal monetary reform and flourishing international trade, the traditional sectors of industry were thoroughly rejuvenated. Wages and social security could be improved without jeopardising exports. Unemployment was low. The basic outlines of socio-economic consultation had been drawn. The rapid recovery of Belgium was met with general admiration and was termed an "economic miracle" (van der Wee, 1985: 88). However, it was a deceptive phenomenon. By the end of 1948, an international recession took hold which had dire consequences for Belgian exports (Mommen, 1994: 82-86). Likewise, the rapid increase in the price of Belgian products, occasioned by wage growth and social security contributions, was to the detriment of export trade. Thanks to the country's initially favourable

6 AMSAB-Antwerpen, Louis Major Papers, 3, s.d. [1947-1948].

position, higher costs were not a problem at first. However, Belgian industry ran into trouble when the continuing recovery of the European economy gave rise to stiffer international competition: it was simply priced out of the market. In the 1950s, Belgian industrial production stagnated and unemployment began to rise.

The Belgian government responded defensively, preoccupied as it was with other issues. In 1950, the controversy surrounding the King brought the country to the brink of civil war. The mobilisation prompted by King Leopold III's return led to homogeneous Christian Democratic governments. Up until the elections of 1954, the Christian People's Party (Christelijke Volkspartij or CVP) was able to realise its main policy objective, i.e. a generous subsidising of Catholic education without even the need to compromise. A large-scale economic renewal programme was not to be expected from these conservative CVP governments, as was apparent merely from the distribution of portfolios. Jean van Houtte first held the post of Finance Minister but, after a cabinet reshuffle, became Prime Minister. The Catholic banker Albert-Edouard Janssen succeeded him as Finance Minister. Both men adhered to budgetary orthodoxy. Economic Affairs had been in the hands of Duvieusart since 1947, with the exception of a short period in the early 1950s when Albert Coppé held the office. In the economic field, the CVP continued the course that had been outlined since the coalition with the socialists (1947-1949) and the liberals (1949-1950).

Three steering principles were applied: a stable currency, stable prices and a balanced budget (Bismans, 1992: 471-477). These factors were related to the struggle to safeguard the position of Belgian industry in the international market. Towards the end of the 1940s, economic developments led to inflation which the Belgian government, discretely aided by the National Bank of Belgium, tried to contain with a deflationary policy. The National Bank, a strong monetary authority, played a prominent role in economic policy making because it had to watch over the stability of the currency. The Bank's strategic position gave it considerable opportunity to stamp its view on the whole of the government. The Bank was led by the conservative Maurice Frère, a faithful adherent of economic orthodoxy (Bismans, 1992: 458-464). Frère evinced special anxiety about Keynesian deficit spending because it increased the public debt and tended to threaten the value of the currency. He also disparaged the possibilities of the internal market for the sale of Belgian products and aimed exclusively at exports. For that purpose, the prices had be kept as low as possible.

The deflationary policy encompassed stricter controls on the granting of credit by banks. In order to keep exports going, the Belgian government had, until 1950, granted credit on a large scale. At the same time it was determined to balance its own budget. This meant that granting credit was to the detriment of domestic investments and subsidies. As a result of these measures, unemployment rose.[7] The deflationary policy, on the other hand, came in for international criticism. According to the OEEC and the EPU, Belgium was sacrificing its economic expansion in order to attain price stability (Kirschen, 1951: 198). The Belgian government and most Belgian economists rejected this criticism.

The preoccupation of the Belgian government with exports by the traditional sectors was an indication that it did not consider the economic apparatus to be fundamentally obsolete. This is also apparent from the allocation of Marshall Funds. Practically all financial aid was destined for the modernisation and re-equipment of the steel industry and the marginal coalmines (see Kurgan-Van Hentenryk, 1993: 157-172). Some people in government circles were aware of the new industries, but an expansion policy aimed more directly towards investments in the dynamic sectors of durable consumption goods never really materialised. Consequently, while the Netherlands was realising its industrialisation strategies and renewing its infrastructure, Belgium was left with a pre-war production apparatus and infrastructure.

The position of the Belgian government *vis-à-vis* the economy remained largely unchanged in the first half of the 1950s. It concentrated on guaranteeing the best possible external conditions for trade and industry to flourish. However, this situation would gradually change as unemployment increased. The government began to implement a more expansion- and employment-oriented policy, but the "expansion act" of 1953 did not really go beyond that. An active government intervention was not being considered (Morissens, 1964: 5). Illustrative in this respect was the debate on the Keynesian adage of "full employment". A memorandum of the Economic Affairs Ministry called this ideal unattainable in Belgium because it required an active role on the part of government, which in its eyes would go against Belgian mentality: "Le Belge manifeste un attachement profond à la liberté, attachement qui n'a d'égal que sa méfiance à l'égard des interventions étatiques".[8] This memo, for that matter, was not intended as a ministerial "*bêtisier*". Former Prime Minister Gaston Eyskens of the CVP was probably closer

[7] The supremacy of price stability was marked in the trade cycle policy by the significant fact that struggles against inflation, initiated during periods of boom, went on long after the downturn had started and coincided with measures taken in order to promote employment.

[8] KADOC. Fonds Dries Dequae. Note pour le Comité Ministeriel de Coordination Economique. Plein emploi et stabilité financière, s.d. (1953).

to the truth when he stated that, given the political situation in Belgium, a full-employment policy was unattainable.[9]

The absence of a general economic policy was also apparent from the co-ordination of the government apparatus. The different administrations with economic competence were hardly integrated, and co-ordination was achieved only in isolated decisions, without any programmatic link. Little progress had been made in this respect since the end of the 1930s. A Ministerial Committee for Economic Co-ordination (MCEC), which was chaired by the Prime Minister, saw to the objective of economic co-ordination (van Orshoven, 1972: 591-623). An Interministerial Economic Commission in which high-ranking civil servants from various departments were represented prepared the activities of this Committee. In the 1950s, the epicentre of economic decision-making was with this departmental commission,[10] chaired by Snoy d'Oppuers. The influence of the administration, with its traditionalist economic views, thus remained quite considerable. The Commission's attention focused almost exclusively on the general issue of import and export trade. There was hardly any co-ordination with Social Affairs. It was not until the early 1950s, when it emerged that certain regions were affected by chronic unemployment, that the MCEC took measures. In 1952, a Department of Planning and Economic Expansion was established within the Ministry of Economic Affairs. However, this body achieved very few concrete results, as a "plan" was clearly lacking.[11]

Meanwhile, in terms of the perception and diagnosis of the economic state of affairs, Belgium had lost considerable ground. The construction of the national accounts is illustrative in this respect. In comparison to the Netherlands where, in the early 1950s, the national accounts were successfully applied in a programmed manner, a great deal of work remained to be done in Belgium. However, responding to the large-scale campaign that the OEEC had conducted to this end, the Belgian government had become convinced of the need for national accounts. In 1949, the Minister of Economic Affairs Duvieusart installed a so-called National Income Commission. Its task, however, proved more complex than had been anticipated. This was largely due to the shortcomings of the statistical apparatus. The relevant statistics for different economic variables were simply lacking. Furthermore, the National Institute of Statistics was seriously understaffed. The political will to provide

---

9 KADOC. Fonds August Cool. Beperkte commissie van het economische programma, 3.11.1953.

10 Rijksarchief Brugge, Fonds Achiel Van Acker, Nr. 1627, Note concernant quelques aspects de l'Activité du ministère des Affaires économiques, s.d.

11 *Idem*.

material support was simply not there. The question therefore arises whether the Belgian government was genuinely convinced of the purpose of national accounts. To an extent, national accounting implied a new way of conducting economic politics. It required policymakers who were willing to apply the results obtained when outlining policy measures. The first accounts were not published until 1953 by the private *Groupe d'études de la comptabilité nationale* of the Solvay Institute. In the official commission, progress was very slow, so that by the end of the decade there were still no official accounting data available (see Van der Wee and Dancet, 1986, 150-155).

There was also a close interaction between the traditional economic policy pursued by the government and the process of social and economic consultation. On the one hand the consultative function, which was intended to assist government and parliament in developing economic policy, was clearly on the defensive in the 1950s (Vercauteren and Wijnens, 2002). The Central Economic Council was not involved systematically in economic policymaking. Which topics were submitted to the Council by the government was determined largely by current events and, for the time being, a systematic confrontation on the essence of the economic development factors between the government and the professional organisations failed to materialise. The reason lay in the fact that the objectives of the Law of 1948 presupposed the existence of a truly co-ordinated economic policy. The objectives that had been formulated were, in other words, too ambitious. On the other hand, being in the state that it was, the Belgian economy was hardly able to support a consultative system that ensured a regular increase in real wages. Thus, "social" and "economic" policy were increasingly at odds.

Contradiction and Controversy over Policy

The increase in purchasing power that workers had obtained after World War II was more or less seen as an irreversible accomplishment in the early 1950s. This was largely a result of a change of course on the part of Belgian employers, among whom the modernist faction had gained the upper hand over the more conservative wing (Luyten, 1996: 170-171). However, the implementation of the principle was far from co-ordinated. After 1948, a transitional year marked by the introduction of the automatic linking of wages to the consumer price index, free wage formation resumed. In the early 1950s, these negotiations were conducted mainly at company level, which led to widely diverging wages and sometimes resulted in strikes (Vercauteren, 2007: 191-202). Wage increases came on top of the expansion of social security, as contributions – particularly from employers – steadily rose. Moreover, the government enhanced the position of the trade unions by granting social perks. This policy of "abundance" had economic implications. The Belgian economy, which continued to rely on exports of semi-finished products, was priced out of the markets. In order to safeguard the competitive position of the country, its economic structure needed to be adapted and modernised. Trade unions as well as employers' organisations grew increasingly aware of this vulnerable economic situation, which eventually led to the Joint Declaration on Productivity in 1954 (Vercauteren, 2007: 161-168; Devolder, 2005. See also Bertrams, 2001: 191-235). In this protocol, employers and employees pledged to work together to improve industrial output. Increased productivity was seen as a means of financing the creation of more jobs, higher wages and better social conditions. This was, in a nutshell, the philosophy of a Keynesian policy based on economic growth, sustained effective demand and income redistribution. However, this declaration was hardly more than an intention. There was no sign yet in the 1950s of the Fordist wage relations whereby social benefits are connected with productivity.

From the mid-1950s, the empirical validity of government policy would be challenged on numerous occasions. The central idea was a plea for an active expansion and employment policy. The focus was very much on the new industries, productivity increase and full employment. However, opinions were quite divided on what were the appropriate means to achieve these goals. The left wing of the socialist union resurrected De Man's concept of planning (Meynen, 1997: 287-294). In 1954, a report presented by André Renard, the leader of the leftist metalworkers' union, contained a comprehensive analysis of the problems the Belgian economy was facing at the time. The report called for structural reforms, with the introduction of a kind of "flexible" planning by the State and the nationalisation of basic industries. In a second report, published in 1956, sharp criticism was formulated of Belgium's holding capital, which continued to invest in traditional sectors and was held to account for the fact that the Belgian economy was lagging behind (on Renard's influence see Francq, 1990; Devolder, 2006: 281-286; ABVV/ FGTB congress reports). The same evolution was unfolding in Christian workers' circles, albeit that here the holdings were held largely responsible for Flanders' under-industrialisation. Gradually, the Christian trade union had put aside its mistrust of state interference (Pasture, 1992: 279-280). It was felt that, with the aid of the government and an injection of foreign capital, full employment could be achieved in Flanders. In this context, the Christian trade union argued that economically oriented planning was required. Within the CVP, a Keynesian perspective grew around the progressive *La Relève* group. Meanwhile, the study department of the party was working on proposals aimed at improving the functioning of the advisory bodies. Among other things, the merger between the Central Economic Council (the "economic" aspect) and the National Labour Council (the "social" aspect) was now put on the agenda (Vercauteren and Wijnens, 2004: 243). Even the Federation of Belgian Industries came up with a "pour une Politique d'Expansion". More moderate in its judgement than the two trade unions, the employers' organisation did not hide its interest in the Keynesian ingredients either. Although the cry for an active expansion policy was resounding ever louder, the government nevertheless took little concrete action. However, the political power balance made it impossible to carry through far-reaching policy reforms. In the second half of the 1950s, the ideological divide stifled any economic renewal.

Ideology Paralyses and Divides (1954-1958)

The education policy pursued by the Christian Democrats in the first half of the 1950s was perceived by the socialists and liberals as a veritable declaration of war. When, in 1954, the Christian Democrats lost their majority, a coalition government of socialists and liberals was formed under the leadership of Van Acker. This marked the start of the so-called "school war" (*Schoolstrijd/ guerre scolaire*) (Tyssens, 1997: 41-110). The programme of the new government was aimed at modernising the educational system by breaking the monopoly of Flanders' Catholic schools. In a sense, this anticlerical stance cut off the socialists from economic policymaking. The socialists acquired the Social Affairs portfolio, whereby they tried – unsuccessfully for that matter – to gain control of the social security system with assistance from the right wing of the socialist trade union (Pasture, 1992: 126-135). The liberals, for their part, obtained all economic and financial portfolios. Both the Minister of Economic Affairs and the Finance Minister were allied to the country's holding capital, so that the liberal economic principles were safeguarded (Ricquier, 1983: 38; also Witte, 2000: 54). Nevertheless, a few Keynesian-inspired viewpoints were introduced into economic policy, albeit in a watered-down version. For example, infrastructure development was stimulated through public investment and new expansion laws were proclaimed in 1955 and 1957. However, there was no question of the government pursuing a dynamic growth policy (Bismans, 1992: 500). And yet the Belgian economy was growing relatively slowly, despite the favourable international economic situation.[12] The traditionalism of the economic groups that dominated large

[12] To explain the anatomy of the decline of Belgian industry, economists pointed at factors such as defensive investment, insufficient home demand, cost-push inflation,

industry remained the government's yardstick. Industrial change was however "an evil" that could be postponed but not avoided.

By the end of 1957, after two years of growth, the Belgian economy had moved into serious recession caused by falling exports and a general slowdown in the steel and coal industry (Mommen, 1994: 99-111). The coal crisis and the ensuing closure of pits had made painfully clear how investments had been ill directed. Moreover, the integration of Belgium into the EEC required an accelerated modernisation of infrastructure and the production apparatus. The renewal of its economy had proven insufficient. Unemployment was rising sharply. The unemployment rate increased from 116.810 in 1957 to 199.209 in 1959 (Pasture, 1992: 285). Early in 1959, the planned closure of many mines in Wallonia provoked a social upheaval. The "performance crisis", which had been largely occasioned by an accumulation of policy failings, heralded a new phase in Belgian socio-economic policy. The early 1960s would see a real breakthrough of Keynesianism.

The Struggle for Hegemony

After the elections of June 1958, the CVP, led by Gaston Eyskens, established a minority government which would succeed in concluding the so-called School Pact. As a result, the major ideological differences had been resolved allowing the government to concentrate on an economic modernisation drive. From 1958, pleas were heard from Christian Democrat and socialist circles for a planned and regionally differentiated economic policy. In December 1959, the BSP, under pressure from its left wing, adopted Renard's programme for structural reform (Meynen, 1984: 32-39). However, the ball was now in the court of the CVP. In the election campaign of 1958, Christian Democratic reformers had argued for a Keynesian "Keynote Plan" (*Sleutelplan*). This programme had been prepared by the party's left wing (Tindemans, 2002: 47). Eyskens, a professor of economics at the University of Louvain, who had been arguing for a programmed approach to economic policy since the early 1950s, now saw an opportunity to realise his plans. It was evident that the time for change had come from the shift in power that occurred from the administration to the ministerial cabinets (Bismans, 1992: 521). Several cabinet members were associated with the progressive Christian Democrat journal and think tank *La Relève*, including the Minister of Economic Affairs, before the liberals joined the government towards the end of 1958.

---

and an unfavourable pattern of exports. For instance Lamfalussy, 1961; Kindleberger, 1967: 74-76.

Notwithstanding the presence of the liberals, the government launched important reforms. In July 1959, several national and regional expansion acts were passed. This legislation was a great deal more consequential than the previous expansion laws of 1953, 1955 and 1957. For the laws of 1959 had in common that they provided for direct state intervention in the financing of investments through interest subsidies and reductions in the burden of taxation. New politics required a fresh set of policy tools. In October 1959, the government founded a Bureau for Economic Programming (BEP). At the same time, a number of changes occurred that marked a new phase in socio-economic relations (Vercauteren and Wijnens, 2002). This turnaround was realised through an accelerated institutionalisation of tripartite deliberation. The fact that the government was now intervening directly in the economy gave rise to the political necessity of deliberation between the government, the trade unions, and the employers' organisations. A National Committee for Economic Expansion (NCEE), established in November 1960, was charged with the tasks of regularising and accelerating economic expansion, creating additional employment and increasing the standard of living. In other words, unlike the consultative councils, the new body was about consultation that was at the same time negotiation and which was supposed to result in draft agreements to be approved by government and the professional associations. In this manner, the consultative function was supplemented from 1960 with deliberation. Moreover, in May 1960, leading entrepreneurs and trade union leaders signed up to a first long-term "social programming accord" (*sociaal programmatie-akkoord*), which cleared the way for more co-ordinated collective bargaining based on mutual trust and productivity gains (Luyten, 1996: 174-179). From an institutional perspective, the changes were quite impressive. However, their implementation would prove a different matter.

The change of policy met with quite a lot of resistance, so that there remained a wide gulf between theory and practice. The right wing of the CVP could not reconcile itself with the reform and the coalition with the liberals also put the brakes on the renewal. The Economic Affairs portfolio was, after all, managed by the industrialist Jacques Vanderschueren. The BEP only came into being after serious social unrest in 1959. For psychological reasons, the government chose to speak of programming rather than planning, as the latter term was felt to evoke an image of far-reaching state intervention (van Meerhaeghe, 1962: 41). Moreover, in the course of 1960 the government was weakened by two significant problems. First, there was the aftermath of the decolonisation of The Congo. Second, due to the economic crisis, the government was facing serious financial problems. In order to decrease the deficit on its current budget, Eyskens incorporated several fiscal, administrative and social reforms into the so-called *Eenheidswet* (Unity Law). This measure demonstrated that the methods of traditional economic policy continued to have an appeal (Bismans, 1992: 536). After all, they had a deflationary impact. At the same time, it was obvious that these policy options were barely tenable. A broad social basis was lacking, especially in Wallonia which had been hit hardest by the recession. A general strike, dubbed the "Strike of the Century", ensued (Meynen, 1978: 481-513). It lasted for over five weeks, throughout the winter of 1960, with Renard playing a prominent role. While this strike would not prevent the introduction of the law, it did result in the fall of the government and would prove to be a catalyst for the transition to Keynesianism.

The Keynesian Era: A New Dawn for Planning in Belgium?

Ideas did not suffice for a change in policymaking. The switch to Keynesianism could only succeed with support from a sufficiently strong coalition. The fall of the Eyskens-government created the right environment for the left wing of the Christian Democrat party to make overtures to the socialists. A "travaillist" Centre-Left government came to power, which could count on the backing of the two large trade unions (Hoflack, 1989: 66-89). The fact that the socialist Antoon Spinoy was appointed as Economic Affairs Minister provided an important impulse for the economic renewal (Gaus, 1989: 1018-1020). Socialist technocrats who had been closely involved in the ABVV programme for structural reforms played an important part in the conceptualisation of policy.[13] Under the new team, the institutional framework for an active government policy was further developed. A case in point was the establishment in 1962 of a National Investment Company, which until then had not been possible because of the opposition of the leading financial circles. For the first time in Belgian history a full-scale programme of neo-capitalist planning was put into practice. At the same time, the method of "economic budgets", which entailed an annual adaptation of the plan to the state of the economy, was introduced. Furthermore, the government intended to link its economic programme with an income policy. The latter implied that all social benefits were generalised, taking into account the plan, which encompassed a prior calculation of new social benefits for the various income categories. In other words, the economic and the social aspects had to be coupled. To this end, the government tabled a draft law for the establishment of a

[13] The majority of these technocrats, however, were won over by neo-capitalist reforms.

Socio-economic Council (SEC). However, both the income policy and the establishment of the SEC were never realised, primarily because the ABVV was not prepared to make trade union activism subordinate to economic criteria (Vercauteren and Wijnens, 2004: 257).[14]

The question arises how planning was conceptualised in Belgium. As in most other western countries, the concept of planning in Belgium was indicative. The main purpose of the BEP was to develop medium-term economic policy plans, as indicator for the general direction of Belgium's economic policy. The first plan (1962-1965) aimed at a global growth rate of 4 per cent, by improving production and export structure. Following the example of the Netherlands, a macro-economic model was constructed (Paelinck and Waelbroeck, 1963). Nonetheless, the model was more preoccupied with input-output tables than with full-scale econometric modelling. In many respects the Belgian planning package bore close resemblance to the French concept of consultational planning. What the plans were concerned with were the actions of the public authorities in their relationship with the private sector. The plans were formulated after an extensive process of tripartite and bipartite institutional consultation. The idea was that the dialogue created an atmosphere of co-operation in the execution of the plan, so the persuasion to execute what was in the plan was mainly located in the psychology of the parties.

The picture that arises from the Belgian planning experience of the 1960s is not clear-cut, because planning has, as yet, hardly been studied at all by historians. As it was, planning had to cope with several difficulties.[15] The BEP was given neither the means nor the manoeuvring space that it required to fulfil its assignment. Staffing was inadequate and, moreover, politicised. The government had preferred to set up the BEP within the administration, as part of the executive power. The majority of staff also held a position with a cabinet, which was already an indication that the government did not consider the BEP as such to be particularly important. Moreover, under the centre-left coalition that came to power in 1966, the preference for planning would wane. Furthermore, the planners had too little accurate statistical data at their disposal, despite a significant improvement since the 1950s. To make matters worse, the consultative procedure was quite laborious.

All these factors influenced the planning negatively. The facts were undisputable. For example, the second plan (1966-1970) was submitted to parliament with two years delay. Both the first and the second plan

---

14 On the initiatives to establish and income policy, see: CRISP, 1964 and 1968.

15 For an overview, see among others: CRISP, 1962, No. 153 (I); 1963, No. 211 (III) and 1971, No. 520-521: 2-5; Van Waterschoot, 1965; Van Bocxlaer, 1972: 370-371.

were insufficiently operational. They were made up largely of a series of general economic considerations. Sectoral and, more importantly, regional planning were largely lacking. This was not surprising as the traditional sectors, mainly located in Wallonia, were experiencing tough times. The economy of Flanders, on the other hand, was renewed. However, nobody dared to express this issue in figures. The necessary regional approach to Belgium's economy was thus inappropriately complicated by inter-community differences. Indeed, the latter proved a real obstacle. Moreover, besides "economic" programming, there was also the aspect of "social" programming. These two different aspects were not properly geared to one another, so that the two-tier approach remained intact, despite a switch in economic policymaking.

The Keynesian turnaround did not herald a new dawn for economic planning or programming in Belgium. That is not to say that it was insignificant. Besides the informative and co-ordinating influence on the government and on the social partners, the holistic perspective on the economy was gaining in popularity in leading circles. Planning in Belgium therefore can be viewed as an exercise in macro-economic education for politicians and civil servants alike. As a theoretical concept, it tied in with the broader picture of professionalisation and technocratisation. Nonetheless, planning was not a key concept in Belgian economic policies. In Belgium and elsewhere, the 1960s were marked by rapid economic growth and increased mass consumption. Consensual social programming smoothed this transformation. The generous Keynesian support policy, which attracted foreign multinational investment through subsidies and tax incentives, was the real catalyst for Belgium's rapid recovery. As R. L. Hoggs puts it: "This was the easiest way out for Belgium. Foreign investors and companies, new to Belgium, were uncluttered by its historical experience and were ready to invest in new things" (Hogg, 1986: 185). Industrial decline in Wallonia however was not reversed, because the multinational companies preferred to invest in Flanders. In an effort to retain a regional balance, the Belgian government subsequently implemented its support measures with too great a conviction. In the longer term, the language rift would stand in the way of any significant economic renewal.

Concluding Remarks

Which elements were working against the process of institutional change in Belgium? Perhaps the most important point to be advanced is that the historical matrix of Belgium weighed down institutional change. The message that "history matters" indeed provides for a compelling understanding of policy continuity in Belgium. Firstly, Belgium was an old industrial country. The economic structure was based on traditional sectors (coal mines, steel, textile), dominated by powerful holding companies, producing semi-finished, industrial products with a low degree of added value which were largely exported. From the onset of World War II, the Belgian economy was still largely determined by its 19th century origins. The likelihood of defensive investment was greater in Belgium than in younger industrial economies, for there was a wider scope for improving what already existed. This was more so as Belgian industry suffered less war damage than its neighbouring countries. A quick recovery favouring the traditional sectors hid a fundamental weakness, which would only become apparent in the course of the 1950s. In Belgium's case, the need for a new long-term economic strategy was greater and therefore its absence more serious than for most other countries. Government policy was however intimately connected with the nature of Belgian capitalism. Governments and captains of industry held an identical view of the management of the economy. Therefore, deeply entrenched economic liberalism made it difficult to contemplate Keynesian economic intervention as a permanent phenomenon in Belgium. As long as Belgian capitalism was able to withstand foreign competition, the government could lean on the existing policy instruments and favour investments in traditional sectors. In the 1950s, liberal economic policy proved to be insufficient as the structural rigidity of the Belgian industry became obvious.

Secondly, from the end of the 19th century, Belgian society was strongly pillarised. On the level of politics, pillarisation mainly revealed itself in a Christen Democratic Party, a Socialist Party and a Liberal Party. Due to the pillarised culture there was a strong tendency towards consensus politics in Belgium. Particularly after World War I, the formation of any single-party government had become virtually impossible. Because coalition governments were governments of compromise, policies implemented were slower and less visible. Moreover, after World War II, rifts in Belgian society would make policymaking a highly charged affair. As a result of the "Royal question" and the second "school struggle", the main concerns of the governments up until 1958, no important changes in economic policy occurred during their tenure of office. Also, due to ideological differences, overtures between the progressive wings of Christian Democrats and socialists also failed to succeed. Instead, in the socialist-liberal coalition governments, economic policy was of a liberal character. This was intertwined with another historical reality.

Thirdly, the reformist tradition of Belgian socialism has also to be taken into account. As the increase in social benefits was their trademark, reformist socialists were less concerned with an economic doctrine and long-range program. Hendrik De Man and André Renard, both claiming to spearhead new economic policies, were more or less categorised as "heretics". The pragmatic socialist leaders, who gained the upper hand after Word War 2, were faithful to traditional economic policy. Certainly, the mainstream of the Christian Democrats also adhered to traditional economic doctrines. Nonetheless, socialists spearheaded economic reconstruction and their success in managing the post-war period made a return to economic liberalism possible. The pragmatic approach to reconstruction gave birth to a two-tier policy which was quite evident from the division of political power and from the twofold structure of Belgium's consultative economy. Subsequently, attempts to establish a socio-economic council in Belgium failed to succeed. The socialist trade union wanted social policy decisions and social bargaining to be dependent on the union's position of power, rather than on economic parameters.

In sum, the interplay of the above mentioned factors ultimately determined the likelihood of path-breaking reform in Belgium. The picture that arises from the process of institutional change can be circumscribed as "muddling through". Up until the late 1950s, there were hardly any over-riding medium or long-term economic objectives. The governments were preoccupied with tactical, short-term improvisation. Gradually they designed a more active expansion policy, but in absolute terms, this policy was still meagre. The inadequacy of economic consultation and Belgium's lagging in the development of the perception and diagnosis of the economic state of affairs were clearly intertwined with the traditional economic policy. The humdrum type of decision-making also characterised social policy and social consultation. Moreover, social and economic policy proved to be contradictory. From the mid 1950s onwards, leftwing political trade union and, to a lesser extent, employers' circles embraced Keynesian economic management. Economic planning was rediscovered. Yet alternative ideas were not suffice in affecting a change in policymaking. The agent of change capable of bringing about the transition to triggering a Keynesian policy was a sufficiently strong Centre-Left coalition. In the early 1960s, institutional change in Belgium was quite impressive. Belgium became a consultative economy in the true sense of the word, with a Fordist system of labour relations and a government committed to a Keynesian policy. The introduction of economic planning as a policy tool was closely related to the desire to give rapid economic growth a higher priority than it had been previously enjoyed. Nevertheless, planning did not unlock the door to sustained economic growth.

References

Bertrams, K. (2001), "Productivité économique et paix sociale au sein du Plan Marshall. Les limites de l'influence américaine auprès des industriels et syndicats belges, 1948-1960", *Bijdragen tot de Eigentijdse Geschiedenis*, Vol. 5, 9, p. 191-235.

Bismans, F. (1992), *Croissance et régulation. La Belgique 1944-1974*, Brussels: Palace of Academies.

Bocxlaer, F. van (1972), "De evolutie van de economische planning in België", *Economie*, Vol. 36, 7-8.

Claeys-Van Haegendoren, M. (1972), *Hendrik De Man. Een biografie*, Antwerp-Utrecht: De Nederlandsche boekhandel, p. 188-193.

CRISP (1962), "La programmation économique (I)", *Courrier hebdomadaire du CRISP*, Vol.153.

CRISP (1963), "La programmation économique (II)", *Courrier hebdomadaire du CRISP*, Vol. 211.

CRISP (1964), "Les tentatives d'élaboration d'une politique des revenus en Belgique (I)", *Courrier hebdomadaire du CRISP*, Vol. 259, 389.

CRISP (1968), "Les tentatives d'élaboration d'une politique des revenus en Belgique (II)", *Courrier hebdomadaire du CRISP*, Vol. 260, 390.

CRISP (1971), "La programmation économique (III)", *Courrier hebdomadaire du CRISP*, Vol. 520-521.

Dambre, W. (1985), *Geschiedenis van de ondernemingsraden in België*, Antwerp: Kluwer.

Devolder, C. (2005), "To innovate or not to innovate. De bedrijfswereld en de productiviteitsopvoering, een opportuniteit voor het ondernemingssyndicalisme? (1944-1980)", Unpublished PhD in History, University of Ghent.

Gaus, H. (1989), "Antoon Spinoy", in: H. Gaus (ed.), *Politiek biografisch lexicon: Belgische ministers en staatssecretarissen, 1960-1980*, Antwerp: Standaard Uitgeverij, p. 1018-1020.

Hansen, E. (1978), "Hendrik de Man and the Theoretical Foundations of Economic Planning: The Belgian Experience 1935-1940", *European Studies Review*, Vol. 8, 2, p. 235-257.

Hemmerijckx, R. (1995), "De socialistische vakbeweging en het Sociaal Pact", in: D. Luyten and G. Vanthemsche (eds.), *Het Sociaal Pact van 1944. Oorsprong, betekenis en gevolgen*, Bruxelles: VUB Press, 1995, p. 227-245.

Hemmerijckx, R. (2003), *Van Verzet tot Koude Oorlog, 1940-1949, machtsstrijd om het ABVV*, Brussels: VUB Press.

Hoflack, K. (1989), *Theo Lefèvre, staatsman*, Antwerp-Baarn: Hadewijch.

Hogg, R.L. (1986), *Structural Rigidities and Policy Inertia in interwar Belgium*, Brussels: Palace of Academies.

Keulemans, D. (1990), "De institutionalisering van het sociaal-economisch overleg. De wet van 20 september 1948 houdende organisatie van het bedrijfsleven", in: E. Witte, J.C. Burgelmann en P. Stouthuysen (eds.), *Tussen restauratie en vernieuwing*, Brussels: VUB Press, p. 189-223.

Kindleberger, C.P. (1967), *Europe's Post-war Growth: the Role of Labour Supply*, Cambridge: Harvard University Press.

Kirschen, E.S. (1951), "La déflation belge de 1948 à 1950", *Industrie*, Vol. 5, 4.

Kramer, S. (1978), "Belgian Socialism at the Liberation: 1944-1950", *Res Publica*, Vol. 20, 1, p. 116-124.

Kurgan-Van Hentenryk, G. (1993), "Le plan Marshall et le développement économique de la Belgique", in: E. Aerts, B. Henau and P. Janssens (eds.), *Studia historica Oeconomica: liber alumnorum Herman van der Wee*, Louvain: University Press Louvain, p. 157-172.

Lamfalussy, A. (1961), *Investment and Growth in mature Economics. The Case of Belgium*, New York: St. Martin's Press.

Luyten, D. (1988), "Wetgevende initiatieven met betrekking tot bedrijfsorganisatie in de dertiger jaren in België", *Belgisch Tijdschrift voor Nieuwste Geschiedenis*, Vol. 19, 3-4, p. 587-654.

Luyten, D. (1995), *Sociaal-economisch overleg in België.sedert 1918*, Brussels: VUB Press.

Luyten, D. (1997), *Ideologie en praktijk van het corporatisme tijdens de Tweede Wereldoorlog in België*, Brussels: VUB Press.

Luyten, D. (2001), "De bedrijfsorganisatiewet: werknemersparticipatie of instrument van de syndicale economische democratie?", in: M. Stroobant (ed.), *De bedrijfsorganisatie aan de vooravond van de 21ste eeuw*, Brussels: Intersentia Rechtswetenschappen, p. 27-47.

Luyten, D. and G. Vanthemsche (eds.) (1995), *Het sociaal pact van 1944: oorsprong, betekenis en gevolgen*, Brussels: VUB Press.

Luyten, D. and R. Hemmerijckx (2000), "Achiel Van Acker, architect van de Belgische welvaartstaat?", in: M. Galle and S. Loccufier (eds.), *Facetten van 100 jaar politieke, economische en sociale geschiedenis: herdenking geboorte Achiel van Acker, 1898-1998*, Brussels: Van Acker stichting/VUB Press, p. 19-46.

Meerhaeghe, M. van (1962), "La planification indicative", in: *Les problèmes de la planification*, Brussels: VUB Press.

Meynen, A. (1978), "De grote winterstaking 1960-1961", *Belgisch Tijdschrift voor Nieuwste Geschiedenis*, Vol. 9, 3-4, p. 481-513.

Meynen, A. (1984), "Structuurhervormingen en algemene staking, 1958-1961", in: *Vooruitlopen op het Vlaamse socialisme. Vijfentwintig jaar Links*, Louvain: Kritak, p. 32-39.

Meynen, A. (1997), "De economische en sociale politiek sinds de jaren 1950", in: E. Witte (ed.), *Politieke geschiedenis van België van 1830 tot heden*, Brussels: VUB Press, p. 287-294.

Mommen, A. (1994), *The Belgian Economy in the 20th Century*, London: Routledge.

Morissens, L. (1964), "Economic policy in Belgium", in: E.S. Kirschen (ed.), *Economic Policy in our Time. III. Country Studies*, Amsterdam: North Holland Pub.Co.

Orshoven, J. van (1972), "Het ministerieel comité voor economische coördinatie", *Res Publica*, Vol. 14, 3.

Paelinck, J.H.P. and Waelbroeck, J. (1963), *Programmation économique et modèles économétriques de croissance: analyse des relations sous-jacentes au premier programme d'expansion 1962-1965 du Bureau de Programmation Economique*, Liège, Bibliothèque de l'Institut de Science Économique de l'Université, No. 3.

Pasture, P. (1992), *Kerk, Politiek en Sociale Actie. De unieke positie van de christelijke arbeidersbeweging in België, 1944-1973*, Louvain-Apeldoorn: Garant.

Pasture, P. T. (1993), "The April 1944 'social pact' in Belgium and its significance for the post-war welfare state", *Journal of Contemporary History*, Vol. 28, 3, p. 695-714.

Peiren, L. (1995), "De houding van de socialistische beweging tegenover de realisatie van het Sociaal Pact tussen 1944 en 1948", in: D. Luyten and G. Vanthemsche (eds.), *Het Sociaal Pact van 1944. Oorsprong, betekenis en gevolgen*, Brussels: VUB Press, 1995, p. 247-287.

Ricquier, J.C. (1983), "Jean Rey: Portrait et Souvenirs", *Revue Générale*, 38.

Tindemans, L. (2002), *De memoires: gedreven door een overtuiging*, Tielt: Lannoo.

Tyssens, J. (1997), *De schoolkwestie in de jaren vijftig. Van conflict naar pacificatie*, Brussels: VUB Press.

Vanthemsche, Guy (1982), "De mislukking van een vernieuwde economische politiek in België voor de Tweede Wereldoorlog: De OREC (Office de Redressement Économique) van 1935 tot 1938", *Belgisch Tijdschrift voor Nieuwste Geschiedenis*, Vol. 13, 2-3, p. 339-387.

Vanthemsche, Guy (1998), "Les mots et les actes. 100 ans de pratique réformiste en Belgique", in: H. Le Paige and P. Delwit (eds.), *Les socialistes et le pouvoir. Gouverner pour réformer?*, Brussels: Labor, p. 57-102.

Vercauteren, G. (2007), *In naam van de sociale vooruitgang. De rol van de overheid in het sociaal overleg in België*, Leuven: Acco.

Vercauteren, G. and I. Wijnens (2002), "A Consultative Economy in Different Guises. National Socioeconomic Consultative Institutions in Belgium: Theory and Practice (1948-1968)", paper presented at the 'Fourth European Social Sciences History Conference', The Hague, 28 February 2002.

Vercauteren, G. and I. Wijnens (2004), "Een twee-eiige tweeling? De institutionele scheiding tussen het federale 'sociale' en het 'economische' overleg (1944-1983)", *Belgisch Tijdschrift voor Nieuwste Geschiedenis*, Vol. 34, p. 231-287.

Waterschoot, J. van (1965), *Fünf Jahre Wirtschaftsprogrammierung in Belgien*, Kiel.

Wee, H. van der (1985), "De Belgische economie in de maalstroom van een halve eeuw, 1972-1975", in: L. Tindemans *e.a.* (eds.), *Gaston Esykens 80*, Tielt: Lannoo, p. 59-118.

Wee, H. van der and G. Dancet (1986), "De Belgische nationale boekhouding, 1920-1985: geschiedenis van haar berekenings- en reconstructiemethodologie", in: V. Van Rompuy (ed.), *Actuele economische problemen: theorie en politiek*, Louvain: University Press Louvain, p. 145-168.

Witte, E. (2000), "Achiel Van Acker: premier van 'paarse' regeringen (1945-1946; 1954-1958)", in: M. Galle and S. Loccufier, *Facetten van 100 jaar politieke, economische en sociale geschiedenis*, Brussels: VUB Press.

Witte, E., J.C. Burgelman and P. Stouthuysen (eds.) (1990), *Tussen restauratie en vernieuwing. Aspecten van de naoorlogse Belgische politiek*, Brussels: VUB Press.

Notes on Contributors

Doreen Arnoldus has been Assistant Professor in Economic and Social History at the University of Leiden and conducted a post-doctoral research project at the Vrije Universiteit Amsterdam on the Dutch consultation economy in the second half of the 20th century, which will lead to the publication of a book in 2007. She is the author of *Family, Family Firm, and Strategy. Six Dutch Family Firms in the Food Industry* (Aksant, 2002) and also published on consultants at Dutch banks.

Peter Berger is Associate Professor at the Vienna University of Economics and Business Administration (Wirtschaftsuniversität Wien). Previously he taught Economic and Social History at Leiden University and the University of New Orleans. Berger published extensively on the League of Nations' financial reconstruction work in Austria during the 1930s. In 2007, his concise history of Austria in the 20th century (*Kurze Geschichte Österreichs im 20. Jahrhundert*) was published by the WUV Universitätsverlag Wien.

Karel Davids holds the Chair of Economic and Social History in the Faculty of Arts and the Faculty of Economics of the Vrije Universiteit, Amsterdam. Previously he has been Assistant Professor in Social and Political History at the Erasmusuniversiteit Rotterdam and Research Fellow of the Royal Netherlands Academy of Arts and Science at the University of Leiden. His publications in English include a book co-edited with Jan Lucassen, *A Miracle Mirrored. The Dutch Republic in European Perspective* (Cambridge UP, 1995) and several articles on the history of technology, industrial districts and consultation arrangements in the Netherlands.

Greta Devos is Professor of Economic History at the University of Antwerp, where she is Director of the Center on Business History. She has published extensively on business history, studying in particular businessmen, employers and employers' associations, as well as the history of ports and the shipbuilding industry.

Claude Didry, sociologist, is Research Director at the French CNRS. He is co-director of the UMR (Mixed Research United) IDHE "Institutions and Historical Dynamics of Economics" in Paris and director of the IDHE of Cachan. His specialisation is the development of industrial relations and labour law in France and Europe since the 19th century. His publications include *Naissance de la convention collective. Débats* *juridiques et luttes sociales en France au début du 20e siècle* (Éditions de l'EHESS, 2002) and the edited volumes, with A. Mias (eds.), *Le Moment Delors. Les syndicats au coeur de l'Europe sociale* (P.I.E.-Peter Lang, 2005) and, with Bénédicte Zimmermann and Peter Wagner (eds.), *Arbeit und Nationalstaat. Frankreich und Deutschland in europäischer Perspektive* (Campus, 2000).

Anton Hemerijck is Director of the Netherlands Council for Government Policy (WRR) and Professor in Comparative European Social Policy, Department of Public Administration at the Erasmusuniversiteit Rotterdam. He studied economics at Tilburg University and received his doctorate from Oxford University in 1993. He was a Senior Researcher at the Max-Planck-Institute for the Study of Society. He has published widely on issues of comparative social and economic policy between 1997 and 2000, including *A Dutch Miracle* with Jelle Visser (Amsterdam University Press, 1997) and *Why we need a New Welfare State* with Gøsta Esping-Andersen, Duncan Gallie and John Myles (OUP, 2002). Forthcoming is *The Future of Welfare in European Welfare States* (OUP, 2007) with Maurizio Ferrara and Martin Rhodes.

Patrick Pasture is Associate Professor of History at the University of Leuven, where he co-ordinates the RU Modernity and Society 1800-2000 (MoSa) and Visiting Professor in the European Program of Drew University (Brussels). He has been Visiting Scholar at the IISG in Amsterdam, the CHS (Paris I) and the University of Pennsylvania. He mainly studied European labour history. His latest books include the edited volumes, with Lex Heerma van Voss and Jan De Maeyer, *Between Cross and Class. Comparative Histories of Christian Labour in Europe 1840-2000* (IISG/ Peter Lang, 2005) and, with Michel Pigenet and Jean-Louis Robert, *L'Apogée du syndicalisme. Les syndicalismes en Europe occidentale pendant les Trente Glorieuses* (Sorbonne, 2005).

Ruggero Ranieri has held a research post at the Vrije Universiteit Amsterdam and teaching posts at the London School of Economics, the University of Essex and the University of Manchester, where he was Senior Lecturer in the history of European integration and Jean Monnet Professor in History from 1999 to 2004. Currently, he is Visiting Professor at the University of Padova and President of the Uguccione Ranieri di Sorbello Foundation in Perugia. His research interests range from the history of European integration to the development of the steel industry in western Europe to the economic history of post-1945 Italy. He has co-authored *The Frontier of National Sovereignty: History and Theory, 1945-1992* (Routledge, 1993) and is co-editor of two volumes on the European steel industry.

Jan Peter van den Toren studied Economics at the Erasmus University Rotterdam and obtained his doctorate in Leiden (1996). He is Fellow at the Amsterdam Institute for Advanced Labour Studies (AIAS) at the University of Amsterdam, where he was an Extraordinary Professor of Industrial Relations from 1998 to 2002. Currently he is Advisor to the Prime Minister in the Netherlands and secretary of the Dutch Innovation Platform.

Gregory Vercauteren studied History at the universities of Antwerp and Ghent, and obtained his PhD in History in 2005 at the University of Leuven with a monograph on the development of social consultation in post-World War II Belgium (*In naam van de sociale vooruitgang. De rol van de overheid in het sociaal overleg in België*, Acco, 2007). He has been scientific collaborator at the Katholieke Universiteit Leuven, but is currently employed as a scientific collaborator of Heemkunde Vlaanderen vzw.

Ivan Wijnens (1973-2006) studied History at the universities of Antwerp and Leuven. He was employed as a scientific collaborator and research and teaching assistant at the University of Antwerp, where he prepared a PhD on economic consultation in post-World War II Belgium, until his untimely death on 10 May 2006.

"Work & Society"

The series "Work & Society" analyses the development of employment and social policies, as well as the strategies of the different social actors, both at national and European levels. It puts forward a multi-disciplinary approach – political, sociological, economic, legal and historical – in a bid for dialogue and complementarity.
The series is not confined to the social field *stricto sensu*, but also aims to illustrate the indirect social impacts of economic and monetary policies. It endeavours to clarify social developments, from a comparative and a historical perspective, thus portraying the process of convergence and divergence in the diverse national societal contexts. The manner in which European integration impacts on employment and social policies constitutes the backbone of the analyses.

Series Editor: Philippe POCHET, Director of the Observatoire Social Européen (Brussels) and Digest Editor of the Journal of European Social Policy.

Recent Titles

No.59 – *Changing Liaisons. The Dynamics of Social Partnership in 20th Century West-European Democracies*, Karel DAVIDS, Greta DEVOS & Patrick PASTURE (eds.), 2007, 265 p., ISBN 978-90-5201-365-7.

No.58 – *Work and Social Inequalities in Health in Europe*, Ingvar LUNDBERG, Tomas HEMMINGSSON & Christer HOGSTEDT (eds.), SALTSA, 2007, 538 p., ISBN 978-90-5201-372-5.

No.57 – *European Solidarities*, Lars MAGNUSSON & Bo STRÅTH (eds.), SALTSA, 2007, 355 p., ISBN 978-90-5201-363-3.

No.56 – *Industrial Relations in Small Companies. A Comparison: France, Sweden and Germany*, Christian DUFOUR, Adelheid HEGE, Sofia MURHEM, Wolfgang RUDOLPH & Wolfram WASSERMANN (eds.), SALTSA, 2007, 229 p., ISBN 978-90-5201-360-2.

No.55 – *The European Sectoral Social Dialogue. Actors, Developments and Challenges*, Anne DUFRESNE, Christophe DEGRYSE & Philippe POCHET (eds.), SALTSA/Observatoire social européen, 2006, 342 p., ISBN 978-90-5201-052-6.

No.54 – *Reshaping Welfare States and Activation Regimes in Europe*, Amparo SERRANO PASCUAL & Lars MAGNUSSON (eds.), SALTSA, 2007, 319 p., ISBN 978-90-5201-048-9.

No.53 – *Shaping Pay in Europe. A Stakeholder Approach*, Conny Herbert ANTONI, Xavier BAETEN, Ben J.M. EMANS, Mari KIRA (eds.), SALTSA, 2006, 287 p., ISBN 978-90-5201-037-3.

No.52 – *Les relations sociales dans les petites entreprises. Une comparaison France, Suède, Allemagne*, Christian DUFOUR, Adelheid HEGE, Sofia MURHEM, Wolfgang RUDOLPH & Wolfram WASSERMANN, 2006, 243 p., ISBN 978-90-5201-323-7.

No.51 – *Politiques sociales. Enjeux méthodologiques et épistémologiques des comparaisons internationales / Social Policies. Epistemological and Methodological Issues in Cross-National Comparison*, Jean-Claude BARBIER & Marie-Thérèse LETABLIER (eds.), 2005, 2nd printing 2006, 295 p., ISBN 978-90-5201-294-0.

No.50 – *The Ethics of Workplace Privacy*, Sven Ove HANSSON & Elin PALM (eds.), SALTSA, 2005, 186 p., ISBN 978-90-5201-293-3.

No.49 – *The Open Method of Co-ordination in Action. The European Employment and Social Inclusion Strategies*, Jonathan ZEITLIN & Philippe POCHET (eds.), with Lars MAGNUSSON, SALTSA/Observatoire social européen, 2005, 2nd printing 2005, 511 p., ISBN 978-90-5201-280-3.

N° 48 – *Le Moment Delors. Les syndicats au cœur de l'Europe sociale*, Claude DIDRY & Arnaud MIAS, 2005, 2nd printing 2005, 349 p., ISBN 978-90-5201-274-2.

No.47 – *A European Social Citizenship? Preconditions for Future Policies from a Historical Perspective*, Lars MAGNUSSON & Bo STRÅTH (eds.), SALTSA, 2004, 361 p., ISBN 978-90-5201-269-8.

No.46 – *Restructuring Representation. The Merger Process and Trade Union Structural Development in Ten Countries*, Jeremy WADDINGTON (ed.), 2004, 414 p., ISBN 978-90-5201-253-7.

No.45 – *Labour and Employment Regulation in Europe*, Jens LIND, Herman KNUDSEN & Henning JØRGENSEN (eds.), SALTSA, 2004, 408 p., ISBN 978-90-5201-246-9.

N° 44 – *L'État social actif. Vers un changement de paradigme ?*, Pascale VIELLE, Philippe POCHET & Isabelle CASSIERS (dir.), 2005, 2e tirage 2006, ISBN 978-90-5201-227-8.

P.I.E. Peter Lang – The website

Discover the general website of the Peter Lang publishing group:

www.peterlang.com

For the avoidance of doubt, input of the whole or any part of this publication into any generative artificial intelligence model, chatbot, program, software or technology is expressly prohibited without the prior written consent of the publisher.